MOSTLY WE HAD IT GOOD
A BABY BOOMER'S JOURNEY

First published in 2017 by Elbow Publishing

Copyright © Tim Albert, 2017

The right of Tim Albert to be identified as the author of this work has been asserted by him in accordance with the Copyright, Designs and Patents Act, 1988.

A catalogue record for this book is available from the British Library

ISBN 978-0-9574090-6-4

Cover design by Su Jones and Paddy McEntaggart

Photographs © Tim Albert except where others are acknowledged.

Interior design and typesetting: Sally Ellis

Printed and bound in Great Britain by
TJ International Ltd, Padstow, Cornwall

MOSTLY WE HAD IT GOOD
A BABY BOOMER'S JOURNEY

TIM ALBERT

Also by this author

Medical journalism: the writer's guide

Winning the publications game

An A-Z of medical writing

Write effectively: a quick course for busy health professionals

To Uncle Eddie and Uncle Peter,
and the others whose sacrifice
during the second world war
made this book possible

Contents

Prologue   1

1950s: the unwinds of war   3
*In which I discover the joys of family life
– and the anguish of losing it*

1.1   An attraction of opposites   5
1.2   Common people   10
1.3   The castle   13
1.4   The lingering shadows of war   17
1.5   Oy Vey Maria   19
1.6   My other mummy   22
1.7   Queen and Empire   25
1.8   Exile, for undisclosed offences   31
1.9   Beyond the Christmas truce   36

1960s: a tale of two certainties   41
*In which I endure schooling, enjoy education
and find my views moving to the left*

2.1   Another decade, another hilltop   43
2.2   Last of the first   47
2.3   Meanwhile in the real world...   51
2.4   Three long years   55
2.5   Free at last – but for what?   61
2.6   The joy of learning   66
2.7   The American dream   72
2.8   A degree of success   77

1970s: brave new world, soon perhaps 81

*In which I embark on the reporter's trade, mix with
the big boys, lose one love and gain another*

3.1	A cub in the classroom	83
3.2	On the local beat	86
3.3	Short shift on the tabloids	92
3.4	The lower rungs of the freelance ladder	96
3.5	A home of my own	101
3.6	Blood and guts	104
3.7	Clashes behind the Iron Curtain	107
3.8	Education observed	110
3.9	Shifting with the big boys	114
3.10	Back to school	120
3.11	A specialist, briefly	122
3.12	Burnt by the sun	126
3.13	Lost and found	132

1980s: health care blues 135

*In which I learn about the world of doctors, import a soulmate,
and wander into the new digital age*

4.1	Regrouping	137
4.2	A new direction	139
4.3	Doctors discovered	142
4.4	For better...	146
4.5	...for worse	149
4.6	Happy Christmas – you're fired!	154
4.7	In the wilderness	157

4.8   A wage slave again   161
4.9   An editor's chair   165
4.10 Into Europe   171
4.11 The slow drip of the new   175
4.12 The NHS under attack   178
4.13 Out again   182

1990s: fronting up   **185**

*In which I become a small businessman and try to persuade
doctors that clear writing might have its advantages*

5.1   Reinvention   187
5.2   The joy of selling   190
5.3   Tilting at windmills   193
5.4   French cricket   199
5.5   The newsletter pandemic   202
5.6   A mended heart   206
5.7   The business rises; the business falls   208
5.8   A clock strikes   211
5.9   Science to the rescue   214
5.10 On the move   218
5.11 The downs and ups of a peripatetic trainer   221
5.12 Deeper still in the wonderful world of science   225
5.13 Equilibrium   229

Postscript, January 3, 2000   232
Acknowledgements   234

Prologue

My family has a squirreling gene. For more than three decades I have hosted
'stuff' handed down by various family members: my great grandfather's
rimless round spectacles, for instance, and a phrenological analysis of his
character ('Your brain is large for a man of your size and weight'); scrapbooks
and photo albums bulging with multi-coursed menus from transatlantic
voyages; a subdued blue Chinese gown my grandmother went in to the opera;
an Indian club and a tutu (no explanation for either); two top hats and a
bowler my father wore.

Even more precious, as far as I was concerned, were boxes stuffed with
written material. From my father came letters written as a child, duplicated
community newsletters from the General Strike, letters seeking work in 1945
and particulars of the house he bought in 1947. From my mother came her
school leaving certificate and a school scrapbook at one end of her life, and
a complete record of who came for dinner and what she cooked them at the
other. And of course a complete collection of my school reports.

The fruits of my own squirreling are also there: angsty adolescent poems
from my school's 'literary' magazine, diaries of my own travels, articles written
as a journalist (many on health and education), business reports and training
material from my second career as a trainer and owner of a small business.

For many years these papers laid around my home, ignored. But, as I started
to think about my next writing project, it occurred to me that the inspiration –
and information – I needed was already around me.

The task of putting it into some kind of order has taken longer than I
thought. But the journey has been fascinating. I have been inspired to
remember and review what happened decades ago. I have discovered new
things about my family, myself and our world, both then and now. I have also
come to appreciate my extraordinary good fortune of living within what now
looks like a lucky bubble, and a short-lived one at that.

Tim Albert
Leatherhead, April 2017

1950s: the unwinds of war

*In which I discover the joys of family life –
and the anguish of losing it*

Time line

1945   End of war in Europe; nuclear bombs end war with Japan

1948   The British National Health Service is set up

1949   George Orwell publishes *1984* – a dystopian view of the future

1950   Start of Korean War; first credit card is introduced; Labour prime minister Clement Attlee is re-elected with a majority of five

1951   Festival of Britain takes over London's South Bank; Winston Churchill is elected prime minister; first colour TV broadcast in the USA

1952   The Great Smog envelops London; King George VI dies; polio vaccine is created

1953   Everest is conquered; coronation of Queen Elizabeth II; Stalin dies; DNA is discovered

1954   Food rationing ends; report says cigarettes cause cancer; Roger Bannister breaks four-minute mile

1955   Rosa Parks refuses to give up her seat on a bus in the southern United States; Anthony Eden becomes prime minister

1956   Suez crisis; the spies Burgess and Maclean surface in Moscow; John Osborne's play *Look Back in Anger* is performed; Clean Air Act; Britain's first nuclear power station opens at Calder Hall

1957   European Economic Community is established, without Great Britain; Sputnik goes into space; Harold Macmillan replaces Anthony Eden as prime minister

1958   M6 Preston bypass is first UK motorway; Mao Zedong launches Great Leap Forward

1959   Harold Macmillan leads the Conservatives to their third general election victory; Fidel Castro becomes president of Cuba

1.1: An attraction of opposites

My father started life as an Edwardian toff, albeit a Jewish one. His first memory, he told me, was the smell of straw laid out in the streets to deaden the sound of horse-drawn carts and to ease the sufferings of a sick neighbour. The family lived in some style in a detached house at 133 Gloucester Road in Kensington, bought from the author JM Barrie in 1902. Surviving photos show a classic Victorian interior: rugs, antimacassars and aspidistras, and solid wooden furniture cluttered with pottery from the Far East

There was a full complement of servants – the 1911 census lists cook, valet, parlour maid, nurse and under-nurse – and my father claimed that he never knew which of these brought him the cup of tea he found on his bedside table when he woke up each morning.

His father, Alfred Samuel Albert, was a businessman, though what that business was at first is unclear. Born into a family of dentists in 1849, he went to America and back, allegedly making and losing a couple of fortunes. When he finally married, in 1905, he was part-owner of Scrubbs Cloudy Ammonia, a precursor of detergents: 'Only a few drops will soften even the hardest water', claimed the advertisements at the time. His first son and 'darling boy', my father Alfred Sydney David Albert, was born in 1906.

I have photographs of the young Sydney, as he came to be called, wearing a dress and a straw hat and standing on a bench. I have another, taken some 10 years later, where he poses with his younger brother, each wearing a dinner jacket with a floral buttonhole, each holding in elegant fingers a fake cigarette.

An entangled bundle of dance cards records his social life in Kensington and the West End. They are delicate affairs, tied to a small pencil, some with intricate line-drawings of Pierrots or butterflies, and inside a programme of dances (printed) and dancers (pencilled). A surviving card from the Great Central Hotel, for instance, has the young Sydney scheduled to do two foxtrots with 'D. Hargreaves' and a one-step with 'McCall'.

His idyll was short lived. My grandfather died when my father was 10, possibly from cancer though again the record is unclear. Times got harder. His mother, determined to turn him into an English gentleman, sent him to Charterhouse, the public school in Surrey, where he was forced to wash in cold water and (worse, in his view) to help build the Church of England chapel. At a reunion in the 1960s he was asked if he was that skinny boy who sat at the end of the table and had to eat the bones. Yet he was a good pupil, winning prizes. One of these, awarded at his prep school, is *The Hawaiian Archipelago: six months among the palm groves, coral reefs and volcanoes of the Sandwich Islands* by Isabella L Bird. It remains on my bookshelf, unread.

He spent a treasured year at Grenoble University, where he acquired fluent French and a long-lasting love for French food, French wine and French tobacco. He turned down a place at Oxford University in favour of becoming a solicitor's articled clerk on the strikingly contemporary grounds that it was more prudent to take an offered job rather than embark on three years of costly study. He was admitted as a solicitor in 1929 and became a property lawyer.

As far as I can tell, he enjoyed the 1920s and 1930s as they were best enjoyed. He was photographed going to the opera: he is wearing top hat and tails; his mother a coat and fur hat. He is smiling; she is not. Another of his photographs shows a long line of Tiller Girls seated at a bar, one long leg folded carefully over the other; they are all smiling. He met the dancers on his regular holidays in France, where he acquired an appetite for casinos. Years later, when I took him to a casino in the Bahamas, he complained loudly that he could play roulette only in French.

During the Great Strike of 1926 he volunteered as a bus conductor. For many years, equivocal about my father being a blackleg, I kept quiet about this part of his life. But looking through the duplicated news sheets he had carefully collected, it's clear he felt that these were inspirational times – fighting the good fight for freedom against the Bolshevik menace. He canvassed for the Conservatives in Baron's Court, and his circle of friends came out of a high political drawer. One later became chairman of the 1922 backbench Tory MPs committee; another would become the second Baron and his son a government minister and Privy Councillor.

When war came, he became what his post-war CV described as 'Civil Assistant, attached General Staff, War Office'. This bland phrase masked the fact that he worked for MI5, using his knowledge of the law and of French to screen refugees coming into the country. Not surprisingly he talked little of his experiences, though he did admit to declining an invitation to attend the execution in March 1944 at Wormwood Scrubs Prison of the German spy Oswald Job, sent to Britain under cover of being a French refugee. The gruesome invitation was in recognition of his role in breaking down Job's cover story with forensic questioning – with the help, I suspect, of a bit of advance warning from an intercepted and decoded German message.

He regularly received Enigma decrypts, and his second wartime story told of when his colleague Mr Jones left his briefcase stuffed with these secrets on the top of a bus in Oxford. My father was with him at the time and, according to family legend, the two of them waited calmly until the bus had finished its next trip. They then retrieved the briefcase, untaken and unopened. They could have lost Britain the war.

My father's mind may have been on other things at the time, since he was courting. The object of his affections, soon to become his wife (and later my mother), was different in temperament, religion and class. Margaret Pauline Young was born in Bristol, one of five children, from what the family claimed was 'yeoman stock'. They also claimed kinship with the craftsmen who carved the screen at St Mary Redcliffe in the city, and with the Victorian reformer John Bright.

The family moved to London, where my grandfather became a publican. He lost his job: according to one aunt because he 'lent' money out of the till, and according to the other because he drank the profits. Thereafter he had a succession of modest jobs, ending up as storeman in a paint factory during the week, and applying himself to the Football Pools every Saturday in the hope of restoring his fortunes. His wife bore three girls and two boys, and supported him throughout.

But the driving force – and chief bread-winner – of the family was my grandmother's sister, Alice Payne. Great Aunt Alice (known to the family as Auntie Al), was a tough late-Victorian working woman who earned a good wage, climbed mountains (I still have a stick she bought in Switzerland, complete with vicious spike and tiny plaques of the places she visited), and had a clear and independent mind.

This led her not to campaign on poverty or votes for women, as many of her contemporaries were doing, but to join the Roman Catholic Church. She was inspired by Cardinal Newman and, according to my Uncle John, struck a deal with her sister that she would support the family provided the girls were brought up as Roman Catholics. For much of her life she worked at Asprey, the Bond Street jewellers, where she presided over 'holy corner', a small section selling upmarket Catholic goods such as ivory crucifixes and leather-bound gold-embossed bibles.

My mother was the middle child. She was more delicate than the others, having had rheumatic fever when young. But she excelled at the La Retraite convent in south London, ending up with a school leaving certificate showing passes in eight subjects and credits in four others. A report stuck into the red leatherette wallet containing this certificate gives her attendance as *excellent*, her punctuality as *very good*, but her conduct only as *good*. This undermines the notion, told to me on several occasions by her siblings, that she was the goody-two-shoes of the family.

She found a good job as a secretary in the London law firm of Penningtons, and started to work for my father. She moved with him when he joined MI5 but spoke even less about her time there than he did. They worked at Blenheim together, where many MI5 officers were based.

For some of the time, according to the heading on one of her letters to my father, she was billeted at Keble College. It was there, according to a recent history of MI5 by Christopher Andrew, that the bursar was driven to write for compensation for 28 coffee pots, 740 plates and 104 dishes that the billeted secretaries had smashed. I doubt my mother had a part in this. (Christopher Andrew, *The defence of the realm: the authorized history of MI5*, Allen Lane, 2009).

My father proposed in July 1943 and on August 21 they got married in the Catholic Church in Putney in what a short notice in the *Times* described as 'quietly'. The surviving photo shows my parents with wide grins, alongside my mother's younger sister Stella as bridesmaid and my father's friend and accountant Jim Clement, a dashing Colonel in uniform, as best man. My father's mother stayed in Hove but sent good wishes in a telegram.

A respectable 11 months later, on July 8, 1944, my brother David arrived with a bang. Soon after his arrival in Westminster Hospital, or so family history relates, a V1 exploded in the neighbourhood and blew out all the windows. There is some circumstantial evidence for this story. When I was born two and a half years later in February 1947 in the same private wing, a friend wrote to my mother: 'I'm sure it must have been such a relief to you both not to have to worry about air bombardments this time'.

What she did have to worry about was a combination of one of the hardest winters for many years and persistent shortages of fuel brought about by the Labour government's post-war austerity programme. 'The whole place is in candlelight,' wrote Great Aunt Alice in a letter to the second-time mother. 'What a government. A more incompetent crowd one could hardly find'. And there was sympathy that I had not turned out to be a girl, though one friend pointed out the compensations: 'You will find two of the same sex quite a relief as regards clothes and, later on, school fees!'

I was soon taken home – to what my Auntie Stella described in a letter as a 'grand apartment' at 27H Bramham Gardens, Earl's Court. My arrival caused an incident. When David was born, my parents kept his pram in the hall – until Mrs Worsfold, the caretaker who lived in the basement, started to report complaints that it was blocking the entrance. As a result, my parents had started to take the pram up to their flat each day in the lift. But my arrival demanded a new and larger pram, which was too large for the lift. My father wrote to the agent to ask if he could go back to keeping the pram in the hall.

'I should perhaps say that Mrs Worsfold has, in the past, suggested that the other tenants did not like the perambulator to be left in the hall; from my inquiries, however, I do not think that this is the case, and now that we have ceased to keep our perambulator there, her daughter keeps hers in the place where we used to leave ours.'

The perambulator war was never resolved. A decision was made that had far-reaching consequences.

1.2: Common people

My parents decided to move to the suburbs. My father agreed with the property agent at Bramham Gardens that he would renounce the option of staying on in his flat as a controlled tenant - in exchange for £100 (£3,500 at today's prices) to 'cover moving expenses'. They started looking for a family house five miles and a world away in Wimbledon village.

A large factor in their decision was the 93 bus route, which in one direction could take my mother to the house in Putney where her family still lived, and in the other could take my father to Wimbledon Station. From there it was 20 minutes on a Southern Region train into Waterloo. Here he could catch the line to the city – commonly called 'the drain' – where he had become a partner in a small firm of solicitors called Lawrence Messer, in a side street just across from the Bank of England.

Wimbledon village was already a magnet for the professional classes, rising above the less prosperous suburbs that provided the chauffeurs and daily helps that kept them comfortable. A Victorian horse trough and drinking fountain stood guard at the top of the steep hill, a reminder to travellers that they had come up in the world both physically and socially. Behind them a vaguely ecclesiastical-looking bank was the first in a line of High Street shops and services: bakers, butchers, a dairy, estate agents, fishmongers, chemists, banks, electrical suppliers, jewellers, and a cobbler's.

Half-way down there was, appropriately, a dog leg at the Dog and Fox, at that time a grand hotel and site of regular Masonic balls. Then came more shops, until a small department store and the Rose and Crown. A few yards further on, across the road, a tall, white-stone war memorial stood apart in a neatly tended plot.

The memorial looked out over one of the village's greatest assets: Wimbledon Common. This was not one of those sedate city parks with clipped lawns and ordered flower beds, but 1,100 acres of unkempt grassland, criss-crossed with paths and dotted with sycamore and oak and maple and silver birch. Within five minutes you could feel well away from city life; in the early 1950s one couple travelled the five or so miles from Chelsea each weekend to stay at their 'country cottage' on the common's edge.

At the heart of the common stood a windmill where Baden Powell was said to have written part of *Scouting for Boys*, and from a nearby office rangers in tweed jackets and bowler hats set out on regular horse-back patrols to ensure that the bye-laws were being respected. There were small ponds for collecting tadpoles and sailing model boats, dirt tracks for riding horses, and two nine-hole courses for playing golf, though the bye-laws required golfers to wear red jackets as a warning to unsuspecting ramblers of potential airborne dangers. It must have seemed a long way from Earl's Court.

On one corner, where the common meets village, stood a line of horse chestnut trees, the largest one of which, standing on the nearest corner, my father came to call the tree of life (of which more later). Opposite this tree was the start of Lingfield Road, a name clearly derived from a not-too-distant agrarian past, though more recently the street had been taken over by an eclectic mix of housing, including a freestanding Georgian house, vast Victorian villas, a 19th century Spanish-style home, and a block of flats built in the 1930s.

My parents' attention was caught by a house just three down from the common, offered for sale at a price of £5,850 by a Captain Maxwell Richmond. My father knew little other than he was a naval man and left for South Africa soon after the contracts were exchanged. I have since discovered that he had already distinguished himself by being the captain of the destroyer that took the British cabinet to France in 1940, and later became an admiral and a knight.

The house was one of a pair built at the end of the 19th century on land carved out of an estate and now locally listed as being of architectural interest. It is a square and sturdy affair, of brick and stucco with shutters on the first floor that we never shut. I have the estate agent's particulars: the headline **Attractive Detached Family House** is followed by a burst of enthusiastic prose. This is not surprising since Ron Downham, the estate agent who wrote the description and later became a good family friend, lived directly opposite. The house, he wrote, was:

'splendidly situated on the highest ground and gravel soil only 50 yards from Wimbledon Common in the best residential district, which is much sought after owing to its convenience for the High Street shopping centre, which is just round the corner, Churches of all denominations, bus routes to Wimbledon Station, and King's College School.'

It obviously suited and my parents bought it. A surviving pile of carbon copies of my father's correspondence shows how meticulously the move was planned. In one exchange my father tells the fuel officer that he was 'very anxious' to be allowed extra boiler fuel because he had a baby 'liable to bronchitis'. He wrote: 'My Doctor considers that it is still essential that my baby be kept in a warm atmosphere in the winter, and I enclose a Medical Certificate to this effect'.

A photograph taken at the time shows me as a particularly chubby and robust-looking child. But I had a role: helping to keep the family warm.

1.3: The castle

My first memory was of being stuck. I had been stored away in my wooden cot one Saturday afternoon, and was whiling away the time with some basic experiments. One was to see whether I could get my arm through the bars of the cot: I could. The next, to discover whether I could get the arm back through the bars, was less successful. I could not. So I started to cry.

My predicament caused some consternation in the Albert household, since my father's practical skills were as basic as the half-dozen tools in the cellar. He sent out to Messrs Gibberd and Sons, builders and decorators, less than a hundred yards away on Wimbledon High Street, and they despatched a carpenter who managed to saw me out. I stopped wailing; the cot was repaired.

The incident, one of the two unhappy childhood memories I still recall, took place in the early centre of my operations – the 'nursery'. It had brown linoleum on the floor and a broad ledge crossing the whole length of the rooms underneath the windows. I would sit on the ledge and stare at the formal garden and grand house behind, or crouch underneath in games of make-believe.

This is where I stored my toys, which I loved and abused. Teddy lost hair when I tested my hairdressing skills; the bendy green-jacketed golliwog lost bits of rubber at the extremities, exposing his wire skeleton; Muffin the Mule lost a leg; and the Pelham puppet – a strange androgynous figure with orange hair, green trousers and red checked shirt – was never knowingly untangled.

The outside world intruded via a brown Bakelite radio, mounted high on a shelf. My favourite programme was *Listen with Mother*, a 15-minute programme of songs, stories and nursery rhymes at a quarter to two every weekday. This was the source of my first recorded quip.

'Are you sitting comfortably,' we were asked.

'No I am on my potty', I replied.

I don't remember this, but the story was often repeated. It was from this same radio in February 1952 that I heard that the King had died. It was two days before my fifth birthday, but I was old enough to understand that this was an Important Event. I am sure I stood up as the announcement was made.

In the next room was what my father called, in his briefing letter to the decorators, the 'night nursery'. The Victorian nomenclature was soon dropped and it became 'the boys' bedroom'. This was where I spent time with my brother David, talking in the comfort of darkness. We each had a single bed, separated by a plain white folding table, on which a light-brown wooden clock with curved Art Deco corners ticked the minutes away. Downstairs in the hall an 18th century bracket clock chimed away the hours. The clock marks time for me still.

Across a little hall were another two bedrooms, one for my parents and one for guests. Between the two sets of bedrooms was a bathroom and a separate lavatory. It was definitely not a *toilet*, which I soon learnt was a word used by those who lived down the hill.

This room played a pivotal part in my second unpleasant early memory. The key to the lavatory door went missing, and a story emerged that it had been flushed down the pan. I was questioned by the great interrogator (though not tortured), and in a fit of hyper-honesty said I couldn't be sure whether I had taken the key, or not. This was taken as a plea of guilty, and I was slapped, on the leg, once. The key was later found. I am still unsure what lessons I derived from the experience.

On the top floor were two rooms intended originally for the servants. For the first few years they were occupied by au pairs: Mitzi came over from Austria, Bridget from Ireland. One of the rooms was long and thin, with a bed at one end and a bath at the other. There was no lavatory, though, as staff were expected to go down four flights of stairs to use the one outside the kitchen door. If they had a chamber pot I never saw it.

The ground floor, well-ordered and spotlessly clean, was for grown-ups. At first it was sparsely furnished, with light-brown armchairs grouped around a long, low stool and a superior wooden-cased radio. The dining room was dominated by a sideboard with deep whorls of old oak, on which stood two bowls of fruit and a silver-plated bell-shaped cocktail mixer from Asprey, given by Great Aunt Alice to my parents as a wedding present. It was a curious choice for the middle of a war, but I suspect she felt my father already had the basic requirements of a gentleman and needed a touch of *louche* luxury.

Every evening my parents would sit down sharp at 7.30 for a three-course dinner (it was definitely not called supper), and they would talk. By this time, I had been sent up to bed with strict instructions not to come down. I tried to flout the rules, particularly if there was company. I rarely succeeded in staying downstairs long.

In those early days, I had little cause to stray out of 'our' part of the house and into what the estate agent's particulars called the 'excellent domestic offices' at the back. Here my mother operated with the help of the au pair and later a daily help. The 'lofty and well-lighted kitchen' was stuck in the 1930s: a board on the wall showed which electric bell had been pressed to summon staff; a mangle was used to squeeze the water from the washing; a wooden frame on a rope and pulley continued the drying. Just off the kitchen was a pantry with tins and packets of food (there was no refrigerator of course) and a scullery with an elderly gas cooker.

Outside the kitchen door (or 'tradesmen's entrance' as Ron Downham had written) were a lavatory and a garden shed. It was in this area that a rat once took up residence, later dispatched by a man from the council. The peculiar smell of the shed stays with me, and I still associate it with vermin.

The formal exit into the back garden was from a separate door, leading onto a tiny lawn, suitable only for French cricket. The front garden was equally small, and dominated by a copper beech tree that 60 years on is still there although, like most of my generation, now firmly clipped and thick of girth.

As time moved on I ventured out from this castle, first riding in the controversial perambulator, later using my own chubby legs – though my freedom was restrained by a pair of reins. My mother and I walked round the shops in the morning and onto the common in the afternoon. Our normal route took us around the pond, though on fine afternoons we would continue across to Cannizaro Park, an 18th century mansion that housed a council-owned old people's home (now inevitably a luxury hotel). We would stroll past the fountain and the parrot cage, through the trees, round the pond and up to the sunken garden where we would sit on a bench and eat our Sunny Spread sandwiches. Life couldn't have been better.

In the autumn of 1952 the walks became longer, and went in the opposite direction. They took me to the nursery school run by Mrs James from her Victorian villa at the bottom of the hill. I coped, since it was for the morning only and I could wear my own clothes. I played the triangle in the school band. I also got married to Pamela, plighting our troth before our classmates with a Plasticine ring, but we soon drifted apart.

It would never have worked, though. She would have had serious competition for my affection from my mother. Around her I felt secure, supported and loved; it was a precious gift for which I surely failed to show enough gratitude. Sometimes she would allow herself the luxury of an hour in the afternoon sitting in her armchair with a copy of *Woman's Own*, but most of the day she spent on the move in our service.

Would she have liked to have had a job? I am not sure it is a meaningful question. It was not what she was there to do: she had her duty to look after her husband and her children, and in that order.

I was too young to realise how unconfident she was. After my father had died I came across some letters she had written to him around this time, saying how she fears letting him down. In one, written on a rare occasion when he was working away from home, she says:

'This note is really to tell you I am very sorry for my behaviour these days – and I know it is <u>awful</u>, but I don't seem to be able to help it...perhaps with the spring (?) weather I shall feel less weary, moody and depressed. Whatever you think, don't think I don't love you any more – I do, tremendously...'

What was that about? No-one now will know. But I am pretty sure my mother was sensitive about the difference in class between her and her husband. (Though I am equally sure Great Aunt Alice was delighted that she had married a man who might have shopped at Asprey.)

About that time a tragedy intruded into our home, though I was not aware of it at the time. I don't know the exact date, but one night in the early 1950s I was awakened by the sound of strangers tramping up and down the stairs. The next day I learnt that they were ambulance men, and that they had taken my mother to hospital. A few days later David and I were taken to see her, propped up wanly in her hospital bed.

It was to be several years before I was told that my mother had given birth to a still-born boy. Grief in those days was private, and not shared with the children.

1.4: The lingering shadows of war

About 350 bombs fell on Wimbledon during the war, according to records in the village museum. They destroyed 800 homes, injured 1,000 residents and killed 150 more. As I travelled on the top of the 93 bus I could look down into the gaps between the houses – carpets of rubble topped with free-standing walls patched with scraps of wallpaper and etched with angular shapes of bare plaster showing where staircases had once linked floors of a family home.

My cousin Angela, elder by five years, recalls exploring some of these sites with her sister. Her main memories are of the brightly coloured flowers that were growing. I suspect she remembers them so well because most other colours were muted: tan skirts and grey flannels, black saucepans and brown Bisto gravy, smoky yellow formica.

Death had punched painful holes into the lives of almost every family and these drab hues complemented the mental scars. Our parents' pain was commemorated on a side table in our drawing room: a photograph of my father's brother Eddie and a drawn self-portrait by my mother's brother Peter. Eddie, at outbreak of war a solicitor on the south coast with a wife and young son, had joined up as an RAF supplies officer and was drowned at sea, his ship torpedoed by a German submarine. Peter, a commercial artist whose drawings of cathedral interiors are still prized by his descendants, trained as a gunner for bomber command and was shot down over Germany on his first flight.

Each year my parents, along with many of our neighbours, walked the short distance to the war memorial to watch the survivors, chests heaving with medals, parading alongside boy scouts little younger than they were. Later, once the RAF memorial at Runneymede was completed, they visited regularly to remember their loss.

A bundle of letters sent to my father on his engagement provides vivid evidence of what they had gone through. One friend wrote:

> 'The outside world is very brutal, as you know and a really good home defence is one of the few things that make life bearable at the moment and I am very glad for you that you have it.'

Another congratulates him, but swiftly moves on to her own concerns:

'Did you know that Andrew has been missing since April 15? He is a pilot officer and was on a raid to Tunisia – his plane did <u>not</u> return. I haven't given up hope of course, but it is very anxious and worrying...I just can't face the idea of his not being alive.'

Our parents, their relatives and friends had done extraordinary things, though most of them kept quiet about them. One of our neighbours left France at Dunkirk and went back on D-Day. Over the road lived a Canadian pilot who had fought with the legless pilot Douglas Bader, made famous in the film *Reach for the Sky*. My first headmaster, Father Bernard Egan, was a paratroop padre who had been dropped at the ill-fated battle of Arnhem, carrying a walking stick instead of a weapon, and captured after several days tending the injured in a cellar. In a previous campaign, he had been awarded the Military Cross for 'extricating' a troop dropped by mistake behind enemy lines.

More extraordinary, looking back, were the deeds of those gentle women into whose warm hands we trustingly slid our own. My mother's best friend Olga spent large tracts of the war listening to phone conversations between London and Dublin, pulling out the plug if she suspected a breach of national security. A friend who as a sixth former lodged with a Polish family told me of her shock when one evening she realised that the mother, at her age, had been running messages for the Resistance.

Another mother, matriarch of some long-standing Belgian friends and a woman of great elegance and dignity, had calmly lifted the phone one day to tell someone – no-one knows who any more – that a trio of SS tanks were sheltering in a copse near the village. Within the hour they had been bombed and destroyed. (It boggles the mind. What do you say: *'Pardon monsieur. Il y a des chars allemands dans le bois. Est-ce-que vous pouvez les ecraser?'*). Another friend's mother, a dignified, kind and maternal woman, had been awarded the MBE, though no-one really spoke about it until she had died.

'What was it for?' I asked her husband.

'For organising mess facilities during the war', he replied. Oh yes?

Our parents and our friends' parents were not just relieved to have survived; I am sure they felt guilty. Our neighbour, who had been through both Dunkirk and D-Day, used to say that he only reached his post-war position 'because all the good people had been killed'. By the time we arrived they were living quietly, savouring their safety, and nourishing the baby boom. The whole nation, it seems, was suffering from post-traumatic stress syndrome.

1.5: Oy vey Maria

Wimbledon village on a Saturday morning in the 1950s would have made a fine backdrop for a gentle Ealing Comedy. Middle-aged men in sports jackets and cavalry twill trousers strolled along gently, lifting their trilby hats at women of their acquaintance. These women walked with more purpose, scarves on head and wicker shopping bags in hand. Jovial tradesmen sold them their wares with a merry quip. The butcher's boy threaded through on his bicycle, loaded with joints of meat for the Sunday lunch, and a file of horses clopped its way to the common from the stables by the Dog and Fox, leaving a trail of gently steaming manure.

But underneath, the place seethed. Years later I learnt that some long-standing residents had boycotted certain shops because they had engaged in the black market during the war; others patronised them for the same reason. The divisions were sharp between residents and incomers, between middle and lower classes (and the various subdivisions thereof), and between those who attended the different Christian churches. There were two chemists, for instance: one was a leader of the Catholic community and attracted a broadly Catholic clientele; the other across the road drew in the Protestants.

My mother ran into difficulties soon after she moved. One of her rare stories was when, as a newcomer, she was invited to the smart house at the end of the road for a party of young mothers and their babies. It turned out to be for Church of England mothers, and though she never told me the details she clearly felt she had been badly treated.

Her upset continued. For years a neighbour who had been at that party would blank my mother at street cocktail parties and veer across the road to avoid speaking to her. What triggered it – my mother's class, her religion, her husband's racial origins, her shyness – we never found out for sure, though I suspect religion was the cause. One neighbour, apparently, was heard to say how sorry she was for the Albert boys: half-Jewish, half-Catholic.

For me the Jewish bit never came into the reckoning. My father may have been Jewish racially, but this was no longer his identity. His father's position, as expressed in his will, was clear: 'My wish is that my children be brought up in the Jewish faith and my hope is that they will perpetuate that faith by marrying therein'.

But his widow, still relatively young when he died, had other ideas and sent the two boys to an Anglican public school, Charterhouse. Both my father and his brother 'married out'. He did retain warm memories of Jewish culture from his early life, though they did not go much further than fond memories of interlocking networks of aunts and cousins – and an occasional craving for *gefilte* fish.

For my mother, on the other hand, Faith was the St Peter's rock on which her life was built. We had fish (not *gefilte*) on Fridays and fasted from midnight on Sundays, when we would scamper along the 'slips' – narrow passages between large Victorian houses – to the Church of the Sacred Heart, a gaunt flint-fronted church run by the Jesuits, which was always packed.

Our year passed according to the main festivals. My father occasionally turned out with us at Christmas to attend midnight mass. But he demurred when it came to the three solemn ceremonies of Easter: Maundy Thursday, Good Friday and Easter Sunday. Those services seemed interminable. On Good Friday my mother disapproved of us doing little more than think holy thoughts, though when I was a little older we always had a good dinner in the village's smartest restaurant the night before.

The possibility of friction between my parents' beliefs had been dealt with firmly by the Catholic Church. Any member of its flock entering into a 'mixed marriage' had to sign a formal agreement that all offspring would be brought up a Roman Catholic. My father signed and stuck to his word, giving us tacit support for our belief. Later, when I asked about his beliefs, he said he was an agnostic.

My Catholic education started in earnest when, after a year at Mrs James's nursery school, I was sent to the Ursuline Convent. At that time it took Catholic boys for two years, though it seemed an uncomfortable arrangement for all concerned. I wore a white shirt and striped tie, and had to stay all day.

I received my second recorded laugh when I called one of the nuns Mother Mary Woodwork, and under her supervision built a toast rack and painted it livid green. Its compartments were, to put it mildly, non-aligned, and the trouble I had constructing it explains why I haven't attempted to make anything with my hands since. Only a mother would have seen any value in it, and mine kept it until she died.

In my second year at the convent I made my first holy communion, the only boy among girls wearing white dresses and veils in a childish parody of marriage. I took easily to religion, and bought little prayer cards allowing me to sponsor an African baby. I found the idea of the missions particularly attractive. The prospect of bumping along rutted tracks in my Land Rover to bring the Word to save unknowing people from the horrors of Hell made me change my career choice from railway porter to White Father.

But saintliness was not everywhere. In the playground, Ian Calnan forced me to give him a sweet every morning playtime so he wouldn't hit me. That stopped when I summoned up courage to complain. But I found the nuns even more frightening than him, as they forced me to eat vile mixtures of mincemeat and onions, ladled out of large pots. The more they forced them on me, the more I retched. These experiences set me up with life-long aversions to being bullied and eating onions; they have made me unpopular in some quarters still.

At the same time, I developed an acute sense of sin. One elderly nun, black-robed and white-wimpled, held me spellbound as she told of the horrors of hell: it would be full of bodies writhing in pain, lapped with tongues of fire, being punished for the horrible deeds they had committed. I could see these horrors plainly, though as I learnt more I found some comfort in the notion that there were two levels of sins – those that would take you straight down to Hell, and those that wouldn't.

I spent much of my early life trying to keep out of hell, and this included accepting a rather good deal that if you went to mass on the first Friday of each month for nine months you were guaranteed a place in heaven. I did 18 months, just in case. Sadly, I never really embarked on the life of debauchery that this would have now excused, but perhaps that was how it worked.

My anxiety levels were such that once, when reciting my sins in a tiny confessional, I saw the grille starting to swim before my eyes. At that time, I was convinced that my time was up, and left mid-repentance, telling the priest I thought I was about to die. As I write this I am struck by the fact that the priest did not follow me out to check I wasn't imagining it. Perhaps it happened all the time.

For my first two decades, I accepted unthinkingly that Jews were the wicked people who had killed Jesus, with no-one reminding me of my half-share in that group. It was not until I was in my 20s – and my father's American friend Dick Goldwater pulled me up for telling an anti-Semitic joke – that I became conscious of my twin heritage. I realised that, had I been born a decade earlier, and had Hitler succeeded in his plans to conquer Britain, my father's lineage would have consigned me to the gas chambers.

I got a shock in the 1990s when, at an Anne Frank exhibition, I came across a photograph of a group of Jewish schoolchildren, all presumed killed in the death camps. One of them, a bemused boy with neatly parted hair and round spectacles, was my doppelganger.

1.6: My other mummy

My short-lived Plasticine-ringed paramour Pamela had another rival for my affections: Nannie. Not, as nowadays, the 'other granny', but a woman whose life was devoted to rearing other people's children. She was an important figure in my early life, as she had been in my father's before me.

By the time David and I came to know her, she was in her late 60s, and would regale us with stories of her simple childhood and her experiences as a nursing aide. She would also speak of wheeling my father in his pram around Kensington Gardens, apparently on easy terms with the balloon seller, probably because she had made it clear they lived in the house of the creator of Peter Pan.

Her real name, though we rarely used it, was Florence Buckingham and she had become part of the Albert household shortly before the first world war. Her signature appears on my grandfather's will made about that time. When my father and uncle grew too old to need her full-time care she went to work with other families, though the bonds remained: I still have bundles of letters that my father wrote to her while he was in his twenties.

During the second world war her role in the Albert family changed from paediatrics to geriatrics, and she moved to Hove to be a companion to my grandmother who had moved out of London. When we were born, she was assigned temporarily to help my mother – and reassure my father. She spoilt us terribly and we loved her.

For two weeks in the summer we were entrusted to her care at the seaside in Hove in a private hotel one street up from the beach. It was a sprawling Victorian mansion, with plenty of high-ceilinged rooms that had been turned into guest bedrooms. The dining room was down a narrow flight of stairs into the basement where the separate tables were carefully laid, each with a little dish full of squirms of butter; cook taught me how to do these and for a while it was, along with bashing the gong, my regular task.

The proprietors were two women in late middle age we called by their surnames, Jay and Hackman - one short with orange hair and both smelling of an unfamiliar talc. They had been theatricals in the West End and the stairs to the dining room were lined with photographs of Edwardian actors in historical costume and dramatic poses.

Nannie took us to swimming lessons at the King Alfred Baths, completed just before the war and then converted into a land-based training centre for naval volunteer officers. It was HMS King Alfred for the duration, and received fame of sorts when the Nazi propaganda machine claimed to have sunk it. There David and I perfected our doggy paddles in warm sea water. After our lessons, we walked on towards Shoreham, past crumbling wooden groynes where waves gurgled to a halt, to a small park where you could hire little motor boats for five minutes or so, and putt-putt serenely in a shallow pond, captains of our own ship.

Sometimes we walked the other way, past the Regency terraces into Brighton and onto the West Pier. Never comfortable with heights, I savoured the thrill of walking along it away from the shore, looking down through the wooden slats at the frothing sea below. I worried whether the wood would hold; I still do whenever I go on a pier. But I loved the penny arcades: wooden boxes where you could flip silver balls round and round and round before they fell down and you lost your penny; cyclists or horses that would race shakily along a slot, provided you turned the handle fast enough; and creaking mechanical tableaux where you could see kings losing their heads or ghosts rising and falling in graveyards. I also tried the battered contraptions that allowed you to peer in at Edwardian women in poses of mild provocation. I was unimpressed.

In between we made duty visits to Granny Albert. She lived in a grand, red-stoned mansion flat on the Drive, opposite a rather superior private hotel which she visited each day for her lunch. Her flat was full of treasures, which were out of bounds to sticky juvenile fingers. After she died it was discovered that we were not the real problem: nearly every piece of the china that her late husband had painstakingly collected while his funds were high had been chipped and cracked by her cleaner.

She kept toys for us in the bottom drawer of an elegant chest of drawers: wooden bricks in a wooden cart, lead farmyard animals in a straw box, and a wooden solitaire board with a boxful of glass marbles. I preferred peering into a display cabinet containing some 40 miniature ivory figures: Chinese characters climbing up ladders, playing musical instruments or charming serpents.

David was also enthralled by them, and we disagreed from an early age over who would inherit them (the rights of my cousin Anthony were never considered). In the event we were spared conflict when, in the mid-1970s, they were stolen from the house in Wimbledon. We never found the culprits, though it may have been my brother David, who has them still in a secret cellar. The prime suspects remain a group of well-organised burglars who were tipped off about the collection by an informant working in the major auction house that had provided my father with a valuation just a few weeks before.

My grandmother died in 1957. My mother told me of her death as she walked me briskly back from school. Neither I nor David were at the funeral. We still went to Brighton though, staying with Nannie in her bedsit; we called it Liberty Hall.

My father later moved Nannie from Hove to Wimbledon, where she lived in a care home which he paid for. As she approached her 80s she 'went funny' (Alzheimer's was not a term we used in those days) and died in one of the large mental hospitals in Epsom. In her obituary notice in the *Telegraph* my father described her as 'a faithful Albert family retainer'. I was not allowed out of school to attend the funeral.

She left behind a much-loved nephew she called Bobby, a policeman in London and then a probation officer in Coventry. We knew him slightly; he and his wife May visited – a solid middle-class couple – and my father did legal work for them. We knew Bobby had a friend who was a famous writer, and later, when David was at Cambridge we were all invited to his rooms in King's for tea. It was EM Forster. At the time, I was bored by the event, thinking him a rather dull old man. Now I rue the chance to have chatted with a familiar of the likes of John Maynard Keynes, the Woolfs, the Lawrences (DH and TE), Christopher Isherwood and more.

Biographers now agree that Bob Buckingham (as they call him) was the love of EM Forster's life, and that together with his wife May he made up a curious *ménage a trois*. I can't imagine what Nannie would have made of it; after all what they were doing was illegal. But we knew enough by the mid-1960s to snigger when she told us in all innocence that Morgan was fond of young men.

1.7: Queen and empire

In 1953, the year I turned six, the browns and greys of austerity gave way briefly to the golds and reds of pomp and celebration. Our country was back on top of the world, literally when it came to the conquest of Everest (yes, Sir Edmund Hillary was a New Zealander and accompanied by a Sherpa, whatever that was, but we took the credit). At about the same time a British doctor ran the four minute mile; more glory. Sweets were no longer rationed, giving us licence to buy as many sherbet fountains and gobstoppers as the pennies of our pocket-money allowed.

The Coronation of Queen Elizabeth II took place on June 2. But preparations had gone on for months beforehand, and we children were a primary focus. One spring afternoon we crocodiled down to the Odeon cinema to see a film about Her New Majesty, and I received a plastic commemorative medal and a commemorative spoon, one of 9,000 spoons for the Borough of Wimbledon. The spoon, of 'best quality 20 years silver plate', still polishes up beautifully after 60 years.

There were endless competitions. David and I entered one for the best home-made crown and fashioned our entries out of purple cloth and yellow-crayoned paper, but failed to get a prize. We also made decorations for the street: our contribution was to take a bit of gold paint we found in the cellar and write on a piece of plywood ERII JUNE 2 1953. Somehow I obtained two toy Coronation coaches, which became prized possessions.

On the day itself we crossed the road and let ourselves into the house of Ron Downham, the estate agent who had sold us our home. He was not there because he had managed to get prized grandstand tickets to see the procession pass along the Strand.

But he was one of the few people in the road to have a television and made his house available to us and to our best friends. We watched enthralled as the coronation of this young woman, younger even than our parents, proceeded on a tiny, grainy, screen. We marvelled at the plumed Field Marshalls on horseback, at assorted royalty (some in unaccustomed shapes and colours) in carriage after carriage, and at the columns of troops in exotic uniforms from all over 'our' empire.

When the processions had run their course, we wandered across Wimbledon Common where, according to the 12-page programme, festivities included a cricket match, dancing to brass bands, parades of cadets, gun salutes, searchlights and a torch procession. I cannot recall them, though I do recall the bonfire, the hog roast, and Bertram Mills's circus. For years afterwards I hoped that the circus would come back, but it never did; after that we only had funfairs.

The festivities left us bursting with pride, as they were intended to do. Not long before the event our teacher pulled out a globe and pointed to the red bits, of which there were many: these belonged to us. We had our royal family, our parliament, our free health service, our sporting prowess (most sports had been invented by us, we were told), our sense of fair play and of course our incorruptible policemen.

We valued duty, loyalty and hard work. If we happened to live 'up the hill' that was because we deserved to; the poor remained poor because they lacked the drive to be otherwise. On the common I met a boy called Donal who lived in a rare council flat in an alley off the High Street and went to a council school. We played cricket together on the common – but we knew we were different and stayed out of each other's houses; within a year we had lost touch.

Race was not an issue for us, though we knew from our books that others had different skin colour and different ways of living. I no longer have my copy of *Little Black Sambo*, once a prized possession but now universally condemned. The book tells of a little Indian boy who gave his clothes to tigers, who found them so entrancing that they rushed round and round, and turned into butter.

But I still have *The little boy and his house* (Stephen Bone and Mary Adshead, 1950, JM Dent and sons, London) which tells of a little boy who goes round the world with his uncle looking at houses.

> 'Black men in Africa build houses of GRASS AND STICKS,' said the Little Boy's Uncle.
>
> 'Is it hot in Africa?' said the Little Boy.
>
> 'Yes,' said his Uncle.
>
> 'Then let's go there,' said the Little Boy.

So they went to Africa and it was VERY HOT INDEED and they found a black man called M'popo who was building a house of grass and sticks...'

We rarely came across these people so the stereotypes stayed. The first black man I met was a student in London and through the church had been invited to a Christmas drinks party. For the rest of the party season the scars on his face were a talking point.

My father's politics were as would have been expected. He read the *Telegraph* and the *Daily Express* and for a while the *Economist*. The household rejoiced when that nasty Mr Attlee went, and St Winston Churchill became prime minister again.

But we still took advantage of the new welfare state. Each morning I would drink a bottle of sticky orange juice, provided free. A few hours later I would down a third of a pint of milk direct from the bottle, slightly more than my young stomach wished to take. My parents had no time for the Labour Party, but they were not going to refuse the services it had introduced.

A year after the Coronation, my life took a more serious turn. I left the convent. This meant that I stopped being educated with girls, a deprivation that would last a decade and handicap me for life. I joined the Jesuits who ran the Wimbledon College Preparatory School, called Donhead after the name of the house it occupied. David had been there for two years, carving out a reputation as a brain box, but as I joined he moved up a level, as my parents saw it, to a preparatory boarding school in Hampshire.

At the end of my first term I came top of the class. My report glows: 'A good term's work has brought its own reward of the highest place in class. He has always worked with enthusiasm and has made excellent progress.' What I did not realise until I started to research for this book is that my mother had taken out a pencil and carefully written my brother's scores above mine. Overall I was down. He had scored twice as many points in English grammar than I did, but I did better in doctrine, history and nature study. This was clearly the first sign of a lifelong habit of seeking out niches in which I could prosper.

I never reached the heights of first-in-class again. My subsequent reports were good but not outstanding. One noted 'good powers of concentration' and called me an 'industrious and enthusiastic worker'; another (the maths teacher) said I was 'inclined to be lazy'.

I started to dislike the school, perhaps because I was being bullied but I can remember no details. To ensure I turned up, my father used to walk me to school along the common, making up nicknames – the bumping lady and the coatless wonder – for those coming in the opposite direction. Later he took me down the hill on one bus and then along to the school in another, a journey that must have added nearly an hour to his own journey.

Outside school my life started to diversify. My mother bought a Broadwood upright piano which was inserted into the dining room. Once a week I would pack my music into a leather music case and walk the fifty yards down Lingfield Road to a three-storied Victorian semi where Miss Potts ran a flourishing business teaching piano and el-o-cu-tion to the young of the neighbourhood.

I thought she was ancient, though she continued to ride up and down Lingfield Road on her panniered bicycle for another 30 years. Everyone said I had great promise as a pianist, with my Grade One examiner writing: 'Small hands occasionally faltered but it was sensitive and musical in intention'. But although I went on to take another four grades, playing the piano never really appealed.

What did appeal was drama. The early signs of this attraction were seen in the circus shows I insisted my cousins should watch as I bounded on and off the pouffes in my grandparents' house in Putney. Later, my best friend at Donhead was enrolled with Miss Potts in an attempt to improve his diction, and I was enlisted for free as a companion.

I took el-o-cu-tion seriously, winning the form prize for reciting a poem ('The night was falling on the ground...') and playing Puck in a small excerpt of *Midsummer Night's Dream* ('What hempen homespuns have we staggering here...'). This piece was performed by some older girls under Miss Potts's tutelage, and it gave me my first crush – on the Fairy Queen no less. I was entered into the Wimbledon Music Festival as one half of a sketch called *Darby and Joan* and won a bronze medal: 'Darby showed to be a stalwart throughout' said my first review.

By this time, the au pairs had gone back home, and we were allowed to extend up to one of the top-floor bedrooms. David swiftly turned it into a train room, where he fed his passion, first with a clockwork set and later with an elaborate electrified layout that spread round three of the four walls.

This passion extended to real trains as well, and as we got older we were allowed to walk together down the hill to stand on the railway bridge to spot the trains: slow locals puttering along from Dorking and Chessington South, expresses swooping in from Portsmouth, Southampton and Winchester. David knew how to recognise the incoming trains, though we disagree these days as to whether it was through the way the lamps were displayed or the numbers on the front carriage. My role was undefined, and my main activity tugging his sleeve to ask if we could go home yet.

I carved out my own niche by collecting toy soldiers. My garrison included a quartet of Greek guards in skirts, a Salvation Army band, four Swiss soldiers wearing Germanic helmets, two squads of plastic French troops (white officers, black men), and two General Montgomerys (which made the chains of command confusing when I conducted my campaigns). But I still complained that I was bored.

One birthday, Great Aunt Alice gave me a book written by an American called G Warren Schloat Jr, with the title: *What shall I do?* (John Murray 1951). It was packed with pictures of small boys with crew cuts showing how to walk on tin cans, make a miniature chest of drawers out of matchboxes, or model Californian mission stations out of a square piece of soap. Most of them were well beyond my level of skill and our resources (they required unfamiliar items like saltboxes and shellac), but we did put the recipe for fudge to good use.

When I got my first bicycle, I raced over the paths and round the pond (albeit slightly tentatively after the winter of 1953 when it was dredged and dried as a suspected source of polio). Paedophilia was not a public issue, and the two well-publicised murders that took place on the common – one of a gay man and the other of a young mother, as her son looked on – were decades in the future. By today's standards my parents would be considered extraordinarily lax in the freedom they allowed me, but they had a different attitude towards risk-taking. After all, what were the dangers of walking alone when you have lived through cascading bombs and rockets, listening for an engine, which was the sign of imminent danger?

The one traumatic event I suffered came from the best of intentions. Like many parents at the time, mine accepted the advice that slicing off my tonsils would improve my health. One morning, having done my homework conscientiously the night before, they told me that I would not be going to school, but to hospital. They had already talked up the experience: it would be fun with lots of girls and boys to play with and plenty of ice cream.

I had a dreadful experience. I still remember being wheeled by strange people in gowns to the operating theatre, groggy from the pill they had given me. Then they clamped a rubber mask over my nose, bringing with it a sickly smell of rubber and gas before I fell, mercifully, into an agitated sleep. (For years I was unable to watch the scene in the Douglas Bader biopic *Reach for the Sky* where the camera focuses on a throbbing anaesthetic machine while our hero's legs are cut from him.) When I woke up I had a searing pain in my throat. Far from enjoying ice cream, I vomited at the first taste of food.

The experience gave me nightmares for months, a fear of the dark, and a lifelong fear of surgical procedures. I also realised, with a shock, that adults could not be trusted.

1.8: Exile, for undisclosed offences

The photograph, taken in September 1956, shows me bursting with hope. I am nine years old but look younger. I stand in our back garden with my father's beloved delphiniums behind me, wearing the full dress uniform of my new school: polished black shoes, long socks (pulled up nicely, but not for long), creased shorts, grey jacket tightly bound on all three buttons - and a blue, badged cap. The creased white handkerchief in my top pocket shows that I care about style. I know my life is about to change, though I do not yet realise how much I will hate it.

Shortly after the photo was taken I left home for Waterloo Station where, along with my mother and brother David, I walked across the station to the Portsmouth line. I had done this walk before: David had been doing this journey three times a year for the past two years, and I had always been brought to see him off. I had found it most exciting.

Halfway down the platform a group of boys, wearing the same uniform as ours, milled around, fuelled by the holiday-end Tizer and sherbet lemons. They were outside a carriage that other passengers were clearly avoiding, deterred by notices stuck on the windows: *Reserved for Douai Junior School.*

I knew some of these boys already. The Groundwater brothers had stayed at our home because their father worked in south east Asia for Shell; they seemed far too grown up for the shorts they had to wear. With them were fair-haired Hodgson, Farrow from Ecuador, and Wilson whose glasses, in my memory, are forever stuck together with Sellotape.

But my brother's friends paid me scant attention. This was school time and I was small fry and new. I introduced myself to those who, like me, were setting out on this adventure for the first time: a Tye, an English, a Lightly, a brace of unrelated Murphys. Before the train had eased out of the station we learnt that first names were now surplus to requirements. I had changed from Timothy to Albert 2.

A short 10 minutes after departure we raced, cruelly, back the way we came, with familiar landmarks such as the black and white striped Ely's Furniture Repository, Wimbledon Station and our train-spotting bridge whooshing backwards into the past. An hour later, we decamped at Petersfield Station into a couple of motor coaches, which wound their way slowly through hairpin bends up to Ditcham Park.

This was a large redbrick manor house, sitting amid its own farm on the top of a hill, with a cinematic view over fields, copses and quarries across to the Solent. The house was formerly the seat of a prominent Catholic family and during the war a naval convalescent home. It was now the home of Douai Junior School. During term time, it contained some 70 boys, most of whom would go on at age 13 to Douai School, 40 miles away in Berkshire.

My parents had chosen it because it was Roman Catholic, small and relaxed. For years they gleefully told the story of their first visit. On arrival a white-jacketed manservant showed them into a grand oak-panelled room. Dominating the space was a large tiger rug, with teeth bared. As they waited they saw through a window a monk, tousle-haired and distracted, black robes flying, wheeling an old pram filled with logs.

He turned out to be Father Edward, the headmaster, a bustling figure who presided over a small community of monks: white-haired Father Clement who taught us Latin (and according to my brother took pot shots at pheasants out of the classroom windows); Father Augustine with sleek black hair who taught us French; curly-haired and severe Father Stephen who tried to teach us mathematics; and Father Aidan, the quiet one who taught us Doctrine. There was one woman teacher, Miss Herrington, who taught us English. She wore tweedy dresses, made us declaim melodramatic poetry, and on Sundays chivvied us on long walks through the woods.

I soon realised that the metal beds, long wooden refectory tables and communal washing facilities were well below the standard of the home comforts I was used to. I also soon realised that I missed my parents. A few weeks into the term, I woke up dreaming that I heard the noise of the taps as my father ran his morning bath. I had a great swell of homesickness. I found little sympathy.

I had expected to be one of the oldest in the bottom class, but found myself, largely on the strength of my brother's reputation, one of the youngest in the next class up. I am not sure the decision did me any favours because for the next four years my academic career can only be described as mixed. I did well in French, Doctrine and music, where the word 'talented' made a rare appearance. I also had my moments in English. Miss Herington wrote: 'Still vague on some points of grammar but spells well', and also: 'produced some amusing verse parodies' ('Oh young Lochinvar he has come out of the west/he wore his pants and not his vest').

I did not do so well in Latin: 'The exact discipline is perhaps somewhat severe for his rather wayward temperament', said one report. Maths was even worse, and one year earned me a particular vicious comment: 'He knows that he has brains and is somewhat conceited about them and feels that he need do no work'.

This had the desired effect: I fought back and that year (and that year only) won the mathematics prize. The book is *Life in the Deep* by Maurice Burton DSc, (Phoenix House 1958) a curator at the Science Museum, part of a series intended 'to suggest careers for the young scientist of tomorrow'. Like my father's prize before me, it remains unread.

My reports are peppered with comments such as 'works sporadically', 'can do well when he tries', and 'outside interests often claiming his attention'. In line with this judgement, my strongest memories are of life outside the classroom. One of our favourite games involved lying on our backs on the shiny, wooden floors in one of the formal panelled rooms. We then pumped our feet to propel ourselves back and forth in races and bumping competitions. That soon stopped, thanks to splintered bums, and in my case splintered spectacles.

Once the weather got milder we took up an even more dangerous craze: roller- skate car-racing. This involved speeding up and down the school drive on our wheels with no padding and no helmets, pulling behind us on a piece of string a Dinky Toy racing car weighted with Plasticine. Competition was stiff and grazed knees common. Fortunately the drive was rarely used by real cars and there were no major fatalities.

In poor weather we huddled in craft rooms gluing and painting Airfix models of Stukas and Spitfires. In better weather we acted out games of war. The gnarled apple tree on the edge of the lawn doubled as a Lancaster bomber from where we carried out bombing missions over Germany. A fallen tree in the woods became a destroyer in which we fought off U-boats attacking our convoys in the north Atlantic. The ha-ha ditch, once we had covered a section of it over with a roof of leaves and branches, became a tank in which we cruised across the Libyan desert and through the Normandy hedges.

There were more minor injuries. One summer I missed my hold parachuting out of a tree (probably over Arnhem) and ended up breaking my arm. It earned me two trips to Petersfield Hospital and got me off piano practice, so on balance I deemed it worthwhile.

Sports figured highly, orchestrated by Father Augustine – Gus outside his earshot – still in his mid-thirties and the youngest and most glamorous of the monkish quintet. He was a fine cricketer who could send a cricket ball racing to the boundary simply by blocking it. We had younger sporting heroes, too, some of whom came in pairs. The sturdy Groundwater brothers would swerve and crash through opponents in rugby matches; the two long-limbed Wichmans outsprinted and out-jumped everyone; the Jeffery brothers underpinned the cricket teams with their bowling - one whirling in with crossed arms and legs, the other loping in with loopy spin. I can still mimic their actions.

I loved sport but was useless. Part of the problem was my eyesight: without my NHS spectacles, I could see little of the action. I was also small. At age 11 I was only 4 foot 4 inches, which made me feel vulnerable, and not just on the sports pitches. I learnt to divert derision with a quip and later to cry quietly into my pillow.

The staff tried to introduce some homely touches. Gus had a black Labrador whom we would pet constantly. We would sit in his room as he played *Fine Kleine Nachtmusik* on his gramophone. We would also sit, but less still, as he read us ghost stories (which I have blocked out) and comic classics (which I have not). I still reread the account of the fast bowling blacksmith appearing over the brow of the hill to terrorise the awaiting batsmen (*England their England*, AG MacDonell, 1933), and the story of the three friends and their dog hopelessly lost in the maze at Hampton Court, trailing an ever-growing line of other lost souls past an upturned cream bun (*Three Men in a Boat*, Jerome K Jerome, 1889).

Gus also kept a model railway set in the basement, though we were rationed in our use of it.

We were not allowed home during term time, but our parents were allowed two visits. Clearly the monks had decided that more contact would upset us, though I think it would have made the deprivations easier to bear.

My parents did not drive, so they would take the train to Petersfield and stay overnight at the Red Lion, travelling to the school by taxi. We would go back to the inn for a Sunday fireside lunch, or take the train to Southsea or even Brighton, where the joys of a pier, and sometimes even Nannie, would be waiting. Sometimes they persuaded friends to drive them down. My status went up briefly when Ron Downham, our estate agent neighbour, drove them down in his open-top Sunbeam Talbot. We went together to a local village fete, and when we drove back I sat on his knee and he allowed me to steer along the private drive.

We were made to write home once a week. Most of what we reported was humdrum, though we did have the odd prized event such as a visit from the film star John Gregson (star of British-made films such as *Genevieve*, *The Lavender Hill Mob* and *Battle of the River Plate*) whose clever son was in the year below. One summer evening we looked out of our windows to see fire engines from Petersfield racing up the drive. It was (sadly, we felt) only a practice, though we were lowered on ropes in a practice evacuation. Once we woke up to find a dead cow on the lawn; it had managed to cross the ha-ha and grazed on poisonous yew. For most of us, it was the first time we had seen the death of anything larger than a fly.

My parents wrote back, separately, also once a week. Most of their news was humdrum too: family members they had seen, parties they had attended and once the death of a neighbour. But they did have one exciting adventure, which my father meticulously noted.

It started with a phone call late one evening, on a day that a Romanian diplomat had been expelled for 'undiplomatic activities'. A man with a thick accent asked if he could speak to Arthur. My father denied knowledge of any Arthur at that address and the conversation ended in some confusion. Minutes later the phone rang again. It was, said the voice, Inspector Barrington from Scotland Yard who had heard about the previous call and asked for details. Not long after this came a third call, this time from a man introducing himself as Walter Partington of the *Daily Express*.

There followed a flurry of activity. My father rang Scotland Yard (Whitehall 1212) and established that Inspector Barrington did not exist. He spoke several times to the sergeant at Wimbledon Police Station. And he sent my mother next door to make some other phone calls, and perhaps to keep her out of any danger since the bogus inspector had said he was sending someone round. After that things went quiet.

My parents were shaken and puzzled by the incident. They never got to the bottom of it. Was it a hoax? An attempt by a newspaper to manufacture a story (one of their friends worked for the Beaverbrook press)? Or was it a real brush with the world of espionage my father assumed he had left behind? I thought it a wizard adventure, and one that brought home to me how much I was missing, stuck on top of that hill in Hampshire.

1.9: Beyond the Christmas truce

I quickly realised that confinement has one compensation: the unconfined joy when release comes. The journey home from my prep school for my first Christmas holidays lodges in my memory as a moment of near-uncontainable happiness.

We stopped our classes the day before, packed up our worldly goods (mainly clothes), and spent the afternoon playing trains in the basement with Gus. After a restless night and a hurried breakfast, we filed back into the same buses that three months before – and a lifetime it seemed – had disgorged us onto this isolated spot. The coach retraced its path past the lodge and through the hairpin bends to Petersfield Station, where we piled into compartments freshly re-stickered: *Reserved for Douai Junior School.*

Our train then raced through the wintry Hampshire countryside, into the outer London suburbs, under our very own train-spotting bridge, through Wimbledon Station and past Ely's Furniture Repository. We raced through rows of grimy terraced houses in Clapham and the small Victorian-built factories that dotted Battersea, all spewing smoke into the grey, still morning. I was back in the real world, among people whose lives were not confined to a hill-top in Hampshire.

Our parents were waiting at Waterloo Station: I had seen them only once since parting so optimistically in September. To my embarrassment my mother kissed me. My father had taken the morning off – though he still wore his bowler hat – and we all ate ice cream together. After this joyous reunion, we returned home to rediscover our possessions. David put his trains on the rails and I liberated my soldiers from their boxes.

We started to get ready for Christmas, the climax of the year. My mother had started the preparations some months before, this time without my help, clearing the kitchen table to stir the suet and dried fruits for her Christmas pudding. We had already sent her our lists 'for Father Christmas' (David had a few years earlier before disabused me of the myth) and she had gone on long shopping trips around the High Street, further afield to Ely's down the hill, and even on the trolley bus to Bentalls in Kingston.

We decorated the house together. My mother threaded the scores of Christmas cards so that they would hang in columns of pink legal tape. We added holly to the picture frames. We put up a tree in an upturned Chinese seat in the hall, draping it with coloured balls and little plastic bells and mock icicles made of lead.

We hung small lights, which this year as every year failed to start until David, now effectively in charge of maintenance, had sorted them out. This usually involved unscrewing them one by one until he found the one that had expired during the year. We also had the usual discussion about what should top the tree. Each year the fairy – a pink and chubby doll with frilly knickers and sparkly lace wings – had to be content with second place, just below the star. It was, my mother insisted, a Christian festival and the Star of Bethlehem had to have the highest place.

On Christmas morning we awoke to find that two large brown woollen socks – a pair that my father kept but never wore – had been carefully placed at the foot of each of our beds. The contents were predictable: a tangerine at the foot; then an assortment of small gifts, like pencils and sweets. They weren't much, compared with what we hoped was to come, but it was a start.

Later, after early church, we took the 93 bus to my grandparents' home in Putney, where, as usual, we met up with my uncle, two aunts and their respective families: six cousins – two older, four younger. As we assembled quietly in the back room, my grandfather slipped out to his room, where he donned a red dressing gown trimmed with cotton wool, wellington boots and a cardboard mask. Then he slipped down again, out of the back door and into the front garden where he would knock on the window.

This year, and every year, my mother and her two sisters gasped in false amazement. The children bobbed with delight, though my cousin Angela, seven years my senior, insists she remained terrified for many years. My grandfather, with his mask jiggling up and down on his face and showing no expression, would make a little speech in a strained false voice, always starting:

'Greetings to you one and all, I come to make my usual call... '

After that came the distribution and unwrapping of presents. The most expensive ones came from our parents, followed by a superior offering from Great Aunt Alice: one of my earliest gifts from her was a copy of *Hawthorne's Wonder Book* with stuck-in colour plates by Arthur Rackham. When I was older, she gave me a carving set that I still use and a monogrammed silver cigarette case that I don't.

We then set the stage for lunch. Men and children undertook the mass clean-up of ripped paper, and distributed glasses of sherry for the grownups, squash for us. Among the women in the kitchen, Uncle Philip, whose family owned a tearoom in Ealing, started to dismantle the turkey. In those days, the food amounted to a feast: turkey, ham, sausages, bacon, two sorts of stuffing, new potatoes from large tins, mashed potatoes, beans, carrots, cabbage, and of course a brown and gloopy gravy based on Bisto. David once told me he ate next to nothing the day before so he could make the most of it all.

For this day only my grandparents used a magnificent blue and gold-rimmed dinner set, Melsary pattern made by Booths of England. I still use it for special occasions: three sizes of plates, soup dishes, oval platters and serving tureens with accompanying saucers. I don't know how my grandparents came to have it, though I assume Great Aunt Alice and her contacts at Asprey (not to mention her aspirations for style) had something to do with it. I also assume they were seconds.

Only when we had finished the first course were we allowed to pull our crackers. They were generally disappointing, apart from the year that they contained miniature indoor fireworks that burnt holes in the tablecloth when we tried to set them off.

Then, with paper hats on head, came the final act in the celebration: the distribution of the Christmas pudding. The lights were turned off (dimming was not an option in those days). We could hear my mother and her two sisters scuffling outside the door. Then one of them flung the door open, holding a pudding ablaze with brandy. It was passed to Great Aunt Alice, who sliced, plated and carefully passed each portion in a clockwise direction. Within moments the room rang to the delighted cries of children finding a silver sixpence buried in their slice.

It was several years after I stopped believing in Father Christmas before I realised that this was also a fix. Great Aunt Alice was forecasting where each plate would end up, and on every child's plate she would quietly slip under the steaming chunk of pudding one of the shiny coins she had carefully collected and boiled.

After that the day wound slowly down. Finally, one of the uncles drove us home - full, tired and laden with presents. Boxing Day was an anti-climax as I played with, and then tired of, my new toys, and within a few days I started to count down the remaining treats before going back to school.

On the last evening of the holidays the four of us went to a carefully chosen show such as *Salad Days* or (less successfully in our opinion) *Kismet*. Before the event we went to a Lyons Corner House, where the queue wound slowly around a glass-fronted kitchen within which white-hatted chefs cooked bacon and eggs. On the following afternoon, we sat through the 40-minute loop of cartoons and newsreel in the tiny cinema at Waterloo Station. Then it was back on the 4.20 train to Petersfield.

I did this journey twelve times in all. On my first night back in my dormitory, as I tried to get to sleep, I went over in my mind what I had been doing one week before. It made the holiday last a little longer. But as the memories faded I settled down to a new nightly routine, counting the days until my parents would come and visit. And after each visit I started to count the days until the next holiday. From my bed I could hear trains passing in the middle distance, racing up to and under our railway bridge at Wimbledon and into the real world it represented. Those same trains could be heard from our house in Wimbledon, and I imagined my mother listening to them as well.

I am sure she found the separation as hard as I did. She was not from the class that banished its offspring for their own good, and it must have been particularly hard to watch her siblings bringing up their own children in their own homes. My father, on the other hand, clearly thought sending us away would be good for our characters, despite having hated it so much himself.

Towards the end of my four years at the prep school I took and passed the Common Entrance examination, earning rather higher marks than expected. Father Edward's final report was guarded: 'There seems to be no doubt that with the will to work he could go far in future studies'. Matron noted that I had successfully completed the course of growth hormone pills that a Specialist had prescribed for me. At 13 years and 6 months I was up four inches, but still only 4 foot 8.

And there was more good news from Matron: my sweaty feet, a frequent topic in her earlier reports, were no longer a matter of concern.

1960s: a tale of two certainties

*In which I endure schooling, enjoy education,
and find my views moving to the left*

Time line

1960   John Kennedy becomes president of the USA; US authorities approve birth control pill

1961   Yuri Gagarin goes into space; Berlin is divided by a wall

1962   Cuban missile crisis; Beatles issue first single: *Love Me Do*; James Bond appears in a movie; Robbins report recommends building new universities

1963   Great Train Robbery; John Kennedy assassinated; first *Dr Who* episode

1964   Sir Alec Douglas-Home succeeds Harold Macmillan; Labour wins the general election and Harold Wilson becomes prime minister

1965   Capital punishment abolished in UK; US sends troops to Vietnam; comprehensive education introduced

1966   Labour wins second general election; England wins soccer world cup

1967   First heart transplant; Che Guevara killed

1968   Robert Kennedy and Martin Luther King assassinated; student riots in Paris and other cities; Tet offensive in Vietnam; Enoch Powell makes speech forecasting 'rivers of blood'; Women's Lib demonstrators disrupt *Miss World* pageant

1969   Neil Armstrong lands on the moon; Edward Kennedy leaves the scene of a fatal accident without reporting it; Concord makes its maiden flight

2.1: Another decade, another hilltop

On a Tuesday early in September 1960, I left behind the long socks and long shorts of my childhood, and donned a two-piece grey flannel suit. I had been given the option of grey herring-bone but I considered that an adventure too far.

As with the previous four years, I had a journey to make. This time, however, it was not from the familiar Waterloo Station, with its electric trains snaking to and from the south western suburbs. It was from Paddington, hissing with steam and stuffed with Victoriana. As David and I dragged our overnight suitcases up the platform, shepherded gently by our mother, I recognised some of my companions from the prep school. Some had made this journey before; others like me were making it for the first time.

It was an older group than I was used to. Their voices were deeper. Many had started to shave, which was not something I was expecting to do for several years. They were bigger than me, with one exception. This particular boy was the same size as me and he had been at the school at least a year; I felt upstaged.

The train we boarded did not speed back through my beloved Wimbledon. Instead it set a firm line towards the west, past the semis of Ealing and the terraces of Reading, deep into the Berkshire countryside showing the first tints of autumn. After an hour or so we came to our destination: a long and empty platform, more of a halt than a station, in the middle of very little. The clue lay in the sign: MIDGHAM: FOR DOUAI SCHOOL.

As in my previous journeys a coach was waiting, and we were driven up a steep and bending road, past a pub, a newsagent, a manor house, a church and its graveyard, and a thatched cottage. As we reached the top of the hill, a squat, square, crenelated red-brick tower loomed in front of us, like a liner coming out of the fog. I had arrived at Douai School, which would be the centre of my life for the next five years.

The Victorian facade was a piece of misdirection. The school's origins went back 350 years to the reformation when a group of English Roman Catholics fled persecution and set up a Benedictine seminary and college in the small town of Douai in Flanders. For years the French government took pleasure in supporting them against the wishes of the British government. But as anti-clericalism gripped France in the early 1900s, the monks and their pupils were expelled. They moved to this hill in Berkshire, merging with a small Catholic school that had been established not long before. When I arrived, a half century later, it was a stable community, with 35 monks in the monastery and 230 boys in the school.

The tower was the official front door, but our entrance was round the back, through some wrought-iron gates and past the lavatory block. We called this important part of our life 'the jakes', a throwback to the slang of the Reformation. It was a cold and draughty place of dripping taps and leaking cisterns, with badly drafted pictures of scrotums appearing, usually briefly, on the cubicle walls. I clearly underestimated it; some three decades later it became a listed building and was converted into up-market and expensive flats.

If this was the school's digestive tract, its spinal column started a few yards away: an enclosed cloister of some 80 yards which served as activity hub and information highway. That first evening it was my first stop. For most of its length hung notice boards, on which were pinned sheets of paper giving our dispositions for the next 12 weeks. Where would I study and sleep? To which sets had I been allocated for my lessons? Which older boys would have power over me as prefects? How many of our Wednesday-night films in the gym would be war films?

On the other side of the cloister, facing the notice boards, were leaded windows through which could be seen a delightful, flower-laden quadrangle. It was strictly out of bounds, and I rarely saw anyone in it. I still don't know what its function was: perhaps it was there as an allegory of the Garden of Eden.

On a corridor off the cloister was the study hall – or in our slang the 'stew', spelt that way on the justification that it was there we 'stewed'. This was a bare-beamed hall containing a hundred or so desks, ingrained with the carvings of previous generations, on which we boys were arranged in order of seniority. There was a gap between the front and back desks, into which that first evening, and all evenings afterwards, the senior boys who had the luxury of their own cubicles trooped in for evening prayers.

As I was soon to discover, a prefect would station himself during periods of study on the raised desk at the side, an observation tower from which he could maintain order and silence. A few decades later this hall featured in the film *Three Men and a Little Lady*, in which a young American girl is consigned by her wicked stepfather to a cruel and old-fashioned English boarding school. It was chosen, I imagine, for its Dickensian overtones.

At the other end of the cloister was another bare-beamed hall: the refectory. This was filled with long tables and long benches, while pictures of stern and long-departed abbots looked down on us from the high walls, hung between the odd painting (or reproduction – it was too far up to tell) of Flanders in winter.

As new boys, our allocated tables were nearest the door and furthest from the kitchen. The food was brought to our tables by Irish skivvies, as indeed we called them. Then those boys seated at the top of each table dished out the food to those at the bottom. In an early lesson in social responsibility, at the end of each week the boys at the top moved down to the bottom while all the others moved up a place. With a slightly different social message, the fourth formers had to serve the prefects' table – rushing up mid-meal whenever one of them raised a hand to fetch them a jug of water or extra knife. Thankfully that was the closest we came to the public-school tradition of fagging.

Past the refectory, and accessed through another cloister, was the monastery. This was strictly out of bounds, except on rainy Sunday evenings when prefects marshalled us through in a long, dry column to the abbey church for Sunday services. There were no restrictions on traffic in the other direction, however, and the monks filled all the leading roles in the school: headmaster, deputy headmaster, housemasters, bursar, subject teachers, rugby coach, cricket coach. They filled an important informal role as well, materialising like Harry Potter dementors in their black habits and hoods, acting as magnets for groups of boys as they defused tensions and encouraged moderately good-humoured debate.

Headmaster since 1952 was Father Alphonsus Tierney, or Alfie as the school called him. He had cut his headmasterly teeth at the prep school, where he presided over what some later described as a country house atmosphere. Like Father Edward, his successor at the prep school, he was a rumpled cleric with a mournful aura, which reached its zenith one day when he realised that the touring theatrical company he had engaged to give a Shakespearean performance were a group of cross-dressing women of indeterminate age. Alfie lived alone in the entrance tower and kept his finger on the school pulse with thrice daily trips up the cloister to the refectory. He had a caring nature and an easy authority and, as I found out several times during my career, a knack of telling you off in such a way that you ended up feeling his pain above yours.

That year he appointed a new deputy, and he turned out to be a particularly gritty chalk to his cheese. Father Hilary Palmer, unlike most of his brother monks, had not been educated at the school. Before the war he had been a student in Paris, during the war he had been a navigator in bomber command, and after demobilisation had decided to become a monk. In his first assembly as deputy headmaster he announced that he would be in charge of discipline. He interpreted his brief with energy, patrolling the school at all hours, administering sharp-tongued admonitions for light offences and canings for others. He swiftly earned the soubriquet 'Paranoid Palmer'.

On my first night in my new school I settled down in my metal bed in one of the junior dormitories. I found the bed surprisingly comfortable, particularly on the first night of term when the sheets were clean and crisp. We each had a small locker (though I am not sure we could actually lock it) for private possessions, but no other personal privacy. We were allowed to bring our own extra blanket, which added a bit of colour; mine was brown.

Mostly we had it good

2.2: Last of the first

As the academic year unfolded, I tucked myself away in my now-familiar position at the bottom of the top stream. That year the stream was well stocked with clever fish, and my then classmates went on to have stellar careers: merchant banker, financial director of a major multinational, diplomat, senior international judge.

We worked in sets of 14-20 and studied traditional subjects, including Latin, but nothing new-fangled like art or drama. My English teacher was Father Dunstan, a short and moon-faced white-haired monk, whose nicotine habit left his fingers yellow and his black habit white-specked with burnt tobacco. He made us learn by heart large tracts of *Twelfth Night*, a practice that fooled me for several years into thinking that the main point of education was committing stuff to memory.

He thought I was lazy and gave me poor assessments. This was important because every second Monday the school assembled nervously in the stew to hear Alfie read out the names of under-achievers, the worst of whom were immediately sent to their housemasters to be caned. I escaped punishment, though came very near to it once. I was saved by what I later discovered had been a clerical error. Probably.

Science was new to me. I started well off the pace and stayed there. Father Wilfrid the physics teacher had come to the monastery with a PhD, and used his skills in such varied tasks as running a ham radio station and organising the monastery's telephone system. But his teaching was dry, and while some found it inspiring I floundered. He wrote in my report: 'Very slow worker; unlikely to make a success in this subject'.

This theme was repeated by the chemistry teacher Mr Tindle, a jolly man with a tweed jacket and a quiff of ginger hair who drove to school in a copy of Inspector Maigret's Citroen car with the double V on the front. 'He has worked well and with interest,' went one of his reports, 'but the pace of the work leaves him somewhat behind most of the time'.

Yet Mr Tindle did not have it all his own way. One morning in class he went off at a tangent to criticise the manufacturers of cloudy ammonia who made a virtue – and huge profits – out of what was an inevitably chemical imperfection.

'Sir', I asked, hand high and suddenly awake. 'Do you mean Scrubb's Cloudy Ammonia?'

'Indeed I do,' he said. 'Why do you ask?'

'Oh,' said I, eyes wide in innocence. 'My father's the chairman'.

I still don't know whether to be embarrassed or impressed. But within half an hour my brother David had sought me out to say that the chemistry teacher had already told the story to the headmaster who had already told him. I still don't know whether David was embarrassed or impressed either.

I tried to get involved in sport but, as at my prep school, I spent most of the time hovering on the fringes without my spectacles, watching fuzzily as the game played out without me. And there was a new problem: the communal showers we had to take afterwards. Being small was bad enough, but much more serious in my view was that, unlike most of my contemporaries, I was yet to show any signs of physical maturity in the nether regions. I was sure I would be teased about it. Whenever possible I used the swimming pool instead of a shower, which allowed me to keep my trunks on.

Despite the generally benign presence of the monks, we bullied and were bullied. There was little physical violence, though the threat was there. The ultimate sanction, it was whispered, was 'blacking': the threat of having your trousers removed and your bottom smeared with boot polish. I don't recall seeing this happen but when I went back 10 years later Matron did ask me if I remembered the day they took my trousers and buried them in the woods. I didn't of course, which means it was either a mistake on her part, or I had suppressed it.

What we had a lot of was what we then called teasing, but which nowadays would be called verbal abuse. I was mocked for my size of course, and in my second year for having a brother who had the temerity to be a prefect. But others fared worse. One boy in our class was particularly badly treated. He was bright and formidably clever with figures but socially awkward. It was said that he had come from a council estate and – even worse – was a socialist who read the *New Scientist*. For these transgressions we mocked him mercilessly.

One group, a few years older than me, was particularly sharp-tongued. One of their leaders, who terrified me, later became a well-known actor (and how I laughed when decades later he turned up on screen as a sadistic SS general). But when I looked at his web site while writing this chapter, I saw that he had written that he had hated his time at Douai because he was bullied. That was how it worked.

At the start of the second year I gave up sciences with great relief, and took up Spanish instead. By this time, the headmaster had decided that the top set, of which I was (still just) a junior member, would take its O-levels early, at the end of the upcoming Christmas term. My chances were not considered good so my father, in a praiseworthy attempt to motivate me, offered £1 for the first O-level pass (those were the days before they were graded) and doubling up thereafter. It was generally assumed that the offer was safe. To everyone's surprise, especially my own, I passed all six of my O-levels. My father paid me £64 (£1,250 in current prices), which he invested in premium bonds and a building society account.

As far as my academic career was concerned it was a false dawn. A small group of high fliers was creamed off immediately on a route to early A-levels and Oxbridge. The rest of us were given a gap half-year, taking one or two more O-levels (in my case Spanish and additional maths) with the rest of the time made up of subjects taken 'out of interest'. The definition of 'out of interest' came from the staff not the pupils, and I have no recollection of what the resulting subjects were.

I spent much of these two terms wandering up and down the cloister being, as Father Denis my housemaster described in a report, 'lost and weepy'. I realised that I not only had qualifications, but was also above the statutory school-leaving age. In the holidays I scoured the papers for jobs and when I found one I liked I pestered my parents to let me apply. The notion was quickly skewered.

So most evenings I would walk to the only pay phone in the building to make reverse charge phone calls to my poor parents, who must have dreaded the call. My state of mind comes through in a poem I wrote about this time for the school's literary (as opposed to official) magazine:

> Lonely but not alone,
> Able to talk yet unable to communicate,
> Tossed like the tinted leaves of autumn onto misty lawns;
> Hurled like a tiny shell over crashing crests,
> And plunged into depths;
> Clutching like the drowning one he was,
> At every little straw,
> To find this, too, eluded him, and left him once again,
> Helpless...

And so on for another 42 lines.

I upped the stakes by threatening to run away, which forced my parents to come down one Sunday to discuss my difficulties with Father Denis. My father brought with him my latest school report; I still have it and on the back he has jotted down some notes. His writing was always difficult to read and I cannot understand what he has written, apart from one word at the end: 'Therapy'. There was (and is) no question mark. Therapy never materialised; instead Father Denis recommended a crackdown. In his next report he wrote: 'Make him do things he does not want to do and make sure he does not get all his own way. I may be wrong but feel a little harsh treatment would do him the world of good'.

My saviour came from Father Martin, teacher of French to the second set and a fervent amateur photographer. He was – and you may start to recognise a current stereotype here – a portly monk with a lisp, thinning hair specked with dandruff, and a sweaty sheen. He took me and another fresh-faced boy into his darkened basement where I became captivated by the miracle of seeing images appear as we swilled bits of paper through the various chemical baths.

Some years later he left the school abruptly, though I have not been able to find out why. But I found him a patient teacher and a good companion, and it was from him that I started to acquire an interest in photography – as well as acquiring skills, friendship and self-respect. I never felt physically threatened by him – and I have no doubt that it was his care and kindness that got me through an extremely difficult time.

2.3: Meanwhile in the real world...

Back home for the all-too-brief school holidays, our daily rhythm played out around our father's routines, which changed little in 25 years. Each morning he took his bath, carefully 'softened' with a teaspoon of that impure Scrubb's Cloudy Ammonia. He then went down to the kitchen to eat his Grape Nuts, bacon and toast, having first flattened his hair with Brylcreem and tied a scarf over his head to keep it in place for the first 30 minutes of the day. We were oblivious to his piratical appearance and probably thought that most people's fathers wore bandanas at breakfast. A friend of mine who stayed overnight was quite perturbed.

'You could have warned me,' he said, once breakfast was over. Other house guests never commented; maybe they were too polite.

On five days a week my father took the train to Coleman Street in the City of London, where he practised as a property lawyer. For lunch he had a Guinness and a Welsh rarebit (later a smoked salmon sandwich) followed by a single square of dark Lindt chocolate, and a 10-minute (he swore it was no longer) snooze in his chair.

When he arrived home in the evenings he headed straight for the bathroom, washed, changed and came downstairs for his drink: a sophisticated Americano comprising one third Campari and two thirds Vermouth, with a flake of lemon peel, all meticulously measured. In his retirement, he poured it an hour early and left it standing until the magic hour of 6.30 when he gave himself permission to start drinking. Throughout all this he smoked, alternating between a pipe and strong-smelling Gauloises cigarettes. His liver and lungs survived the onslaught until he died of what appeared to be a broken heart, but that will come later.

My mother spent most of her waking hours cooking, darning, ironing, shopping. Her job was to enrich our lives. She encouraged David and me to take tennis and golf lessons, and walk together to the tiny cinema in Raynes Park. She also encouraged us to turn off our television in the evenings so that we could play bridge as a family. I partnered my father and David partnered my mother. I usually played my hand badly, which unleashed all kinds of family tensions. I have never played bridge since.

David spent his days working on his model railway. He built wooden trestles that went nearly round the room, painstakingly constructed both trains and rails, and wired up switches to a control board. I understood little of these things, and certainly did not share his passion or his patience.

However, when the trains were running I had an important job. Since the track never went right round the room, I was placed in a curtained-off area at one end. As the trains came in I turned them round and sent them back. We communicated by bells according to the standard code laid down by the Great Western Railway, a copy of which we both had in front of us. From time to time I made the trains crash, mainly for something to do.

I stopped putting my soldiers on manoeuvres and devoted my time to photography. I converted the long, thin room where successive servants had slept into a darkroom, placing my enlarger and trays of chemicals on a board laid across the bath. I spent contented hours sitting on a stool in the orange half-light watching black and white prints emerge, and listening to the BBC Light Programme, the BBC Home Service, and occasionally Radio Caroline. I also bought a floodlight and persuaded the daughter of our daily help to pose for my camera.

On fine days I would walk down the hill and spend a good hour, perhaps more, talking to the proprietor of Creamers, a small photographic store near Wimbledon Station, in the quiet times when he had no customers. He sold me a British camera – a Corfield – and a couple of weeks later the company went out of business. My father suggested he was working on inside knowledge; I hoped he was wrong.

Wimbledon village started to change. A Chinese restaurant and an Indian restaurant appeared; these were accompanied by scabrous stories that a cat had been found in one or other (or even both) of the kitchens. Then came a Steak House, part of a chain, housed in a modern building in an airy space trimmed with wood and brass. It offered a fashionable alternative to the family-run Italian restaurant down the road, and served modish dishes such as prawn cocktails and giant mixed grills. An exotic delicatessen opened, run by an Armenian family, offering delicacies for cocktail parties, such as smoked salmon rolled up and wrapped in brown bread. They also offered a new service: the food could be delivered to the door, along with crockery and cutlery on loan.

A Kenco Coffee House appeared down the hill at Elys Department Store. My mother was particularly impressed by the tomato soup: it looked and tasted like Heinz's soup, but had a glamorous dash of cream and a sprinkling of chopped chives. She started to run her own dinner parties, keeping lists of who had been invited, with whom, and what she had cooked for them. She bought a Hostess Trolley, which at a stroke obliterated the crispness of her roast potatoes.

David began to be invited to parties, and in preparation attended Mrs Thompson's week-long courses in ballroom dancing. I was hugely jealous for a year or so, until I was allowed to join. In a large room over a furniture shop in the High Street, I started to learn how to place my hand firmly in the small of a lady's back to guide her through the waltz or quickstep, or grasp her hand and twirl her with abandon for a burst of *Strip the Willows* or the *Gay Gordons*. It was my first prolonged encounter with the opposite sex since my days in the convent. I found it scary.

Our parents organised the occasional party for us, but they were staid affairs, with a disparate handful of the children of friends and acquaintances rounded up for the occasion. We danced to borrowed records on fitted carpets and ate sausage rolls and vol-au-vents filled with condensed mushroom soup. I still felt acutely aware of looking undersized and young. And I clearly hid it badly: many years later a slightly younger relative told me that his parents had told him off severely after he had remarked to my face that I was 'very small'.

In the middle of the decade our horizons expanded, literally. Until now we had relied on buses and trains and rides in other people's cars. My father had been part-owner of a car before the war, and occasionally spoke of the times he drove my mother around in MI5 pool cars. But for a reason he never explained, he no longer drove. David took his driving test as soon as he could, and my father bought a white Morris 1100 'for the family'. David could use it, but also was required to give my father a ride if he needed one.

By this time, I had been touched by death and disease. Nannie and my mother's parents died while I was away at school, and in all three cases my parents decided I should not attend the funerals.

It was not until a decade or more later that I learnt that the circumstances surrounding the death of my maternal grandmother caused great ill feeling in the family. Shortly before her death she agreed to her daughters' arguments that she should convert to Catholicism. A Jesuit was summoned to do the necessary and my grandfather later followed her example and also converted. My mother, her sisters and of course Great Aunt Alice were delighted, seeing it as a clear sign of the work of God. However, my mother's brother, my Uncle John, was incandescent. He told me later that he had had many conversations with his parents during which they had both insisted they would never consider becoming Roman Catholics. He thought it bullying and treachery and it must have compounded his grief.

Grief of another order appeared when Auntie Stella's third child, Elizabeth, died at the disgracefully early age of seven. I wasn't allowed time off from school for that funeral either. Elizabeth started to have headaches and there are pictures of her squinting through glasses at family parties. The doctors eventually diagnosed a brain tumour. David and I were told the full story, and knew that she was dying. Her siblings Susan and John were not told. When the inevitable happened, they were devastated.

Little did I know at the time that a similar scenario was being played out in my own home. My father had been active, still playing tennis from time to time, but then one of his legs started to feel numb. He went to see a neurologist and the diagnosis was grim. His GP wrote: 'You are suffering from a motor neurone disease', and added the rather weak compensation: 'although slowly progressing, there is no reason why you should not live for well over five years'. Shortly afterwards he received a letter from the insurance company saying that they would no longer accept his life insurance payments.

I was told only that my father had a bad leg and would have to wear a calliper. It was not until several years later that I discovered the diagnosis. I am sure the deception was a kindly attempt to save me unnecessary suffering, and in the event the diagnosis proved wrong. But I would have preferred being included.

2.4: Three long years

In September 1962, for the third year running, I alighted from the Paddington train at MIDGHAM: FOR DOUAI SCHOOL. I was a sixth former.

Being in the sixth form was not then the rite of passage it now seems to be, but it did involve some minor changes. I wore the same grey suit, but with the jacket buttons undone. I ate the same food in the same refectory, though being nearer the kitchen the food arrived earlier. I had privacy, in the form of a tiny cubicle that contained a bed, a desk and some storage space.

My brother David was still around, this time for a final term so that he could apply to Cambridge, and he was now head boy. Father Denis had left; it was reported with ill-disguised glee that he had met a woman. Father Martin replaced him as my new housemaster.

I had a new English teacher: William Bell, a scholarly man with a tilt to his head, a crackle in his voice, and an air of revelling in his reputation as an eccentric schoolmaster. He chose traditional authors – Chaucer, Shakespeare, Pope and Austen – and went through the text line by line; I don't remember many group discussions. One afternoon I primed several alarm clocks and placed them at strategic points around the classroom. Each time they went off, Mr Bell mistook them for fire drills and took us out of the building. For that I was despatched to Father Martin for six strokes of the cane. It was not the hardest punishment I was going to get.

My history teacher had no trouble in keeping my interest. Oliver JG Welch was the heavyweight of the common room, an energetic man with a forked beard, bow tie and the mild halitosis that (as I was to discover to my own cost some years later) comes from smoking small cigars. His sister Dame Werburg Welch was a Benedictine nun and artist of some note, and he had written our O-level textbook and a book on the French revolutionary Mirabeau.

We sat around him in the senior library as he gave formal lectures, pacing up and down while stroking his beard reflectively. These lectures were followed with essays and tutorials. He found some points of interest in my work: 'He has developed a certain sense of historical irony, though this at times degenerates into silly facetiousness.' My note-taking, he wrote, was 'sound, as well as being a work of art'. I should have taken the warning that I was concentrating on form at the expense of substance, but I did not.

In an attempt to find something I was good at, I threw myself into a wide range of activities. I ran the photographic club and organised the annual exhibition. With my eye for the under-populated niche, I had taken up fencing, and made it into the school team where one Saturday, under the watchful eyes of what in those days we called a 'detective', I beat the future Crown Prince of Jordan in a contest of sabres. I made it onto the school stage, in a cameo role as Messenger in *Murder in the Cathedral*, with a blacked-on beard and wearing hired boots with raised heels fresh from the feet of an extra in the recently released Burton-O'Toole blockbuster *Becket*.

On Saturday nights I carried on my great aunt's tradition by selling (though not for my profit) rosaries and prayer cards in a small repository. On successive Sundays I became a keen debater, taking sides on such issues as, 'The pure scientist is not an educated man' and 'It is pointless to follow fashions'. I discovered that I could keep an audience and make them laugh, though not always, which gave the task an edge. In my fourth year, which started in September 1963, I won the prize for most improved speaker.

That year my comfortable world view was challenged, as was so many others, by the assassination of President Kennedy. On the evening of November 22, 1963 I was walking up the cloisters to make my nightly misery phone call (reversed charges) to my parents. Half-way up I met Father Alphonsus coming the other way. He looked shaken and distinctly un-headmasterly. He told me the news. A few moments later, when I got through to my parents, I passed this news on to them. For once my own concerns did not dominate the conversation. My study of history had told me about assassinations, but I had not imagined they would occur in what we assumed was a civilising world.

The national mood was changing, with the aristocrat Sir Alec Douglas-Home replacing Harold Macmillan as Conservative prime minister and the technocrat Mr Harold Wilson becoming leader of the Labour opposition. Deference was replaced by debate and satire.

In the run-up to the 1964 general election the monks persuaded the local Labour candidate, David Stoddart, to come and give us a talk. We behaved disgracefully, shocking the poor candidate (later a government whip and Labour peer) with the vicious way we shouted him down. The few monks in attendance, not natural socialists and wary of a party that questioned the value of their school, gave us tacit approval. Our ringleader, later a prominent businessman, shook with the white heat of rage at the idea that our parents might not be free to buy us an education. David Stoddart had one champion: the scholarship boy whom we had bullied so ruthlessly when younger. We shouted him down, equally fiercely. Later the startled candidate spoke publicly and with some scorn on the rudeness of these expensively educated boys.

I was with the majority then, but signs of rebellion were stirring. I became a fervent member of the smokers' clique, which aligned me firmly with the dissident groups. I had grown to a more reasonable 5 foot 5 inches, but I still looked younger than I should have done. I imagined, foolishly of course, that smoking would make me look like an adult, and not just like a child with a silly habit.

Our leader was Manuel Ravassa from Colombia, son of a prominent Spanish family who had been on the wrong side in the civil war. (I found this out much later – we did not bother with back stories then). We had our favourite haunts: behind the bike sheds if in haste; in the cellar if it was dark and wet; in the jakes if desperate. Father Hilary, the fierce deputy head, set out to stop us, darting in to look under the cubicles in case we had a cigarette in our hand. Once I came out just as he was coming in:

'One day I'll catch you, Albert', he said.

He never did, though my come-uppance came. One afternoon, minutes before the call to tea, I was having a furtive drag behind a hedge when my old prep school teacher Father Augustine, now a housemaster at the senior school, came round the corner on his bicycle. He wobbled when he saw me with fag in hand and guilt on face. He said nothing, but that evening, just before lights out, Father Martin, now my housemaster, summoned me in my pyjamas, and gave me the maximum beating of eight with a cane. It was much more painful than the six I had received before, but curiously I felt proud that I, a self-professed wimp of the first order, had managed to tolerate the maximum punishment without tears. I have no idea whether Father Martin took any pleasure from the incident.

The odd thing was that smoking was not completely banned. Some years before, in less health-conscious times, the school had set up 'smokes' during which sixth formers could go and relax, cigarette in hand, in their housemasters' studies for the last hour before lights out. The tradition continued, though in deference to the latest medical studies smoking was now limited to pipe or cigar. I went every night to the 'smoke' for a sanctioned puff on a pipe, which turned into a surreptitious puff on a cigarette whenever Father Martin was called away. We joshed and listened to music, with some of the keener pop-pickers playing the air guitar and drumming without drums. The serious ones stayed in their cubicles studying.

At night I dreamed of going out with girls, and one evening in my second sixth form year my dream came true. Times were changing and the monks saw fit to arrange a dancing fixture (the only context we could see it in was as a sporting event) with Rye St Anthony, a Catholic girls convent school in Oxford.

For the event my friend Lightly and his stage management team transformed the school gym into a dance hall, using cricket nets festooned from the ceiling, hung with glass balls, and other maritime detritus intended to give a nautical feel. Around the side were tables where Father Romuald the bursar and his catering staff had prepared bowls of Twiglets, sausage rolls and - the latest delicacy - half grapefruits pierced with toothpicks of cheddar cheese and pineapple.

We moved warily around the edge of the gym, weighing up the opposition first then chatting nervously before pairing off and dancing to the Rolling Stones and the Beatles. As the evening wore on, the exchange of partners slowed, as in a game of musical chairs. As the monks innocently (or was it tactfully?) left for a cigarette, Caroline and I went onto the floor for the last dance. It was Ray Charles and Georgia.

The lights were dimmed. I looked at Caroline, she looked at me, and our lips met. It was my first kiss, albeit a chaste and closed-mouth one. My elation was only marginally dented some weeks later by a rumour that she was planning to become a nun.

I moved on, and a few months later found myself exchanging letters with another girl. My fellow-smoker Manuel had fixed this up for me. He was one of the few of my year who could reasonably claim to have a girlfriend, and they plotted together to find me a match. They settled on one of her school friends, who like me was harbouring ambitions of maybe one day becoming a writer.

We wrote for several months, and during one school holiday my mother came across the letters. Although she didn't read them I was embarrassed and threw them out. This was a pity since the correspondence of a teenage Libby Purves, now distinguished writer and broadcaster, would be of considerable interest nowadays, not that I would be ungentlemanly enough to reveal the content.

Girls were not everything; I had to start thinking about what I was going to do when I left school. We had a visit from the Public Schools Appointments Bureau in the form of a retired major who interviewed me and recommended a career in retail. To that end he procured a two-day familiarisation course with Simpsons of Piccadilly, the posh tailors in the iconic building in Piccadilly. I went with a schoolmate, and in the evenings he led me to a club in Soho, he ended up being a prison governor.

Reluctant to commit myself to a career in retail, I decided I wanted to study sociology. This came from my study of history, where I became more interested in the way people lived rather than in wars, treaties and accessions. I duly filled in my university application form, and without any interviews was offered a place at Edinburgh University. I worried because they hadn't seen me, and feared that I wouldn't fit in.

I need not have worried: I failed the grades by quite a margin. So I went back for a fifth year – seamlessly, as if my failure had been expected. In those days the response to failure was to carry on as before but harder, not to ask whether the task should be approached differently. I would dearly have liked to have walked away from that school - and I am sure I would have benefited. But the matter was closed.

On the first evening of my fifth and final year I scoured the notice boards that lined the cloisters and found that once again I had not been promoted to prefect. This was a blow that was not softened by my appointment as public man, a consolation prize of a job which involved walking round the school each night making sure that windows were closed and lights were out.

I did, however, get elected to the Thirteen club, an 'intellectual' discussion group set up by Oliver JG Welch to give pupils practice for university interviews. I went to the Imperial War Museum in my holidays and pored over files and microfiches to write a descriptive piece on the first and last days of the first world war. I won the Abbot's Prize for English with yet another angst-ridden poem, this time a dystopian sonnet about a man climbing up a municipal rubbish dump.

I continued to debate, and was voted most improved speaker for the second year running. The award for best speaker went once again to my friend Stephen Wall - tall, composed and clever, who later became Ambassador to the European Union and John Major's adviser on European affairs. In an improbable development, I was marked as a sportsman by becoming captain of fencing and then awarded my 'colours' as a symbol of my prowess.

By now most of the people I had studied alongside in my first term had left and were at university. I still tucked myself into my usual place behind the academic leaders, but this time they were from the next and younger wave of bright young men. I sent off my application forms again, and was offered a place at Birmingham University. I revised hard, which I interpreted as writing dates on little cards and trying to commit them to memory. I took the exams in the school gym for a second year, and waited.

My last evening did not come soon enough. Before we went to bed, three of us set our alarms for the early hours of the morning. We rose and dressed and wandered the grounds together. It was a clear, balmy night and there was dew on the ground. We reminisced about the past, and speculated about the future. I am not sure why we did it: a final act of rebellion, an assertion that we were now beyond the school's jurisdiction?

Whatever the cause, my joy was unbounded.

The next day I said my goodbyes. The fierce Father Hilary had the last word:

'The trouble with you, Albert,' he said, 'was that everyone was frightened of your tongue'.

If only he had told me earlier.

2.5: Free at last – but for what?

I marked my liberation by spending six weeks on my own in France. My parents had generously paid for me to attend a summer school at Grenoble University, which held so many fond memories for my father. I took the boat train to Paris, then the sleeper to Grenoble. There I stayed in one room in a house overlooking the river and the citadel, with a cable car whining repetitively outside my window. Beyond the citadel I could see the Alps. Every morning my landlady brought me a tray with coffee and croissant at an hour rather earlier than I would have liked. After this, and for the first time in my life, I was master of my own timetable.

Conscientiously, I started to attend lectures, but soon realised that their content assumed rather better language skills than A-level French. So I spent hours in pavement cafes mixing with fellow students from different backgrounds: French, Irish, American, Swedish, Algerian. We listened to recordings of Edith Piaf and Jacques Brel, went up in the cable car for picnics, and ate wholesome three-course meals in a ridiculously cheap self-service student restaurant (definitely a restaurant and not a canteen). I learnt how to hide my embarrassment at my American companions wearing Bermuda shorts, and I developed my skills of marshalling and delivering arguments.

I tracked down the woman who had taught my father French some 40 years before, and paid her a visit. Sadly she had lost her memory. But as I chatted to her husband we established that we had both been educated in the same red-brick buildings in the middle of Berkshire, though his time there predated by a couple of years the arrival of the Benedictines. Clearly my enforced home over the past five years was not going to let go of me that easily.

A few weeks later I headed home: I had been so frugal with my money that I had plenty left for a couple of expansive days in Paris. One evening I signed up for a coach tour for the *Folies Bergère*, which I considered rather daring. The show disappointed and I felt self-conscious.

My return was swiftly followed by two crashes. The first was my A-level results: they had improved only slightly, and were not good enough to take me to Birmingham. The second involved a 10-ton lorry. I was an hour into my first long solo drive, from Wimbledon to Pulborough, on my way to see my school friend Stephen Wall, when I fell asleep momentarily on a black spot bend at Beare Green in Surrey. I was whisked to Redhill Hospital where most of the glass was taken out of my face (one sliver emerged only 20 years later) and I spent the night under observation. I had been lucky.

That autumn I took a temporary job with the photographic company Agfa. This was not much of an achievement since the company was run under licence in the UK by the family business Scrubbs Cloudy Ammonia, of which my father was chairman. But his influence got me only as far as a mindlessly boring job of copying documents. After a few days I put my verbal skills to good use and ended up in what was an early version of a call centre. My job involved taking orders from retailers and sorting out supply problems. There were only four of us and we knew most of the callers so it was fun and satisfying. At one stage I acted as go-between between two of my colleagues; they later married.

After Christmas I took out the history books again. I commuted via the underground to a large house in Holland Park which housed Davies Laing and Dick, a crammers specialising in restoring academic success to black sheep from posh families who had messed up their A-levels. To be on the safe side I arranged to retake history A-level at two different boards.

My education took a new turn when my tutor, a slightly dishevelled former public schoolmaster, suggested one day that I might like reading a newspaper called the *Guardian*. Thus I was weaned off the *Daily Telegraph* and the *Daily Express*, and discovered a new world: Neville Cardus on cricket and music, Alistair Cooke on America, Norman Shrapnel on politics. I asked for the paper to be delivered at home. My parents sighed and paid, and took it as another sign of my accelerating decline.

At the end of the summer my protracted A-level career ended in spectacular failure, with a moderate C for the first set of exams - and then for the second one taken three weeks later, an O (effectively a failure). University was now out of the question. There was no Plan B.

Once the shock had sunk in, I (or more accurately my parents) started to look around for things I might be able to do. We combed the *Evening Standard* for suitable jobs, and one night my mother spotted an advertisement for young people who would be trained as chartered secretaries for the Central Electricity Generating Board (CEGB). It would, they told me, give me a profession, albeit one that until then I had not heard of. I had no counter-suggestion so I went along for the interview, in an office block next to the power station that is now the Tate Modern, and found myself hired.

I soon discovered how boring the world of work could be. It was one of those training schemes that look good on paper but in practice offer little more than sitting at a different desk every couple of weeks to learn about a department that can't find anything for you to do. I learnt some lessons but they were tangential, such as the existence of a whole department doing nothing but move other departments around the building.

I found my level in the basement, working in the reprographic department producing hundreds of different documents a week. It was the blue-collar part of the building and somehow I got on famously with my colleagues. I realised that I still wanted to learn things, so would bring in books from the library that I could read while sitting by the machines, waiting for when the paper had to be unsnarled.

In the evenings and at weekends I tried to make up for all the years of socialising I had missed. I joined the Young Conservatives, the usual destination for people of my age and class who needed to make new friends. We debated, listened to talks, and at weekends whizzed around the lanes of Surrey on treasure hunts. In the 1966 election I went canvassing in some tough flats down by the railway line. The residents were firmly in favour of giving Harold Wilson a bigger majority and another chance; so it turned out were most of the country.

At weekends I played cricket badly for a team on Wimbledon Common. I swept into amateur dramatics, joining a church group where I camped it up in *The Rivals*, playing the country bumpkin Bob Acres as a Kenneth Williams clone. 'He bounced round the stage like an overcharged dynamo', said the review. Our house became the place for post-rehearsal coffees, with my parents clearly relishing the company of young people that sending us away to boarding school had caused them to forgo.

My father was particularly buoyant. He was limping but no longer considered himself dying. His doctors had finally told him that since he was still alive their diagnosis was probably wrong. He never found out what had caused the paralysis, and he ended up blaming a particularly brutal osteopath.

A weekly diet of politics and drama, a daily dose of the *Guardian* and crashing boredom at work made me hanker after journalism. I applied for various posts and was interviewed for a trainee reporter's post in Ealing and a TV cameraman's traineeship for a London commercial station, both without success. I started popping into the office of the CEGB staff newspaper to ingratiate myself with the editor. He sent me off to do some interviews, though in my own time.

Then I had the good luck to meet Monica Morgan. She was probably not more than 10 years older than me, a fellow *Guardian* reader who had joined the CEGB as what we then called the personnel officer. She realised that I was as suited to my new career as a duck to concrete, and started to tease out of me the implications of going back to full time study, perhaps at one of the new-fangled polytechnics.

There was one serious obstacle. My parents had come to the conclusion that any further investment on trying to educate me would be a complete waste of my time and their money, which under the circumstances was quite reasonable. So Mrs Morgan arranged to meet my father for lunch in a pub by Blackfriars Bridge where he agreed, clearly with reservations, that he would support me if I managed to persuade an academic institution to have me.

Among the prospectuses I looked at was one from Surrey University. It had been given its charter that year as one of the new technological universities introduced by Harold Wilson's Labour government. It was being developed from the Battersea College of Advanced Technology, a stolid Victorian institution known for engineering and home economics.

What particularly interested me was a course called human relations. Its goal, according to the 1967 prospectus, was to produce social studies teachers and social workers. It would do this by teaching them 'the structure of society, the functions of social institutions, and explanations of human behaviour... together with the values which direct human relationships and social action'. For the first four terms, students would study philosophy, psychology and sociology, and then continue with two of these for another five terms. It seemed to be what I was looking for.

I drove the few miles from Wimbledon to Battersea for an interview and found myself face-to-face with a genial academic called Malcolm Wicks. He was an occupational psychologist who had been involved in setting up officer-selection procedures during the war and was now in charge of course admissions. We got on well, I soon relaxed, and somewhat to my surprise he offered me a place.

'What about my A-level grades?' I asked.

'They're fine,' he said. 'And anyway we'll take you as a mature student'. I liked this, particularly since I was 20 and still being asked on buses if I wanted a child's ticket.

Monica Morgan was delighted; my parents perhaps less so. She immediately took me off the training programme, installing me instead as her assistant. For three happy months I prepared exercises for the training scheme she was setting up: quizzes to help the new intake familiarise themselves with the building, and 'in-tray exercises' – fictional letters designed to expand their communication and problem-solving skills.

I visited her and her husband for several years but eventually the visits and the Christmas cards dried up and we lost touch. I have since tried to trace her without success; I owe her a lot.

That summer I crossed the Channel again, hitch-hiking with my friend Mike to the south of France. Unlike during my visit to Grenoble two years before, my immediate future was assured. I just had to make the most of it.

2.6: The joy of learning

My new and exciting journey started on the seashore of Greece. Not literally, but conjured up in my imagination at the start of my first philosophy lecture at Surrey University. On a gloomy weekday in October 1967, I and some 35 others filed onto the tiered seats of a wood-panelled lecture hall in which cohorts of engineers had been learning their trade since mid-Victorian times. At the front, owning the stage, was a white-haired gentleman of distinguished bearing. He was Dr James Welch, a former Royal Chaplain whom someone at this fledgling university had had the good sense to have co-opted as a lecturer on philosophy. His first lecture started:

'Imagine a Greek man standing on a cliff looking at the setting sun, and wondering where all this beauty had come from... '

I was hooked. Over the next few weeks he raced with us through the early recorded history of western thought: Aristotle who never stopped questioning until he took his own life; Plato, who planned to educate an elite who would run a perfect state; Diogenes, my favourite, who lived in a barrel and barked at passers-by. Not only had I not met them properly before, but a couple of months previously I had been locked into a job that offered me no challenges, no interest and no joy. Now my imagination was fired and I started to learn in a way I never had before.

Our tutors made it clear that assessment was to be mainly through course work. Instead of memorising the contents of textbooks in order to regurgitate them later under exam conditions, I went to the library – and started to read and listen and argue and write.

Each morning I drove in my black Morris Minor across the divide from middle-class Wimbledon to working-class Battersea. It was the kind of place I had been reading about in my pre-course book-list: a run-down inner city area where streets were being cleared and communities destroyed to make way for high-rise flats. The pubs were exempt from the razing on the grounds that they would be needed to rebuild the communities once the work was done. The college building stood out among the terraces and buildings sites, an island in a neglected backwater.

My fellow students were as unfamiliar as my surroundings. Most of them were men from state schools studying science and engineering. A minority was made up of what the university's 1967 report called 'girls' (though in the following year's report they had been rebranded as 'women'). Most of these were on my course, which had a ratio of 4:1 of women to men.

For once I did not feel like the runt of the litter. This had nothing to do with class or gender. I was a couple of years older than many of my course mates, and I knew I had just had a narrow escape from an unfulfilling life. I attended Freshers' week with great enthusiasm, which grew as the week progressed.

On the first day, as I sat in the lofty assembly hall, I heard David Varney, the outgoing president of the student union, speak enthusiastically of our new opportunities. He was acting president because – and the warning did not elude me – his elected successor had failed his exams and left. The election for his replacement had still to be held.

A few days later in that same hall I was impressed by a forthright speech from a guest speaker, a young-ish Conservative politician called Lynda Chalker. She was roundly booed, which as a Young Conservative I found unsettling. But I did realise that both speakers were of an altogether different calibre from the type of person I had been meeting as a CEGB trainee. Time proved me right. Sir David Varney (as he became) became head of Shell, British Gas and HM Customs and Excise; Baroness Chalker (as she became) was to become Minister of Overseas Development.

I volunteered to help with the *Surrey Guardian*, the university newspaper which came out every two weeks, give or take a day or two. It was run by a small group of human relations students one year ahead of me. They seemed glamorous, living and laughing together in a park-side mansion flat in the smart part of Battersea, and making references to all kinds of subjects that I knew nothing of. Within a couple of weeks, they had tired of student journalism and, for lack of any other candidate (after all, most of the students were scientists and engineers) they appointed me editor. I had rights to a small office in the university annexe, a former secondary school next door.

I launched into the role with enthusiasm and insensitivity. In my first editorial I made what was in effect an attack on my predecessors. Fresh from working with professional journalists at the CEGB, I thought the paper looked amateurish. I thundered:

'We shall need professionalism, not only to succeed but to survive...This will not curtail the freedom of the Student Press. At most it should prevent some of the more irresponsible abuses. Independence and professionalism are not incompatible. Together they make a more powerful and more valuable combination. What use is free speech if one can only express oneself badly?' (Surrey Guardian, 1967).

I took one practical step by persuading the subeditor from the CEGB newspaper to help. One evening Sam Weller (as he really was called) came down to one of the halls of residences where a group of us sat on the floor and made up the pages, under his supervision. The ensuing edition did look much more professional. But my attacks were continuing. A proposed arts festival had failed and the director had resigned: 'The whole affair reads like a satire from a right wing don', I opined.

That was my last editorial and my last edition. I was deposed. The putsch was led by David Varney in cahoots with an ex-vicar turned radical student. I can no longer remember the mechanism of my dismissal, but I do remember being devastated.

It was probably a blessing in disguise. My appointment had come too soon. The task, which came with no resources, was taking up a lot of my time and effort and I was finding it difficult to sustain. I learnt an important lesson: that professionalism was worthless without political nous. And I now had time to concentrate on what I had signed up for – to learn.

So I did. I continued to follow the development of western philosophy, though tragically without the guidance of Dr Welch who died suddenly in the Christmas holidays. I started to do a bit of philosophising myself, agonising over a mini-dissertation on capital punishment. I ended up rejecting the view I had been brought up with: that it was a good deterrent. Instead I came to the conclusion that the state had no right to kill in these circumstances, particularly since at times they killed the wrong people.

The study of experimental psychology took me into pastures new. Our lecturer was a serious young man, until recently a postgraduate student at Aberdeen University. In his first class he gave each of us a duplicated copy of a map of the centre of Bath, and tasked us to come up with a plan to relieve rush hour congestion over the main bridge. At first I didn't understand where that fitted in to psychology, though I soon realised that he was encouraging us to think.

The following week I found myself sticking pins into my fellow student Janice in an attempt to measure the perception of pain. This activity was not what I had expected either, but again I worked out the point. This was what science was – not a compendium of facts to be taught and regurgitated, but a way of increasing knowledge and understanding by asking questions and gathering evidence.

My third subject, sociology, proved to be the most challenging. With new-found keenness I had read most of the recommended books before the start of term, making me realise how little I understood about the world. I soon came to understand how little I knew about writing academic essays.

I wrote the first one for Mr MacDonald, who wore a tweed jacket, had his hair neatly parted, and reminded me reassuringly of a master in a public school. The essay came back covered with withering red-inked scorn. The main direction of the comments was that I should stop churning out platitudes and attitudes, and instead cite evidence and construct an argument.

As my first year continued I began to realise that many of my staunchly held beliefs were just that – beliefs. It finally came home to me that my privileged position was not due to the superior talents of myself and my family, but to the accident of birth. If that were so, then our privileges were clearly unfair. The figures on inequality startled me, particularly those showing how so few people owned so much. Like many others at that time I started to sip the heady cocktail of guilt and idealism, topped with a thick slice of anger at our parents' generation for letting things go so badly wrong, or so we thought.

There was plenty to become concerned about. At home Harold Wilson's government became bogged down in strikes. Internationally, the promise of a better, fairer world seemed further off than ever. We were horrified at the pictures coming out of the American war in Vietnam showing innocent people shot by soldiers or incinerated by napalm. We were terrified by the fact that all over the world those in power continued to develop weapons that threatened, at the touch of a madman's button, to obliterate our so-called civilisation.

Then came the remarkable spring of 1968. Young people – mainly of my age – started to demonstrate in countries all over the world: Spain, Poland, Czechoslovakia, Italy, England, Spain, China – and particularly in the United States. Some marched for better conditions for students while others marched against the Vietnam War. Many demonstrations were brutally suppressed, and again we saw the pictures on the television. In May came the biggest shock of all, when students and workers managed to keep Paris at a virtual standstill for a month. Big changes, it seemed, were coming.

At this point Brian Darling, one of our sociology lecturers who specialised in the sociology of France, cancelled his classes. It was clear where he had gone, and when he came back he seemed to have on his leather jacket the dust of the French cobblestones that had been prised out and thrown at riot police. He told us what our brothers and sisters were doing in the Sorbonne and why. When President de Gaulle made the last-ditch speech that saved his presidency, he talked us through the underlying imagery.

A few weeks later another Kennedy was killed. This time it was Bobby, who was campaigning for the US presidency. I heard the news one morning as I was getting into my car to drive to university, and we spent the first class, with Brian Darling, trying to come to terms with our shock. The distinguished *Guardian* correspondent Alistair Cooke had been on the spot and captured the moment:

> 'An exploded flash bulb maybe, more like a man banging a tray several times against a wall. A half dozen of us trotted to the kitchen door and at that moment time and life collapsed.' (Alistair Cooke, Another American Tragedy, *The Bedside Guardian 17*, Guardian Newspapers 1968).

By now I was regularly attending the weekly student union meetings, where debate was bitter and wide-ranging. Way out on the left was a small and well-drilled group of International Socialists, brimming with anger and making endless points of order. Way out on the right was an isolated Conservative, who wore a black suit and a tie and had his shock of blonde hair cut in the way of the Beatles. The more moderate students were on the left of the Labour party and I began to identify with them.

For the first year I lived at home, where ripples of tension began to emerge, particularly during Sunday lunch. The two lawyers in my family (my brother had decided to follow our father's calling) were critical of the '-ologies' I was embracing. In turn I argued that at least I was trying to make sense of the world, rather than dominate it with a set of man-made rules.

Once over the roast beef and Yorkshire pudding I threw in the line that Marxism was really the economic application of Christianity. I didn't admit that I had tried without success to read the old Communist's writings in the original, but it didn't matter since no one else around the table had read it either. My brother David batted back my arguments with what was then the standard defence: 'It sounds good in theory but it won't work in practice'. My mother failed to hide distress that her offspring were disagreeing so loudly, while my father watched in amusement and, I suspect, some pride. I found it less aggressive than family bridge and certainly more fun.

During the summer vacation I joined the working classes. This was not my choice. One of the founding principles of Surrey University – and probably a reason why it now sits among the top British universities – was that students should get experience of the real world. Part of our human relations course was to do 'routine work' for six weeks in the first summer holidays and produce a report on the formal and informal organisation.

I found a job at Shannons, a traditional family-run business that occupied a large factory just off the A3 between Wimbledon and Kingston and produced a wide range of stationery products. My place was on the shop floor with a team of mainly middle-aged women who made items such as ring binders by pulling levers and pressing pedals on ancient machinery. We were on batch production, which meant that we moved around our section of the shop floor doing different tasks. There were two men in my section, a kindly foreman called Arthur and a less kindly time and motion man in a brown coat who would come round and assess how long each task should take.

One of my jobs was to stamp cardboard covers into the form of a folder. I discovered that you could put two pieces of card into the press at the same time and, with only a fraction more effort, produce two creased folders instead of one. This made a nonsense of the standard timings (and the rate of pay), and I was transferred to another machine where I was allowed to rivet rings in the time-honoured manner. As my sociology books told me, I had reacted in a predictable way to an extremely boring activity, and my fellow workers had reacted in a predictable way by not allowing me to disturb their way of working.

Later that summer I booked in for a few days at a Dominican monastery in Gloucestershire. I was still a church-going and confessing member of the Catholic Church, but my recent discovery of reason and evidence had made me challenge some traditional views. I had some pleasant chats with the monks but my doubts did not disappear. Later I started to read the radical God-as-concept ideas of theologians such as John Robinson, the Bishop of Woolwich. I also became haunted by a small verse published by a fellow student called Fred Pipes in one of the university newspaper publications: 'I believe in God,' he wrote, 'But does he believe in me?'

My mental journeys continued for a second year, but with a few changes. I moved out of the family house to a small flat near Tooting, which I shared with my friend Bernard. The university was now split in two, with half of the departments (though not mine) now placed in what was effectively a building site 30 miles away in Guildford. My new-found social conscience had found an outlet: setting up a social action group within the university.

I was confident that our generation would soon start to change the world. But first I wanted to see a bit more of it.

2.7: The American dream

We were happy to go onto the streets to rail against the American imperialist capitalist running dog pigs – and we couldn't wait to visit them. In the summer of 1969 I flew to New York under the auspices of BUNAC, the British Universities North American Club. They organised the charter flight, provided an excellent guide, and ran a two-day induction course at a New York Hotel.

My first night stuck in my memory for years. I came out of the hotel where we had been booked, strolled up a hot and clammy street, saw smoke billowing out of a subway grill... and then a fire engine rushed past - siren blaring, ladders swaying in the traffic, firemen in their oversized helmets hanging on... I felt I had landed in a movie set.

It's a good memory, except that when I went back to look in my diary I read that this memory was itself a kind of movie, and that the incident with the fire engine did not happen until a few weeks later, and in Canada.

What did happen is that I spent the next few days with my father's recently rediscovered friend Richard Goldwater. He and my father had met on a transatlantic liner in 1938, and then lost touch. Richard was told that my father had been killed in the war. But in the summer of 1968 he had come to England with his second wife Maria, looked in the London telephone directory, made a speculative call to Sydney Albert, Solicitor – and they were reunited. We all went out to dinner and I took the opportunity to persuade him to be my sponsor for my trip to the USA.

Richard was a highly intelligent and well-read lawyer who usually spoke as if addressing a jury. He and his father (then in his 80s) still ran Goldwater and Flynn, the family law firm with a foot in two important New York ethnic camps. The family were staunch Democrats: Richard had served as a New York state congressman, and he kept in pride of place in his apartment a photo of his smiling father arm-in-arm with President Roosevelt at a Democrat convention.

That first weekend they took me out of Manhattan to their yacht in Connecticut. On Independence Day I drank gin, ate shellfish, swallowed Dramamine, watched fireworks from a raft of yachts by a wooded island off the coast – and slept through pitching seas on the trip back.

I had come with a three-month pass for the Greyhound buses, and left New York for Boston. I stayed with a former neighbour whose husband was a housemaster at Phillips Academy, a smart prep school nearby. Among their charges (whom I may have met but probably didn't) was a young George W Bush, who she says was an unexceptional student.

Later I bussed down to Washington where I spent a few days in the office of Congressman Bingham, a close friend of the Goldwaters. I was scheduled to stay overnight with another of their friends, a staffer for Ted Kennedy. At the last minute she cancelled and I had to stay elsewhere. One of her colleagues wanted to go to a party in New England. The colleague's name was Mary-Jo Kopechne, and the party was the one in Martha's Vineyard when she was killed in Kennedy's car after it had crashed off a bridge.

That was not the only slice of history being made around me. A few days later, as we passed through some mountains in Tennessee, the driver of the Greyhound bus snapped on his intercom.

'At this time the first American is due to be landing on the moon', he said.

Whoops of joy filled the bus. The event remained a source of pride throughout the rest of my trip. I noted in my diary the appearance of topical drinks such as Moontinis and Moonhattens, and when I returned to England I brought my brother a globe of the moon.

In Texas some ranchers I had met earlier that summer at a cricket match in England put me on a horse, handed me a rifle and told me to shoot a cactus which, to everyone's surprise, I did. I travelled to Flagstaff, where I teamed up with three English fellow-travellers I had met on the bus: an Englishman called David who was slightly older than the three of us, and Fenella and her younger sister Fiona.

We hired a car together and that night, on the rim of the Grand Canyon, Fenella and I snuggled up together. I travelled on with the sisters to Las Vegas, where my gambling career lasted five throws of the roulette wheel. We met up again in New England some weeks later; even in the days before personal phones, letters and landlines allowed us to make complicated romantic arrangements.

As I rode the buses I read the whole of *War and Peace*, slept a lot, and gawked at the passing deserts, mountains, lakes and cities. I still have five boxes of colour photos, though most of them are landscapes. There are no photographs of me in front of famous buildings, though there is one of me looking terrified on that horse in Texas.

In the buses, usually at night, I met soldiers on leave from the Vietnam war, students travelling to demonstrate against it, a man going home with a new leg, and a 16-year-old girl who, I confided in my diary, told me that the world was in a mess and that there was little anyone could do to change it.

Americans, I found, were extraordinarily generous. People I had just met bought me meals, guided me through museums, and provided me with 24-hours-worth of sandwiches. They introduced me to BLTs and McDonald's hamburgers, neither of which I had eaten before. I was taken to Chinese restaurants where I came across doggy bags and hot towels. I ate three Mexican meals and hated them all.

On several occasions I climbed into the cars of complete strangers for a tour of the city: the highlight was often the deprived and burnt-out scene of still-recent rioting. In Chicago I chatted to a young waitress who, after her shift had ended, took me to a park and showed me where she had been the year before when Mayor Daley's police had waded into protesters during the Democrat Convention.

After four weeks travelling, from east coast to west, I arrived in Pasadena, a hot, smoggy and well-heeled suburb of Los Angeles. My university course had required me to use this long vacation to experience something 'vocational', so I had persuaded my friend Martha, recently relocated from Wimbledon to Pasadena, to see if her father could fix me up with a job on the local newspaper, for which he was the insurance agent. He got me in, but only as far as the advertising department.

Within a few days I talked my way up into the newsroom (my diary doesn't say how, though it was probably through persistent nagging). On my second day in the newsroom I came in complaining about my eyes and nose and chest, and someone suggested I should write a piece comparing Los Angeles smog with London fog. I did and they published it, under the headline: **Blimey! Oh for Some English Fog**. (*Pasadena Star News*, August 21, 1969).

I was taken under the wing of the resident humorist, a middle-aged man with a beard, a generous nature, a talent for comic writing and a proper humorist's name: Russ Leadabrand. He suggested that we should write a joint piece, in which we would independently write answers to a 'questionnaire' he devised (but attributed to professors from the totally fictional Miskatonic University). Questions ranged from 'How do you greet each new day?' to 'Do you think that English women are the world's most beautiful?' I found it hard going, but we ended up each with little pieces to each question and had a joint photograph taken; the article was published on the front page of the Sunday feature section under the title: **Slippery hands across the sea** (*Pasadena Star News*, August 31, 1969)

I then found myself being sent on all kinds of assignments – and writing about them. At an old people's centre I was outplayed by octogenarians in shuffleboard and pinochle (**British Lad Toppled Off 'Centre'**). I attended a Canada vs USA cricket match (**Our Lad Explains Cricket – We Think**). Following an invitation from their press department, I visited the noted higher education institution Caltech (**Our Briton Goes Looking for Famed U.S. Egg-head**). I struck up a friendship with members of the local police force who allowed me to ride in the back of their police cars. We sped, siren blaring, to investigate a call where a gunman had allegedly been seen; we found no trace of one.

I received fan mail. One published letter referred to 'those adorable articles… by the boy from England. Such a darling point of view'. Another came from a 16-year-old who described herself as a 'black aquarian' and, despite being born in Cleveland, was really a displaced Briton who should have been born in Liverpool.

'The deeks downtown give me odd looks when I walk into the stores and say in my poor imitation Cockney (it'll fool them, every time), "Pardon me madame (sic), but could you direct me to the loo", she wrote.

One lunch time a waitress, hearing my accent, asked me if I was that English student who was writing all those articles.

On my last night in Pasadena, with a hired tuxedo and haircut both paid for by the paper, I escorted Beverley, the junior reporter in the Society section, to a grand ball celebrating 200 years of the state of California. The host was the state governor, some second-bit actor I hadn't heard of called Ronald Reagan. In my piece (**Our Tim Goes to the Ball**) I described turning up among the Bentleys and Cadillacs in our red Toyota to be greeted by a fake beefeater and a (probably) fake priest who directed us to the ballroom.

> '…Down in the lobby was Old California. Cellophane-wrapped oranges ripened on plastic trees. A picturesque well with real water glistened in the artificial light. A genuine stagecoach stood deserted, as if it had been ambushed with flowers on its way to the kitchens.

> 'Among these the costumes of the male and female guests looked splendid – and dangerous. Sequinned pants threatened to rip neatly sewn frills; ornate gun belts threatened to rip well-disguised bodices; large sombreros threatened to rip spotless white lace mantillas' (*Pasadena Star News*, September 7, 1969).

On my way back I wrote several more articles about my travels for which the newspaper had paid in advance. When I got home I was sent a cutting in which Russ Leadabrand bade me farewell:

> 'One of the pleasures of this summer has been the visiting in the office with Tim Albert, an English chap, who somehow got on our staff for a few weeks...Next year there will be more Englishmen over here. They'll come because Tim Albert was here and took home with him fond pictures of the Hyperion Sewage Outfall, Wilmington's Backwater and the gravel pits at Irvindale... I wish him Godspeed on his plan to picket the Tower of London when he gets home.' (*Pasadena Star News*, October,1969)

2.8: A degree of success

As the weeks went by my American dream receded, though with one sharp
reminder that the world can be smaller than we often think. A few weeks after
my return, I spent the weekend in Wimbledon and on the Saturday night my
father invited to dinner the sister of his old school friend from Charterhouse.
At one point she started telling us about her nephew.

'He was engaged,' she said. 'To someone called Fenella. But she went to
America with her sister and I think she met someone there at the Grand
Canyon. Anyway she's called the engagement off'.

I probed gently. This was indeed the same Fenella with whom I had shared
some happy times on the rim of the Grand Canyon, at the tables of Las Vegas
and under the autumnal leaves of New England. I blushed, and then kept
quiet.

Back at university I stuck my cuttings into an album, added some
generalisations about humour, and submitted the whole as my summer
project. I concluded about my articles: 'Whatever their artistic value they did
enable me to see a country'. They were also about to enable me to start a new
career.

For this, my third and final year, I lived in a hall of residence in Guildford.
My new home was in a square utilitarian building in the shadow of the
cathedral. There was an angel on top which was lit up at night, and its soft
light seeped through my curtains. My room was comfortable enough, if small,
and my friend Bernard happened to be in the room next door.

This was the university's second year on its Surrey site. The hardships may
have been fewer than in the previous year, when even fewer buildings were
finished and staff and students had to take their meals in a tent. But cranes
still hovered overhead and building sites were still blocked off. As the year
progressed we extended along new roads and into new buildings. By the third
term we had bricks-and-mortar campus restaurants.

But for the whole year there was no student union building and only one
bar, in the administration building. This served students and staff together and
(along with Peter Leggett, the well-respected and inclusive vice-chancellor)
was one of the main reasons why relations between the two groups were
calmer than in many other universities at the time.

In my first term on site I was heavily involved in the community action group, which officially started with 120 students volunteering to become involved in the surrounding communities. The problems we found in Surrey were not like those in Battersea, but there was plenty we could usefully do. Early tasks included tidying the gardens of the elderly and researching what the disadvantaged of Guildford really needed. One late autumn evening a posse of large forwards from the rugby club provided the heavy lifting for a special shopping evening that the Rotary had organised for wheelchair users in the town.

We also supported a young charity called Crisis at Christmas, for which my brother David was one of the first steering group members. At Surrey we organised a teach-in on homelessness in the cathedral and a fund-raising walk up to London. Lord Robens, the chancellor and former head of the Coal Board, saw the walkers off in appalling weather; Peter Leggett, the vice-chancellor, was among the 57 taking part. I sped up and down the A3 checking on their progress and keeping dry.

After Christmas I concentrated on my studies. In psychology I was introduced to Kelly's personal construct theory, which turned the understanding of people away from past and present trauma and onto how they tried to make sense of the world. With Malcolm Wicks, the industrial psychologist who recruited me, I studied practical issues such as careers guidance, selection and training techniques.

As part of our criminology course a group of us visited HM Prison Grendon Underwood, a controversial place since its stated aim was not just to confine prisoners but to help them. Many were serving life sentences for murder, and we were warned in advance not to dig too deeply into the circumstances. They were charming hosts, the food was good, and it was a convivial evening. The women in our party were made particularly welcome.

One of the main events that year was the launch of Apollo 13 in April. I followed its fraught journey back following an explosion within the spacecraft, listening on my small transistor radio in between my final revisions. A few weeks later my radio saw more heavy use as news came through that American students had been shot at Kent State University while demonstrating against the Vietnam War. I, like many students all over the world, was outraged.

My world view was changing but I still wore a jacket and tie (though seeing photographs of the campus at the time I was surprised to see how so many others did too). My taste in music was classical, which is why I was one of the few Surrey University students of the time who does not claim to have been present at the landmark concert in 1968 when Led Zeppelin gave their first-ever performance. I was less worried about looking young, but these anxieties were being replaced by concerns that I came from a privileged class.

Sex was around of course, and there was a rumour that outsiders were allowed to stay overnight, but that if caught the penalty would be a five-shilling bed and breakfast fee. Drugs were around too, but I kept well clear on the grounds that I was having enough problems with my addiction to tobacco. This was not seen as anti-social in those days; indeed the student newspaper reports a pipe-smoking competition sponsored by Imperial Tobacco, with entrants being given a clay pipe and half an ounce of tobacco. The winner puffed for one hour and six minutes.

I had to decide what I wanted to do. A year before I was convinced that I would become a social worker. Now, with the buzz of being a celebrated journalist in my recent memory, I was not so sure. I decided that I should have a shot at journalism first, on the grounds that it would be harder to get into. I applied for the four major training schemes: the *Sunday Times*, the *Daily Mirror*, the BBC and Reuters.

The *Sunday Times* called me up for a preliminary interview in its offices in the Gray's Inn Road. The interview seemed to go well until suddenly the interviewer looked straight at me and asked:

'How do you feel about blood?'

I stammered, and said I probably felt OK. I assume now the question was: 'How is a fresh-faced boy like you going to cope with car crashes and murders?' If he'd asked that I might have done a bit better. But I realised as soon as I had stuttered a confused answer that this particular application had gone as far as it was going to go.

My next set of interviews went better. They were with the *Daily Mirror* group and the selection process took place in a London hotel a few hundred yards from my previous interview. We were put up overnight, given some group work, some psychometric and general knowledge tests, and one-to-one interviews.

There were hundreds of applicants and six places. I got the seventh, but within a few days someone dropped out and I was offered a place. I accepted at once, partly because I had been impressed by the selection procedure and partly because the scheme offered two and a half years working on local papers. This, I judged, would teach me all the basic skills I needed. I was still being considered by two other schemes – the BBC and Reuters – but I thought they offered a more narrow training, and I withdrew.

Not long after my interview came my final examinations. I still have my exam papers, marked with some of the questions I answered then, but certainly couldn't now.

- 'Examine the evidence of the convergence of sociological and psychological theories in current attempts to explain any one type of social deviance.'

- 'Discuss the part played by religious beliefs and religious bodies in Latin America in accelerating or hindering social change.'

- 'The major problem of sociological research is the interaction between the investigator and the individual or social group being investigated. Discuss.'

With my track record on examinations I would have approached this with a certain amount of terror had it not been for an enterprising experiment. A few days before each examination the questions were posted on the notice-board. The idea was that it would reduce the element of chance and be fairer; of course the standard of answers would be expected to be higher. This practice was stopped soon after.

My last exam took place in the morning of the 1969 general election. When it was over I drove back to Wimbledon where I had volunteered to drive people to the polls. Four years before I had been canvassing in the same area for the Conservative party; now I turned out for Labour. We were confident that Conservative governments were a thing of the past and that Edward Heath would not unseat Harold Wilson. We soon discovered that we were wrong. It came as a shock.

A few days later, as we were all winding down after our exams, I ended up around midnight playing *boules* on one of the completed pieces of lawn. I stepped back to admire my shot, not realising that I was in the area where the drop was not one foot but four. I ended up with a broken arm in a sling.

But things got better. When the results came out I had got the 2:1 degree I had been aiming for. Furthermore, and against all my history, I was a Bachelor of Science.

1970s: a brave new world, coming soon

*In which I embark on the reporter's trade,
mix with the big boys,
lose one love and gain another*

Time line

1970 Four students shot at Kent State University; Edward Heath defeats Harold Wilson; Beatles break up

1971 North Sea oil concessions auctioned; UK goes decimal

1972 Miners' strike prompts three-day working week; terrorists attack at Olympic Games in Munich; Watergate scandal begins; President Amin of Uganda expels Asians; pocket calculators introduced; Invicta Airlines Flight 435 crashes in Switzerland; 14 killed in Northern Ireland on 'Bloody Sunday'

1973 US pulls out of Vietnam; Great Britain joins European Economic Community

1974 President Nixon resigns and Gerald Ford becomes president of the United States; Harold Wilson wins two general elections; UN conference on population in Bucharest

1975 Microsoft founded; Helsinki Accords signed

1976 Jimmy Carter elected president of the USA; Soweto uprisings in South Africa; Harold Wilson resigns and Jim Callaghan becomes prime minister; Muppet show premiers; the long hot summer creates water shortages in the UK

1977 Lord Avon (former prime minister Sir Anthony Eden) dies; Elvis Presley found dead; Steve Biko killed in South Africa; first *Star Wars* movie released

1978 Louise Brown, the first test tube baby, is born in Oldham; deaths of Pope Paul V1 and Pope John-Paul I; election of Cardinal Wojtyla as Pope John-Paul II; 912 die in Jonestown massacre

1979 Ayatollah Khomeini becomes leader of Iran; Margaret Thatcher becomes prime minister of UK; Bill Moggridge designs first mobile computer; Lord Mountbatten killed by IRA; Mother Theresa awarded Nobel Peace Prize

Mostly we had it good

3.1: A cub in the classroom

September 1970: another decade, another autumn, another journey. This time I did not take a train, but drove myself in my nearly-new red Austin 1300, guided by a route map provided for me by the RAC as part of their service to motorists. In the back of the car was my growing pile of treasured possessions, including a transistor tuned permanently to Radio 4, a typewriter already showing signs of wear, and a green tweed suit that I thought would help me to blend unobtrusively into country life.

Setting off from the suburbs of Surrey I drove across the Wiltshire plains, past the slabs of Stonehenge, through winding Somerset villages, and then right across the rolling Devon countryside to the county's south western perimeter. This time I did not fall asleep at the wheel. What kept me awake was a combination of frequent stops and the excitement of my imminent transformation from a student wanting to change the world into a journalist wanting to report on those changes.

Late that afternoon I signed in at the Plymouth YMCA and met some of my fellow trainees: the men. Later still, in a local pub, I met the women; with due propriety they had been billeted away from us in carefully selected B&Bs.

There were 15 of us, and we were an eclectic bunch: graduates from traditional Oxford and revolutionary Essex universities, an ambitious young graduate from Belfast who had already cut his teeth reporting 'the troubles', and a school leaver who had played one of the twins in the 1963 film version of *Lord of the Flies* – and who clearly missed being with his brother.

The training scheme was the pet project of Hugh Cudlipp, legendary editor-in-chief of the *Mirror* newspapers and at the time chairman of its parent company, the International Publishing Corporation (IPC). He had decided that the future of British journalism required a training scheme.

He bought half a dozen small local papers in Devon and staffed them with experienced executives, many from the *Sun*'s pre-Murdoch days. He added a couple of experienced trainers from local newspapers. It was one of the few places you could get a sustained training in journalism, and this scheme went on to produce editors of tabloid newspapers (David Montgomery and Tessa Hilton), a Labour minister (Chris Mullin), a prime minister's spin doctor (Alastair Campbell), a prize-winning investigative journalist (Nick Davies), leading thriller writer (Val McDermid), and a chief executive of the Mirror Group itself (David Montgomery).

Our early weeks were anything but glamorous, however, and we were impatient to carve out our careers. One of us rashly put a notice saying PRESS on his car. Within hours, someone else had finessed his gesture by placing a button next to it on the windscreen.

For the first three months we studied full-time. We spent most mornings in a draughty church hall under the lee of Brunel's Royal Albert Bridge in Torpoint being drilled in shorthand outlines by Mrs Furze, a kindly middle-aged woman whose only previous experience had been with would-be secretaries. In the afternoons we decamped to a training room in the offices of the *Sunday Independent*, a regional tabloid newspaper and flagship of the west-country editorial fleet. On some days Mrs Furze taught us touch typing to the rhythm of once-popular tunes.

At other times our journalism trainers, Geoff Harris and Bill Wood, taught us the basic tenets of the reporter's craft: how to record the salient facts in our notebook (and for legal reasons to keep them there for seven years); how to tell the story in the first paragraph then develop it with facts and enliven it with quotes; how to keep our words common and our sentences short.

From time to time we were taken out of the office for some make-believe reporting, such as a mocked-up car crash or an interview with a bomb disposal officer. At other times one of our trainers would take the part of a local dignitary in one of several carefully-crafted exercises, such as this one:

'You have been sent by your paper to the Mechanics' Institute, Massingham, for the weekly meeting of Massingham Literary and Scientific Society, held at 7.30 p.m.

'The speaker is Dr W.J. Makepeice, headmaster of St Adrian's Grammar Schoool, Massingham.

'Take notes in the normal way. You are expected to take a selective – NOT a verbatim – note. Average speed of delivery will be 88 w.p.m., dropping to 72 w.p.m. or rising to 120.

'Will you please then write a story of 400 words, finishing by 11 a.m.'

The unconventional spelling of the headmaster's name was a deliberate trap; several of us fell into it. Our stories were later returned with careful comments at the bottom. Mine included the following: 'I would have liked to have seen fairly high in the story a slightly longer quote...Having been told *what* is happening the reader wants to know *why*...This seems to me to be reporter's comment introduced in the middle of a straight news story – and quite unnecessarily'. Ouch.

I found the training hard. In a waspish article I wrote a couple of years later for the *New Statesman* (well, it had to be waspish for the *New Statesman*), I described it as a slow climb down from ivory towers.

> 'When a police car sirened through it was no longer the fascist pigs maintaining their repressive hold over the proletariat, but a possible page lead for the morning, perhaps even a sex-test-mercy-dash to flog to the nationals. Since the chosen trade was black and white, things had to be seen in black and white. Intelligence couldn't remain a disputed concept, held with learned reservations and references. It had to become simply 'brains' if it was to give the headline the right shape'. (Tim Albert, Learning the IPC way, *New Statesman*, March 6, 1973).

I thought about leaving the scheme and may well have done so had it not been for Mike Tillson. He was a clever, sensitive man with round, rimless glasses and an unfashionable crew cut, who had fought in Italy in the last year of the war, studied in Oxford when it was teeming with gifted ex-servicemen, served as west-country correspondent for the *News Chronicle*, and then taught French and Italian in one of the smarter schools in Exeter. When he moved to Cornwall with his second wife he became a part-trainer, part-reporter.

He was one of the few graduates on the staff (perhaps the only one) and his thoughtful and principled approach to writing was based on the difficulties of balancing the private right to privacy and the public right to know. Over the next few years we had many long chats together. I often wonder how, 40 years later, he would have viewed the practice of phone-tapping by reporters.

As Christmas approached I assuaged my social conscience by organising a weekend fast in a Plymouth Square in aid of Crisis at Christmas. We were joined by various people including an American curate and my friend Joan from university who was now a social worker at the other end of Devon. My colleagues and employers were supportive, and we made the most of our emerging skills to get local publicity.

On the last morning, the Royal Marines came and cooked a gloriously fatty fry-up over little stoves – our break-fast. A few days later we were sent home to be fattened up still more by our families before being released into the wild as cub reporters.

3.2: On the local beat

A few days after the first Christmas of the 1970s I found myself trudging up a winding path on the edge of Dartmoor. Snow was on the ground. Gusts of wind tugged at my new overcoat. I could see the lights of a small cottage just ahead; otherwise the night was country-black.

Suddenly, over my right shoulder, came a rushing of air and a clanking of chains. An intolerant bull? The Hound of the Baskervilles? The Hairy Hand?

It was hairy all right, but a goat, tethered with a chain that jerked it to a halt, just inches from sinking its horns into my urban buttocks. Rampaging goats had not been a hazard on Wimbledon Common and I was terrified. But I trudged on through the snow, fearful and shaken, to where it looked as if warmth and safety beckoned. Finally, reaching the front door, I knocked.

'G-g-g-good evening,' I stammered, with words chosen carefully in the warmth of my car. 'I am from the *T-t-t-tavistock Times*. I am very sorry to hear that you have recently lost your wife and I wonder whether I could ask you a few questions so we could publish an obituary.'

'If you are from that paper that is now owned by the *Daily Mirror* then the answer is: No. Goodnight.' And the cottager slammed the door.

My career as a reporter had begun.

I and three other trainees had been assigned to the *Tavistock Times*, a weekly paper serving a mainly rural community on the western edge of the moors. Duncan was a former member of the National Youth Theatre, who lived in an old flying jacket, moved on to become a TV presenter, and ended up in Hollywood where he was killed in a forest fire trying to save his cat. Chris was a fine linguist and the proud son of a bus driver; he went into television and became head of the London Bureau of *NBC News*. Esther was straight from a Devon grammar school and conscious of being 'only' a school-leaver; she was the most talented writer of us all and later got a first-class degree in English and became a books editor.

The four of us rented a cottage in Lydford, a rambling village on the edge of Dartmoor with a gorge, ruined castle, two pubs and a small private hotel. Our cottage abutted the hotel, with a door that gave us entry into the bar, and we went through it most evenings. There was little passing trade, though once we had to transform ourselves into waiting staff when an all-male group turned up on the wrong night for their dinner and blue film. (Esther was sent back to the cottage while the latter was showing.)

Often there was only one other person in the bar: Farmer Dawe, who at one stroke could imitate a hunting horn and knock back a double Glenfiddich. He told us stories of when he rode across the moor with the 'Mad Axeman' Frank Mitchell, an infamous East End criminal sprung from Dartmoor prison four years previously by the Kray brothers and later killed, probably by them. But we found out no more about the murderer other than he had been a charming person to ride with.

Every weekday morning we drove the six miles over the moor to our office in Tavistock. Over a bacon sandwich and a mug of Nescafe – and under a sign stating ACCURACY IS EVERYHTING – we would scour the *Western Morning News* for births, deaths and any other events that could conceivably be tied in to our circulation area. After we had followed these up, we were sent out to cover the 'diary' engagements.

Court cases were generally dull – shoplifting, drunken assault, non-payment of rates and parking offences – though Esther did once find herself covering a case of lewd activities with a sheep. (This time she was not sent back to the cottage.) But our reports sometimes had unintended consequences, as when I wrote that my local supermarket (in fact the only supermarket) had been fined because of maggots in a pork roast.

'I bet pork sales have gone down this week', I gloated to the manager.

'Not at all' he said. 'They rocketed.'

Council meetings were duller even than court proceedings, at least to us. That was probably because, as newcomers to the area, we had to make sense of heated discussions on where to place a street light or whether a caravan could be kept in the front garden. Councillors took themselves seriously and debated hard and fast, often too fast for us to understand the ramifications. They also went through our published reports with eagle eyes, complaining immediately if we had got something wrong.

When not covering formal events, we were turned out into the streets of Tavistock and surrounding villages to do 'the calls': to vicars, headmasters, duty sergeants, shopkeepers, and of course publicans. They rarely fed us anything more exciting than music exam results and plans for jumble sales.

Years later I heard from one of my professional contacts that while I was covering his patch he had to rescue a neighbour from a coal cellar after his wife found out he was having an affair, and protect another neighbour from a shotgun-toting husband for the same reason. He also had to keep quiet about two local worthies who were found guilty of sheep rustling. They were convicted in a court outside our area and he told me nothing of it for 30 years.

Since I had the most reliable car I was given responsibility for a special edition of the newspaper that went out under the title of the *East Cornwall Times*. The main town was Callington, where a new firm called Ginsters was starting up – making Cornish pasties and selling them to the nation. We weren't sure there would be a market for them.

My patch came with a fiercely independent and untrained local correspondent called Mr Maker (a great source of mildly blasphemous puns in the office) who filed regular reports on the activities of a strict Christian organisation called the Brotherhood. My reports, on the other hand, were secular and sometimes troublesome. One of the most controversial was our campaign for a youth club, which earned me the *sotto voce* threat (not entirely in jest) of being tossed on top of the Maypole.

Around Callington was a selection of hamlets, farms, riverfront and disused mines; it was a long way from the city of my birth. One afternoon in the tiny village of Kelly Bray I started talking with an old woman wearing a straw hat topped with plastic fruit and enjoying the sunshine. Had she been to London, I asked.

'No' she said, 'But I went to Plymouth once'.

I was able to unearth some good 'human interest' stories, mainly thanks to my trainer and colleague Mike Tillson who picked up the gossip in his local riverside pub. One was the army veteran who had just been told that, thanks to a bureaucratic oversight, he was not a British citizen but stateless. Another was the tale of the little old tramp who regularly trudged in his shabby clothes along the main road – for meetings with his stockbroker some 15 miles away in Plymouth.

I also wrote stories that eased my social conscience, and convinced me that local newspapers could be a force for good. I helped a single mother apply for allowances she was entitled to, and persuaded a Normandy veteran to have his amputation re-measured, which increased his income by 70 per cent.

I pushed a wheelchair user around the town, noting that the brand new £7,000 lavatory for the disabled was virtually inaccessible in a wheelchair from the car park. I also found two six-inch steps up to the Old People's Rest Room, six steps up to the council information office and some bone-juddering cobbles outside the rectory. My report did not go down well, but the point was made and largely acted upon.

I had failures, of course. My favourite came when I went to interview a sub-postmaster who was about to retire.

'Have you enjoyed the job?' I asked.

'I can't tell you that,' he replied. 'I signed the Official Secrets Act'. Exit again with empty notebook.

During these ups and downs I was sustained by a gifted trio of colleagues. Jimmy Mildren, a former hospital administrator, was the district reporter for the regional daily, the *Western Morning News*. He often dropped into our office to tip us off about local stories, once he had safely filed them to his own paper.

He guided us in the etiquette of phoning copy up the line to the BBC in Plymouth or the nationals in London. He claimed that Dartmoor Prison was second only to the Royal family as a lucrative source of stories. Esther supported his theory when she found and sold to the nationals a story that newly-installed security floodlights had tricked local birds into singing 24 hours non-stop. The headline writers must have loved the **Jail birds...** opportunity.

Jim Thorington was our staff photographer. A disenchanted Australian electronics engineer who had relocated from Putney, he raced around the district in his battered car with Spuds, his girlfriend and assistant. On assignment he flashed his gap-toothed smile at the about-to-be photographed, and relayed helpful tips and comments to us reporters out of the side of his mouth.

His patience was admirable, though he did have a breaking point. One story went that he got so fed up waiting for a group of dignitaries to arrange themselves for a group photo that he left the building while they were still arguing, no shots taken. On another occasion he allegedly refused to photograph some visiting Japanese on the grounds that during the war they had 'eaten his brother'. I was also told by others that he dipped quietly into his own pockets to help people in difficulty.

My main inspiration was Brian Fogg, our editor. He had gone into journalism straight from school, and had left a prestigious job as editor of the trade newspaper *Tailor and Cutter* to bring up his family in the country. He worked late into the night, thriving on the jostling of the ambitious and often arrogant youngsters passing through Tavistock on their way to London and better paid jobs.

On Friday mornings, after the paper was published, a trail of aggrieved readers would gather in the front office. He spoke with them all, door closed as we strained to hear. Usually he defended us. When necessary he admitted the mistake and apologised. When appropriate we would be admonished. Shortly afterwards he would give us our next assignment, sometimes standing in the waste paper basket to lighten the mood.

Brian was good at reining me in, particularly when it came to the sociological jargon I had spent the last three years acquiring.

'I don't care if you have a degree,' he said. 'There's no point publishing anything if Nellie Sludgebucket isn't going to understand'.

Brian reinforced the point by subediting our rambling copy into crisp stories. Then he added a headline, rarely passing up the chance of a pun. When I wrote a story about the warning to Cornwall County Council workmen to be careful not to cut down the rare bladderwort in the roadside verges, he came up with: **Men who weed in hedge warned**.

It earned him a swift reprimand from head office in Plymouth for (improbably) bringing down the standards of the *Mirror* group. But it did not begin to compete for bawdiness with our rival publication's **Ugly erection in Crapstone**, though this was almost certainly unintentional.

After nine months, trainees were generally moved to another paper, though I managed to swap places with a colleague and stayed in Tavistock. I moved into the centre of town, living in a first-floor flat owned by a local antiques dealer.

I was lonely. Many of the young people were either married, or had left to study or work. There was little social or family life for outsiders of my age, though one or two vicars' wives took pity on me and invited me to Sunday lunch. The most fruitful source of companions were teachers from the local secondary school, but the headmaster discouraged fraternisation and we were banned from the school. Nevertheless, for a while I harboured an unrequited crush on the gym teacher.

The outside world intruded from time to time. In early 1972 the miners went on strike, causing power cuts and a reduced working week. Our contribution to public morale was to publish an article showing how to improvise candles out of beef dripping. We tried it ourselves, and discovered that in this case the cost of light was mild nausea.

A few months later, in August 1972, President Amin of Uganda expelled hundreds of competent and hardworking Asians. A large group of them was flown out of Africa and into Plasterdown Camp, a Royal Marine base on Dartmoor. Brian Fogg gave me time off to go to the camp as a volunteer. I worked with an expelled graphic designer who had reasonable English and together we created and put up a wall newspaper in Gujurati.

I wrote about the experience for the paper, noting that many of the refugees had been stripped of their homes, their jobs, their businesses, their friends and their underclothes.

'...Now they are in a strange land. There are new faces, new customs and for some a new language to learn. Some have little rooms. Others just have a partitioned corner.

'They have a bed, linen, towels, soap and part of a wardrobe. They wear clothes that have been given to them.

'Why are they so pleased to be here? One beamed when I asked him. "Otherwise dead," he said in his broken English.' (Tim Albert, They can still smile, *Tavistock Times*, October 20, 1972)

I also wrote that they were hopeful of finding work and settling down, not realising the contribution these desolate people were to make to our economy over the next few decades. President Amin will appear again briefly in this story. Meanwhile I am about to move on.

3.3: Short shift on the tabloids

In November 1972, as the final part of my training, I was sent on a two-month attachment to the *Sunday Mirror* in London. To replace the green tweed suit that I had worn only a couple of times I bought a flashy brown pinstripe three-piece. The suit turned out to be one of my few successes.

Had I been attached to the *Daily Mirror*, with a daily news agenda to follow, I might have been more comfortable. But on the *Sunday Mirror* the stories were rarely time-specific and often involved probing into somebody's personal life. I was now well aware of the newspaper magnate Lord Northcliffe's remark that news was what someone somewhere didn't want published; all else was advertising. But I wanted to pick my fights with people that mattered.

I reported for duty in a blue and red office tower in Holborn. My colleagues were a mix of those who had recently graduated from the training course and their more grizzled colleagues who had started as copy boys and then worked their way up through hard graft and talent.

One of the first things they taught me was how to fill in an expenses form. In those days there was a tacit agreement between managers and journalists that editorial salaries could be topped up with fictional expenses, which of course reduced the tax bill. There were clear ways of doing this. If you telephoned someone, you put in a claim – no receipt necessary – for going there and back in a taxi. You added a notional tip, making it difficult for a zealous accounts clerk to question your honesty. If you could get hold of a restaurant receipt you would submit it, putting in the name of someone plausible as your guest.

I also got a lesson in serious drinking. At lunch we would cross the road to the White Hart public house, generally known among *Mirror* staff as the Stab (in the back). After a couple of pints we would file out to a nearby Italian restaurant, where we would have a fine lunch washed down by several glasses (sometimes more) of red wine. My colleagues still managed to write crisp, clean copy, but it was too much for me.

Our working week started on a Tuesday, a gentle day used for inquests and assignments and expense reports. The pace of research and writing quickened as the week progressed, and by Friday it was usually clear which stories would make it, and which would not. The latter would be impaled on spikes, with the sharp end bent downwards in a loop so that, it was said, reporters slumping unconscious would not drill it into their heads. To be fair I never saw any slumping.

On Friday evening we turned ourselves into a daily newspaper and a night editor came in to deal with any major incident. On Saturday morning we assembled on a different floor, and sat in rows in the *Daily Mirror* newsroom waiting to be assigned a developing story. Extra reporters were drafted in for the day, including a number of young Australians doing the grand tour of Europe and looking for Fleet Street experience.

One of these was Jonathan King, not the English singer and convicted paedophile, but an Australian reporter a few years older than me. He had worked as a 'jackaroo' on a farm and a reporter on Murdoch's *Australian*, and had just finished a postgraduate degree at the London School of Economics. It was with Jonathan one Saturday evening that I was sent out to a tree-lined suburban street to door-step the neat and tidy house of a bank manager who had committed suicide. One of the neighbours rounded on me:

'Why are you doing this? It's a private tragedy. Let the family cope with this in peace.'

I said nothing, though privately I agreed. A few days later we discovered that the bank manager had defrauded his bank of quite a substantial sum of money. The ethics of journalism were not going to be as clear-cut as I had hoped.

Otherwise I spent much of my time chasing celebrities. I asked Jimmy Savile a question as he was leaving some important event. I have no recollection of the question or his answer, but I do remember feeling patronised.

I spent a happy half hour speaking on the phone to the popular impressionist Mike Yarwood. We were planning to publish a photograph of him holding his new-born baby. I asked him whether he was thinking about naming his child after Harold Wilson, then leader of the opposition and one of his most successful 'characters'. I cobbled his answer into a three-sentence caption denying that his daughter was to be named Harolda. It was the only thing I wrote that eluded the spike.

Fortunately someone had a bright idea that saved my attachment, and possibly also my career. I suspect it came from our news editor Monty Court, a tough hard-news man who went on to edit the *Sporting Life*. The plan was that, with my well-flagged social conscience, I would find it interesting to spend some time in the Readers' Services Bureau.

This was a little-known outpost of the *Mirror* newspapers which occupied the floor of a rather run-down office block several tube stops (or an expensive taxi ride plus tips) away in Camden Town. It had a full-time staff of 20, including teachers and social workers, a barrister and the deputy leader of Southwark council. At its head was a veteran *Mirror* journalist Fred Redman and at his right hand an elegant and competent housing expert called Pamela Duveen, not a natural *Mirror* reader.

The team dealt with 7,000 or so letters sent each year to the *Mirror* papers. These excluded relationship issues which were sent to another department in the same building run under the auspices of the agony aunt Marje Proops. I felt immediately comfortable with the committed and less cynical atmosphere.

In those pre-Google days some of our questions merely sought information: what was the best way to send a cat to New Zealand, and who played the nude bottom in the film *Frenzy?* The latter presumably was to settle a bet.

Other inquiries were more substantial. A pensioner wrote wanting to know why her pension had been cut now that she had moved into her son's house. A young couple wrote to ask how they could avoid being evicted. The staff drafted replies, and also got involved in direct negotiation, ringing up shady traders and intransigent bureaucrats to sort out misunderstandings, injustices, and fraud.

The work of the unit gave me a different insight into the tabloid press: the extent to which some people relied on 'their' newspaper for help when they needed it, and how that newspaper could harness its power to right some serious wrongs. Sadly the unit was closed down a few years later.

In one sense it was surprising that I enjoyed my two weeks there because in that period I gave up smoking. The reason was simple: my chest had started to hurt. It was either give up or go to the doctors. I went cold turkey, drinking glass after glass of water and gradually finding my cravings ease. The hardest part came when I was writing, because I had become conditioned to typing out my copy with a cigarette dangling from my mouth. But I soon felt better and was determined not to go back to the habit. I was also, according to later evidence, laying myself open to a serious medical problem.

At the end of my attachment, in January 1973, I returned to Tavistock for a couple of months until my training contract was over. I discovered that my failure at the *Sunday Mirror* had been counterbalanced by my success in the professional journalism exams. In the diploma run by the National Council for the Training of Journalists, I gained one of a handful of distinctions and was awarded the national prize for the best report written after a 'speech test'. This part of the exam involved an outsider coming in to read from a script that we immediately wrote up under exam conditions. The ACCURACY IS EVERYHTING message had obviously got through.

My success posed a problem for my employers, who like me had realised that I was unlikely to make the grade as a tabloid journalist. Fred Redman offered me a job, but I wanted to write articles, not letters. So I was summoned back up to London to meet one of the directors, who offered me a place on the weekly magazine *New Society*, which IPC also owned. Next to the *Guardian*, it was where I wanted to be.

The magazine had been recommended reading on my university course. I had already made contact with one of the assistant editors and had written a couple of small pieces for them. But the IPC top brass had reckoned without the independent streak of the then-editor Paul Barker. He didn't want to be told what to do by the owners, even if they were willing to add to his budget to give me a job, so he refused to meet me. It wasn't personal, but it was a blow.

I was then offered a place on the *Daily Record* in Glasgow.

'It would be a good jumping off place for the London papers,' I was told.

I remembered being told something similar two and a half years before when I went to Devon. So, like many others before and since, I left the shelter of a small country newspaper to go up to Fleet Street and try to make my reputation.

3.4 The lower rungs of the freelance ladder

Within three days of coming up to London as a freelance I was working on Fleet Street. It wasn't one of the big newspapers - by then only a few were still in Fleet Street anyway - but a small magazine called *Drugs and Society*. It was jointly owned by the publishers Macmillan and the Institute for the Study of Drug Dependence, a joint commercial and idealistic response to what had become a major moral panic.

We had a little office to ourselves, overlooking an ornate clock that overlooked the famous street. Later we were moved into the main building, where I once travelled up in the lift with Harold Macmillan himself, patriarch of the publishing business and the man whom we scoffed at less than a decade before when he told us that we'd never had it so good.

My editor was a tall, charismatic, young woman called Frances Verrinder, who had been running the magazine for a couple of years. She had attracted a talented staff. Ivor Gaber, the deputy who had just left, went on to become a professor of broadcast journalism. John Ezard, who wrote a monthly column on press coverage, was in the early years of a career as one of the *Guardian*'s star reporters. Some of our covers and cartoons were drawn by John Spooner, an Australian lawyer on the grand tour and later long-term cartoonist for the *Melbourne Age*.

Drugs and Society trod a careful and objective line between the various cultures, though it raised eyebrows in some places by including alcohol and coffee on the same terms as glue sniffing and LSD. It also prodded the mainstream media. The *Daily Telegraph*, for instance, was reprimanded for publishing an estimate for the total of drug takers in London schools that turned out to be higher than the number of pupils. There was no apology and for years this figure kept reappearing in newspapers all over the world.

I became part-time temporary news editor, but still had time to write some feature articles. Some of these look remarkably contemporary. In one, for instance, I described how new regulations were allowing immigration officers to turn people away on the suspicion that they took drugs. In another I reported the successful campaign by residents in south Wales to block plans to build a hostel for former addicts. The leader of the protesters defended himself.

'I'm not against the hostel in principle,' he told me. 'What I'm against is siting it in a residential area.' This was to become a familiar refrain over the next few decades.

Sadly the magazine failed to meet the publisher's financial targets and was closed at the end of 1973. Frances left the country and became a family counsellor in California. But she had given me a good launching ground for my career.

My first article to be published in a major London newspaper had its origin in a thought that had been consoling me as I set out on my journey to storm the battlements of Fleet Street. If I didn't make it as a journalist I still had the shorthand and typing skills to find work as a secretary.

I enlisted as a temp with the Alfred Marks Bureau. The two kind ladies who signed me up said that I had excelled in my tests, and they sent me along the next morning to a firm of West End solicitors. I wore my natty brown pin-striped suite, which set off my shoulder-length hair rather nicely.

'Golly,' said Deirdre as I walked in to the typing pool in my natty brown suit. 'The men are taking over. Is nothing sacred?'

As word got around the office that a *male* secretary had turned up, a succession of young – and not so young - men kept putting their heads around the door, using some flimsy excuse such as where to find a fresh paper clip. They looked at me, giggled, and retreated.

'Good grief', said one, unable to contain himself.

After a while the number of visitors dropped off. So did the typing work I was given, though I was tasked with pouring one of my bosses a cup of tea out of a pink china teapot. I was eventually transferred to a department in the attic, where all the staff were women and they had no problem giving me dictation. They did not require me to pour their tea.

I published the story of my two-day foray into the typing pool in an article under the headline **How I failed the sex test** (Tim Albert, *Evening Standard*, April 5, 1973). It had two unexpected outcomes. First came a cameo appearance on the *Today* radio programme, along with Alfred Marks himself who skilfully turned the whole thing into a plug for his employment agency, and why not.

Then came a call from a rival employment agency who asked if I were free to fly out to Bahrain where they were desperate for male secretaries. The rates of pay were tempting, as was the prospect of foreign travel. But I was already building up commitments in London, so I stayed a journalist when I could have become a Sheikh's PA.

I laid down a retrospective marker, however, by taking Deirdre out to dinner.

I started to write regular pieces for *New Society*. The editor might not have wanted me imposed on him as a staff member, but his deputy was happy to give me assignments. I started off with a short piece describing how British native red squirrels were being squeezed out by an influx of sturdier, sex-mad grey squirrel immigrants from America (Tim Albert, Up the Reds, *New Society*, March 20, 1973).

I wrote about collectors of toy soldiers, with the star interviewee being an *Evening Standard* engineer who had 12,000 of them dotted around the rockery and shrubs of his garden near Heathrow (Tim Albert, The Toy Regiments, *New Society*, September 13, 1973). I did some personal research into three new-fangled computer dating agencies. They failed to find any suitable matches, and when I interviewed the owner of one of them (whose company, it turned out, didn't even have a computer), he put the blame on me.

'I don't want to be rude but you are rather small', he said. (Tim Albert, Mates of a machine, *New Society*, June 6, 1974).

My first serious story came out of a major air disaster. In April 1973, an aeroplane flying from Bristol Airport to Basel crashed in snowy mountains in Switzerland. All but 37 of the passengers and crew were killed. What gave the crash an extra dimension was the fact that most of the passengers were women from close-knit friendship groups in and around Axbridge in Somerset.

Fresh from my experiences reporting from small rural villages I wondered how the communities would cope, and wrote about the effects on the affected communities. The response to the disaster had been anything but well organised, and I concluded:

> 'That's not surprising...There's no national team of specialist advisers or workers. No national source of emergency funds. No properly recorded experience on which to draw. If there had been, perhaps we would have avoided a situation where husbands were told that their wives had not survived after all, and where estimates of motherless children fluctuated between 200 and ... 47' (Tim Albert, Grief and Aid, *New Society*, April 19, 1973)

I did not mention in my first article, because at the time it hadn't occurred to me to do so, that the rescue operation had been severely handicapped by the fact that airlines were not required to keep lists of their passengers. That soon changed.

What I did mention was the press's behaviour at the incident, which tested my allegiance to my new trade. Within hours of the crash, several hundred journalists, including 32 camera crews, descended on the small communities. Stories emerged of children being given tissues so that they could cry for the cameras, and of a reporter loudly phoning his copy through from a public telephone in the middle of an open-air memorial service.

He escaped a public beating, but only just, it was reported. Elsewhere, however, a local restaurant refused to serve journalists, and photographers were punched. I quoted Doug Sleight, the *Daily Mirror's* west-country correspondent, as saying it was the worst hostility of its type that he had seen. I reassured myself with the hope that lack of preparation was at fault.

I started to expand into the world of radio reporting. A friend of a friend got me an introduction to BBC Radio London in Hanover Square. After a brief interview with a brisk woman news editor I was offered shifts to write bulletins.

I did not get off to a good start. My first shift was due to start at 9am and I turned up a few minutes before, just to be safe. The newsroom was deserted, apart from a young Chinese-Canadian woman, who seemed surprisingly pleased to see me.

'Come with me' she said, leading me upstairs.

She carried a sheaf of papers and I like to think she took my hand, but that may be the happy fog of hindsight. She took me into a small room, sat me down in a chair, and put the papers on a table in front of me.

'See that red light. When it goes on, start reading. I'm banned from reading the news because I have a Canadian accent, and you're the only other person here.'

Within seconds, it seemed, the red light went on and I started to read. I had no chance to look at what I was reading, and I found that a colony of frogs had occupied my throat. I carried on with my task until, after what seemed like an hour but certainly was not longer than two minutes, the red light went out and I was told to stop.

It was not the start from which confidence was likely to grow, and it didn't. I had a few excursions lugging about a heavy Uher tape recorder, and then using an unguarded razor in an attempt to splice the result into a reasonable interview. But mostly I was confined to bashing out bulletins for others to read. It was unglamorous work, but it taught me how to write a short news story to tight deadlines.

And the stories in London at that time were big. The Provisional IRA was bombing the capital and, being in the West End and working for the BBC, we were in the middle of it. When someone with an Irish accent phoned us or the police to tell us of a bomb we had to stop what we were doing and move out into the street until either it exploded, or we were given the all clear. I never found myself near an explosion, but there was a climate of fear, and soon we were told not to contribute to it by reporting false alarms.

My most frustrating moment in my short broadcasting career came when I lost my chance to give an on-the-spot report of a major news story. I was in my flat when I heard on the radio that there was some trouble concerning Princess Anne's car in the Mall. This was three minutes away from where I was living so I went down, took some notes, and came back to my phone. I rang Radio London. As I started to explain I was interrupted.

'We're really busy. A gunman is trying to kidnap Princess Anne'. And they hung up.

When a vacancy for a full-time post came up, the station manager suggested I apply for it. It was unlikely I would get it (that decision had already been made, it was implied) but the experience would stand me in good stead when the next vacancy came round.

I abandoned radio work after that. I realised that I preferred working on something I could see and touch the next day, rather than something that disappeared out into the air waves. Also, my work as a writer was beginning to fill my time.

3.5 A home of my own

For the first few weeks after I returned to London I stayed in Wimbledon with my parents. It was strange. I had accumulated enough belongings in my two and a half years of independent living that I needed to hire a small van to bring them up from Devon. The room I had used in my first year at university had been turned into a rather formal guest room. I had also got used to living in my own space to my own rhythms.

Thanks to my father's contacts, after a few weeks I found a one-bedroom flat to rent just off St James's Street in the middle of London's West End. It had been designed for Edwardian gentlemen who could escape to their country estate each weekend, and was tiny. I immediately applied a coat of fashionable orange paint to the walls, but it remained dark and smelly. The only window looked out onto a dank inner well, at the bottom of which a large fan extracted strong odours of fish, both dead and alive, from Madame Prunier's reputed restaurant on the ground floor, and moved them into my flat.

It may have been a smart address but I found it a lonely place to be. During the day the streets were bustling. But once the shops and offices closed they became quiet, then deserted. The shops were not much use to me anyway. While I could have bought a trilby hat at Lobb and a case of claret at Berry Bros and Rudd (both companies with royal warrants), I had to drive to the King's Road to do my grocery shopping.

My nearest friend, a colleague from Macmillan the publishers, was a 10-minute walk away through St James's Park. My second nearest friend, a cousin of my Australian friend Jonathan King, was on a houseboat in Chelsea, a 10-minute drive away. The only place I could keep my car was at Leicester Square, so that meant an additional 10 minutes or so on foot each way.

Nevertheless I spent more and more time driving up to Hampstead where Jonathan presided over a lively flat-load of Australians. On one of these journeys I became hopelessly lost. I found myself in a small street between one-storey Victorian terraced cottages, most in a state of dreadful disrepair. Above them glowered the towers of a tall council estate. The area, I discovered later, was called Gospel Oak.

But the street had character, and did not appear unduly grand. I noted that one house was flagged with a For Sale notice. I wrote down the number on the board and the next day contacted the estate agent and made an appointment to visit.

Inside, the house was grim. Paint was flaked and wallpaper was peeling. There was an outside lavatory and a tabletop bath in the kitchen. The pulse of dripping water could be heard in several rooms. But I was hooked: it clearly had history, and I could see it might have a future.

My father persuaded our old family friend the surveyor Ron Downham, on whose TV we had watched the Coronation 20 years before, to look it over. His report went as far as a professional man could go to be discouraging. The only good news was that it was 'quite an attractive type of two-floor Victorian house'. He itemised dry rot and woodworm. The slates were cracked, the lead pipes broken and the window frames rotten. He couldn't get access to the roof but suspected it was in a state of near collapse. It would, to put it mildly, need a lot of work.

Undaunted, I bought it, paying the deposit with the help of a trust fund set up by my entrepreneurial grandfather 40 years before I was born. My father the property lawyer thought I was being foolish, but it turned out he was wrong. I sold it five years later for three times the price; now the houses are changing hands for well over a million pounds.

I commissioned three architect friends to make the place habitable. They had the roof secured and the windows mended. They supervised a massive clean-up, taking out fireplaces, adding a bath and an inside toilet, and a kitchen with all mod cons.

I supervised the decoration and furnishing, though probably I shouldn't have. Since orange was now out of favour, I ended up with brown curtains from Habitat, brown plates from Woolworths, and brown corduroy chairs from a mail order company. I also bought a brown print from John Lewis: it depicted a cross section of the earth with what looked like a sausage in the sky; years later when I sold the picture I made a loss, a difficult thing to do with original art.

A favourite feature of my kitchen was that it was equipped with a sink that could gobble up food rubbish and dispose of it down the drains. One day it became hideously blocked. Once the engineer had sorted it out he told me my mistake.

'I am afraid you can't put artichokes down these, sir'.

I wouldn't have used the word at the time, but I was playing my part in 'gentrification'. One or two original tenants lingered on in the street, but Gospel Oak was becoming a middle-class enclave. On one side of my house lived a consultant gynaecologist and on the other the singer-songwriter

Lyndsey de Paul, who was not friendly and left within a year of my arrival. She felt my builders were deliberately dropping bags of cement to wake her up and get her out of the house so they could see her in her night clothes. She was of course right.

On the corner was Clare Latimer, the cook accused many years later in the press of having an affair with John Major when he was really having an affair with the politician Edwina Currie. Living next to her in two connected houses was the comedian Michael Palin. A few doors down lived Robin Denselow, *Panorama* producer and pop music critic for the *Guardian*, and Liz Forgan, later chair of the Scott Trust, owner of the *Guardian*. I don't think I met her, but it turned out to be a great street for name dropping.

I was clearly in danger of becoming successful: I had a good place to live, good friends and an expanding family – my brother David was now married to fellow Am-Dram enthusiast Kate and nephews were on the way – plus articles in prestigious publications. But there was one problem: I had developed an unpleasant illness.

3.6: Blood and guts

I was still living in the West End when I first noticed the symptoms. I felt the strain of living alone and making my way in a competitive career, but did not feel particularly ill. One morning, however, I found some unpleasant signs that I might be: streaks of blood combined with a clear, glutinous-looking liquid on my stools.

I was still registered with a doctor in Tavistock, so I went to my parents' GP, who prescribed me some diazepam to keep me cheerful and said he would refer me to a specialist.

I had arranged a writing trip to Sweden, then the must-visit destination for left-leaning liberals. I went ahead, keeping to the busy schedule I had organised. My first trip was to a meticulously planned and massive estate which combined social housing with all the social and medical services its inhabitants might want. Everyone I spoke to hated the place.

I then interviewed a university dean whose knowledge of English was so extensive that I had to abandon my shorthand (the outlines would have been too unusual for me to decipher afterwards) and immerse myself in an English dictionary as soon we had finished to make sense of my notes.

As a complete contrast, I interviewed a couple who made their livelihood performing live sex twice a night in the *Cabaret Chat Noir*. I had supper with them in their flat and then went with them to see the show. I offered the resulting article to the *Guardian* but they declined to take it. I don't know whether the piece was ahead of its time, or just too boring. Perhaps the diazepam had made me too restrained.

Soon after I got back to England I was summonsed to see a physician at St George's Hospital, then still occupying its stately corner site overlooking Hyde Park Corner in central London. I waited in a corridor (the social workers had taken over the original waiting room), with a stained three-year old copy of *Country Life* to keep me amused. Later I described the experience.

'If I was feeling ill before I came, I was feeling even worse when they called my name. They put me on the weighing machine (without telling me how much I actually weighed). They made me take off my tie and take off my jacket and take off my shirt and put my jacket on again and take down my trousers.

'I waited once more. Then the specialist came, saw, diagnosed piles and told me he was sending me to the surgeon 'to have a look'. He sailed out leaving me bare bottomed, bemused and more than ever convinced I was about to die.' (Tim Albert, Struck dumb with trousers down, *World Medicine*, May 7, 1975).

I walked back to my flat in a daze. I knew people were sent to surgeons to be cut up and have organs removed, usually because they were cancerous. A family friend had died a few months previously of cancer of the stomach and it didn't take a big leap of despair to imagine I had the same. In my rational moments I knew that at age 27 a cancer was improbable, but the irrational led me to feel that it would be no consolation to die a statistical outlier. As I walked back through the spring flowers, I started to plan my last Christmas.

A few weeks later I got an inpatient appointment. The weekend before, I drove down to Tavistock to stay with a former colleague and feel less scared. It didn't work. The official line was that my hospitalisation was 'for tests', but this bland phrase is loaded with implications for the imaginative.

I signed in at St George's as an inpatient and remained there for eight days, though I was told that I could have gone home for the weekend if only I had asked. Today I would have had all the tests as an outpatient. Most of the time I was bored, though I was cheered up by a visit from my Uncle John who brought not grapes, but kippers. I also made myself unpopular by refusing a sleeping pill.

'Everyone has one here', I was told.

The worst bit turned out to be a barium enema (now less commonly done, thankfully) which involved being starved, purged, then filled from the rear with what feels like a pint or more of chalk you have to retain while a heavy x-ray machine whirrs around your nether regions.

I left the hospital with a diagnosis of ulcerative colitis. According to *NHS Choices* (last accessed 15.04.2017) ulcerative colitis is a long-term condition where the colon and rectum become inflamed. Symptoms include bloody diarrhoea, abdominal pain, a frequent need to go to the toilet, fatigue and weight loss. It is an auto-immune disease and more common among those descended from Ashkenazi Jewish communities (my grandmother suffered from it). Medication may ease the symptoms and bring remissions but, if that fails to work, surgery may be required to remove a section of the colon. It is estimated to affect 1 in every 420 people.

What the patient information doesn't tell you is that, since ulcerative colitis affects the muckier parts of the digestive system, it is not a disease that is widely discussed.

In the meantime I was given a bottle full of large brown pills of which I had to take eight a day, plus several packets of steroid suppositories of which I had to use one at night. I went back to Wimbledon for a few days to be spectacularly spoilt by my concerned mother. I then drove to Tavistock again to recover still more.

It didn't seem to work. I began to feel sicker and sicker. On my second morning I found a rash on my arms and went to a local GP as a temporary patient. He advised me to stop taking the large brown pills and I recovered. No-one had warned me that I might have been allergic.

My symptoms started to settle down, and for the next few years amounted to little more than taking unpleasant medication and having to go to the loo a little more than most. But I now had a chronic condition – and a reason for writing about health services. Not long after, I suggested that the way my consultant had treated me had hidden implications:

> 'This trousers-around-the ankles approach is, I later learnt, a common technique. It is also, in this time of financial emergency, vital to the continuation of the National Health Service. It's founded on the assumption that if a patient's bottom is bare (either actually or metaphorically), he is much easier to deal with.

> 'The practitioner can get on with the next case without having to admit that the service is starved of time, of resources and even of adequate knowledge, and that behind each medical problem lurks a frightened patient.' (ibid)

3.7: Clashes behind the iron curtain

I had little time to wallow in my newly-diagnosed illness. One evening soon after my return to work, one of my news editors, who happened to live round the corner, dropped in unexpectedly. She told me that a group of journalists (including two from the *Guardian*) was planning to fly out to Bucharest to run a daily newspaper at the United Nations world population conference. With just a few days to go, one of the team members had dropped out and they were looking for an available freelance. Could I go? Could I not.

I met my colleagues for the first time at Heathrow Airport on a Saturday afternoon in August 1974. We left in good spirits and arrived in even better ones after the captain's mid-flight announcement – to whoops of joy throughout the plane – that President Richard Nixon had resigned.

In Bucharest I was surprised to find a city that looked remarkably like Paris, but seedier and hotter, with eastern Orthodox churches. We were billeted in an old coaching hotel, with balconies facing an inner courtyard. For the next three weeks we would gather on them in the evening to drink cheap local sparkling wine and share our impressions.

It was a rare chance to visit eastern Europe. An early talking point was how thoroughly President Ceausescu's totalitarian Romania had prepared for the occasion. We found 400 taxi drivers in UN-blue uniforms waiting to give free rides in UN-blue cars to anyone who could prove they were with the conference. We saw dozens of multilingual guides, many of whom were teachers and students of foreign languages, waiting to show us the way. And, once arrived at our destinations, we were shepherded by a cohort of tough but smart ushers who we assumed came from the ranks of the security police.

Our liberal western European ways soon came into conflict with the eastern European bureaucracy. Our newspaper, sponsored by the International Planned Parenthood Federation and with the encompassing title of *Planet*, was to be published over 10 evening editions. But it took four days before we could finalise the agreement with the local paper that had agreed to print it, and five days until any office supplies materialised.

I had my own problem. My task had seemed straightforward enough: obtain a biography of the Romanian foreign minister, himself a former journalist, who was to be the conference chairman. But it took me three days of endless calls, by phone and in person, and my mounting frustration was and always met by bland shrugs of hopelessness. At least it put into perspective the frustrations I had faced trying to wheedle stories out of reluctant Devon and Cornwall parish councillors.

As we were trying to get ready for the conference, a subsidiary event was taking place. This was a meeting of the 'youth' of the world, some of whom looked distinctly unyouthful.

Infact one of them looked strangely familiar. It took only a few moments to realise that he was my old school friend Manuel Ravassa, leader of the guild of smokers, with whom I had shared many happy hours behind the bike shed and who had found me a pen friend of what in those days we called the 'opposite sex'. He was now a firebrand representing Columbia and the developing world against the perfidy of the west. The English public school had a long and sometimes unexpected reach.

Once the conference itself started, our lives moved from becalmed to hectic. The blue taxis were soon whizzing around like dung-happy flies, ferrying government delegates, chiefs of missions, press attachés, and representatives from non-governmental organisations such as the feminist Germaine Greer and the anthropologist Margaret Mead.

The event itself was a three-ring circus. The showcase arena was the Palace of the Republic (blue-roofed of course), where heads of state gave interminably dull accounts of their deeply entrenched positions, usually to a handful of people. One exception was when President Ceausescu of Romania used his moment in the limelight to call for a new world order. The packed assembly greeted his speech with tumultuous applause, though the effect was spoilt when the crowd evaporated as soon as he sat down.

The best theatre came from the Faculty of Law where a Tribune of non-governmental organisations agitated, argued and persistently tried to reinstate recommendations that the official delegates had just rejected. The real business, however, took place in small smoke-filled rooms where professional diplomats horse-traded shamelessly over the draft World Plan of Action.

After my morning stint reporting the plenary session, I returned to our offices to work alongside our chief subeditor Pat Ensor, shortly to take up a job at the *Guardian*. He designed the pages and worked with the printers; I edited the copy and wrote the headlines. I subedited most of the articles, but still found it hard to work out what was really going on.

Our newspaper was well received by the delegates, less so by the Romanian regime. When we were about to go to press with the third edition, a 'workers' delegation' came up from the print room to ask us to modify a caricature of President Ceausescu on the grounds that it was 'artistically unsuccessful'.

The next day a 'cultural deputation' considered that an incidental figure in a cartoon might offend Leonid Brezhnev, then president of the Soviet Union. We agreed with the printers that they could sort that one out by literally defacing the offensive image with a sharp blow from a chisel.

On the fifth day a censor arrived to sit with us. He was a charming, well-dressed man with excellent English and unbending views on what we could and could not write. We had no choice but to accept this imposition, though in practice it affected only minor details.

Throughout the conference the plans of the western countries had been constantly attacked by developing countries, the communist bloc, and the Vatican (invoking higher authority even than the United Nations). The Chinese argued particularly fiercely that the answer to the population explosion was not contraception but self-reliance and independence; the one-child family was still a few years away.

An agreement came just in time, and against the flow of rhetoric. Family planning targets were included, though they were undated and the Vatican was allowed to dissent.

On the last evening we held a splendid party with the printers at their offices, without the censor. As the vodka flowed we exchanged gifts (they received a group caricature done by our cartoonist Richard Willson) and pledged ourselves to international workers' solidarity. As we returned to England and our normal lives, Pat told the story of seeing a pile of already typeset stories sitting on the top of a filing cabinet.

'What are those?' he had asked.

'Next year's news,' said the printer.

3.8: Education observed

When I got back from Romania I found myself writing more and more about education. This was a good area for a freelance, mainly because of the buoyant demand for teachers and lecturers. Their job advertisements supported several weekly specialist supplements, giving plenty of space to fill with editorial.

The thickest of these publications was the *Times Educational Supplement* (*TES*) It was in the same building as the *Times* and a recognised route into the main paper for ambitious journalists. As technically a part of a national newspaper, its journalists enjoyed the same standard of (genuine) expenses: taxis, first-class train travel, multi-starred hotels, top restaurants.

I started going into the *TES* on press days to write up news stories, and then graduated to helping out on the subs' desk. I carved out a niche for light-touch 'I was there' pieces, following the progress of a nativity play through rehearsals to performance, and then flying off to Switzerland with a school party from Kingston to learn to ski. The pupils taunted me: 'Can you be a reporter with a broken arm, sir?'. But they cheered me at the post-trip party when the head teacher presented me with a special medal – not for skiing but for valour.

Not all my pieces were light, and one went so far to earn me the threat of blacklisting by the Department of Health. It was a profile on Her Majesty's Inspectors of schools that had proved remarkably hard to research. One inspector, whom I knew quite well socially, declined to speak to me on the grounds that he had signed the Official Secrets Act. (That excuse again!).

It took me several weeks to fix up an interview with the chief inspector, but when I turned up with my list of questions I was told that this wasn't the interview, but a meeting about whether I could have one.

When I finally got the interview – a stilted affair – and wrote my article, I mentioned the fact that it had taken me several weeks to get a non-attributable interview. I felt it spoke volumes about the culture of the organisation I was profiling. I immediately received a sharp letter, saying that my reference to the meeting 'makes a nonsense of the whole arrangement, since obviously the whole point of a non-attributable meeting is that it should not be attributed... In the light of this reference is there any reason for us to extend these facilities to you in the future?'

Mostly we had it good

In an argument worthy of the highest civil servant I responded that, while it would have been breaking the agreement had I attributed specific bits of information, writing that a non-attributable meeting had been asked for did not do so. The *TES* took my side and the Department continued to talk to me, though I suspect grudgingly.

I found more work across the corridor at the *TES*'s sister paper, the *Times Higher Educational Supplement*, a newer and smaller weekly paper edited by Brian MacArthur. He had made his reputation when education correspondent of the *Times* by phoning contacts before breakfast. He was now a genial and generous editor.

The paper was smaller than the *TES* and opportunities for freelances were greater. Brian entrusted me with a major developing story at Lancaster University. Like my *alma mater* Surrey University, this was one of the new out-of-town campus universities built in the 1970s and it had become a hotbed of dissent. The dissent had turned into violence.

The background was a national rent strike called by the National Union of Students, led by Charles Clarke, later Labour Home Secretary and Secretary of State for Education. The local flash-point came when a cash-strapped and naive student asked the university from which he was withholding money to give him a loan. Not surprisingly the university declined.

At this perceived injustice a group of students stormed into the administration block, injuring a couple of staff members as they did so. The sit-in and the anger lasted some weeks. Bailiffs finally evicted the students on the strength of a High Court order. The university authorities then suspended five student leaders and fined eight others. A special appeals committee later voted that the decisions should be overturned.

I found the university authorities stern and unyielding, and the vice chancellor Charles Carter was particularly difficult to interview; I was told later this was due to shyness not arrogance, as I had thought. I found many of the staff vindictive. And I found the students aggressive, particularly towards me as a representative of the rampaging, capitalist press.

But I did find some calming influences on campus, particularly Paul Smoker, then in a pioneering role as reader in Peace Studies. He told me that the whole affair had been 'worth at least two or three courses in pressure groups, politics, conflict research and so on...'.

At least the Lancaster students had the opportunity of an education. One of the other stories I covered for the *THES* looked into the persistent trade in what we started out as calling bogus qualifications. We ended up, after advice from the lawyers, describing them in print as 'unrecognised degrees'.

I spent a couple of weeks researching the story. I went by train to Sheffield and by car to Ashdown Forest, accompanied by a burly photographer and hoping to get an interview with those running these degree mills. I did not. I then flew up to Edinburgh, had lunch with the UK's authority on phoney degrees, and flew back that same afternoon. Freelance or not, I felt I had now made the reportorial grade.

I wrote a two-part series, focusing on the Sussex College of Technology, the College of Applied Science London, and the National Ecclesiastical University. These were run, respectively, by a former RAF corporal operating under one of his own PhDs, the self-styled Duke de Neuillay, and an equally self-styled Archbishop and Head of the Old Catholic Church of the North of England.

Their 'colleges' offered qualifications 'in recognition of the applicant's achievements', without the bother of an examination or thesis – or even a course of studies or a reading list. The certificates weren't cheap: a degree of Doctor of Humanities, for example, cost £63, equivalent to about £500 now.

A German factory manager paid much more than this because he insisted on a degree ceremony. One was deliberately staged for him in front of phoney knights, phoney counts and a phoney abbess. It did him no good: when the worthlessness of his qualification was discovered he lost his job.

He was not alone. In America the head of a state air pollution agency and the director of a chain of child guidance clinics were both dismissed for phoney qualifications. More incidents were reported from developing countries, though with the added – and rather sad – twist that many of them had spent their life savings on them.

So why no legislation? Senior officials told me that there was a legal difficulty. Less senior ones explained that they could draft a law stating that receiving a degree required more than paying money and turning up for a ceremony. But this, they pointed out, would disqualify all those Oxbridge graduates who, taking advantage of tradition, had upgraded their Oxbridge bachelor's degree into a master's. So the degree mills continued to churn out their certificates, and as I write 40 years later, my in-box is being still attacked with offers of qualifications available for cash, and little else.

I had some more relaxing assignments. One of them involved taking a trip in the Mediterranean on the SS *Uganda*, later pressed into service as a hospital ship during the Falklands war, but then specialising in school cruises. It was a strange 10 days, with children on the lower decks in dormitories and adults in upper cabins living the life of luxury and wishing the children weren't there.

One incident pricked my growing self-confidence. One evening, with the sun long since set, a teacher came up to me.

'Isn't it time for you to get to your dormitory?' she asked.

'Madam,' I said, rising to my full 5 foot 5 inches. 'I am a reporter for a national newspaper.' It was then I decided to cut my hair and grow a moustache.

3.9: Shifting with the big boys

At the start of what turned out to be the long hot summer of 1976, I began to get shifts at the heavyweight national newspapers. The first set came when I was asked if I could do a three-month three-day-a week spell as late night features subeditor (holiday relief) on the *Guardian*.

At the time I was working on the *TES* and I confided the news to the chief sub, who I had come to see as a friend as well as a boss. This was a mistake, as he immediately went along and applied for the post as well. We ended up doing the job in rotation. We looked similar – small, rotund (though in varying degrees) and bespectacled. Luckily, since he was a lot more experienced at subediting than I was, they kept muddling us up.

The *Guardian* was where I wanted to be. I was interviewed and hired by the features editor, Harold Jackson, whose despatches from Vietnam and Northern Ireland I had read with awe not long before. Around him was a jostling group of mainly young writers/subeditors, also familiar to me through their bylines. They were bright and ambitious, exuding confidence and trading remarks that seemed far smarter than any I could make.

Their smartness did not extend to what they were wearing. The uniform was blue jeans and tee shirt. I followed their example, though was mortified one evening when John Ezard, whom I had known since *Drugs and Society* days, quietly told me that even for a subeditor I looked rather scruffy.

In the late afternoon I drove and sometimes cycled the few miles from Gospel Oak to the offices in Gray's Inn Road. My first task of the evening was to work on early features for the next-but-one-issue. It was interesting to see the copy in the raw, and I was pleased to discover that not all my writing heroes knew as much about grammar and spelling as I did.

My main duty was to process the late reviews for the final editions, which came after I had sunk a couple of pints in the break. Often I was alone in the features department, though critics such as Edward Greenfield and Michael Billington, then young bloods, would pop in briefly, take over a desk and quickly bash out a review. They usually flouted the dress code, occasionally turning up in a dinner jacket. Their copy was equally elegant.

I subedited the articles quickly (though there was usually little to alter), wrote a headline and sent the copy downstairs to the typesetters. Then came the difficult bit. I too went downstairs where I would play my part in the nightly skirmishes called stone subbing.

Those were the days of hot metal and cold, tough printers who had got their job through a tortuous combination of patronage and apprenticeship. They sported the weatherbeaten look of people who spent most of their days on the golf course, and dressed much more smartly than we did. They shared none of the political beliefs of the *Guardian* and its writers, and they looked on us as callow and over-privileged youths, often with justification.

Each night we stood facing each other at a table – called the stone because that is what it once was. On it was placed the wooden frame of the page. On one side the compositor inserted the columns of lead lines, fleshing them out with lead strips if the articles were too short, and asking us to cut lines if they were too long.

On the other side we wrote our changes on paper galley proofs and passed them back. We were not allowed to touch the type; that would have triggered a serious industrial problem. It was that kind of relationship.

Pricked by sarcastic jibes from my friends that I was now an active contributor to the *Guardian's* misprints, I started a one-man campaign to clean them up. I soon realised that the problem was not that no-one had seen the errors, but that the paper's resources did not allow enough time or staff for errors to be corrected before the papers were bundled up and sent out to catch the night trains.

I learnt to relax about the misprints, though not before I had fallen into the trap of searching them out rather too intensely. This caused me one evening to miss a rather more important error: the same headline had been duplicated and put on two different stories. I am sure the compositor knew, but he said nothing. Next day Harold Jackson chided me gently, though I had spotted the error and had been mortified since breakfast.

The work ended after three months, and my fellow contractor and I went on a boating holiday in France together. Our rivalry continued at every lock we passed through. Neither of us was offered a full-time position on the *Guardian*, though we were both invited to a rather grand party marking the move of the paper to its spanking-new premises in Farringdon. I picked up other shifts in various parts of the paper and continued with my freelance life.

I started to work for a second national newspaper: the *Observer*. David Astor, its long-serving editor, had retired in 1975 and the paper was undergoing a traumatic period of change. Several journalists took redundancy and those who didn't dare leave found themselves in unfamiliar posts.

One week I found myself doing a day's shift as a reporter, subediting the business pages, writing a careers advertorial, and staffing the night news desk on Saturday night. I was also refused access to a National Union of Journalists meeting on the grounds that the future of the paper had nothing to do with me.

A high point came when I turned up at my usual time, shortly before the first deadline, to find one of the faxes clattering out news from an agency that Lord Avon (the former prime minister Sir Anthony Eden) had died. I had 15 minutes to write the story from agency tapes and library copy; it was my first and only front-page lead in a national newspaper.

The Saturday shifts were a strange experience. At 6 o'clock the full time staff drifted off to the boardroom for a drink, leaving behind them a knot of hardened journalists from places such as the *Times*, the *BBC* and the communist *Morning Star* to guide the paper safely into the morning. When all looked stable, the night editor took a taxi to the Royal Automobile Club in Pall Mall where he stayed the night in the Turkish bath.

One day I discovered that even liberal journalists have their limits. I was asked to write about a London girls' grammar school threatened with closure. As with most of us writing about education at the time, I was in favour of closing selective grammar schools, which we thought gave unfair advantages to the children of the better-off.

I was a little nervous when I was told in the briefing that a couple of senior members of the *Observer's* staff had children at that school. But I went anyway, coming up with what I thought was a good angle that preserved both our positions: an entire school was likely to come onto the market on Monday if the authorities did not back down.

Later that night a senior executive, one of those who had children at the school, phoned me up.

'We have changed your intro', he told me. 'It now reads "Parents at a renowned girls' school in London are fighting attempts to close it down".' I said that was fine, but asked for my name to be removed from the story. Thereafter my work for the *Observer* started to dwindle.

Luckily I had a new place to work: the *Times*. Brian MacArthur, my former patron at the *THES*, had moved back there as news editor and he offered me work as night reporter. He told me that I would be working with the night news editor Colin Wilson (not the novelist), his deputy Brian Forbes (not the film director) and the *late* night reporter Stanley Baldwin (not the deceased prime minister). I thought at first he was joking, but he was not: these were their names.

Mostly we had it good

Sydney Albert (top left) with his younger brother Eddie standing beside him; a young Margaret Young (top); Margaret and Sydney wreathed in smiles at their marriage in Putney in August 1943 (left).

At Auntie Stella's wedding (below) I am held by Nannie with my father on our left. My mother is at the far end next to Great Aunt Alice, and David in the front; Granny Albert with us in Hove (bottom), while the 'two mummies' look on.

Sydney Albert

With our friend Lucy in the nursery (right); the house and copper beech tree as they are today (below right); my First Holy Communion (bottom); pictures of my uncles killed in the war (below).

Our mother with David's prizes on Parents' Day (left); I pose proudly (below) before going off to boarding school; Douai Junior School at Ditcham Park in Hampshire (below left).

The family in a hotel somewhere in France, (top) with my father looking smug after figuring out the time release; Douai School on its Berkshire hilltop (below).

The headmaster Father
Alphonsus hands out prizes
at a swimming gala with his
pipe-smoking deputy beside him
and myself visible under the
cup (top); the study hall (above
right); a sulky captain of the
fencing team (right); the genial
headmaster in his office (above).

Seated at my desk during my short spell as editor of the Surrey University student newspaper (top left); students in jackets and ties stroll among the still unfinished buildings on the Guildford campus (left); my precocious journalistic career revives in California (below).

British Lad Finds Traveling by RTD a Gruelling Task

Long Beach has the Queen Mary and Pasadena has Tim Albert, a British exchange student, and it was natural that the two should meet. Tim's previous research into Southern California going and had hardly prepared him for this, his tempted inaugment — finding out if it is really is a pleasure to ride the RTD bus. —The Editor.

By TIM ALBERT

They told me to keep away from the office on Friday. "Go and see the Queen Mary, and try out the Los Angeles Rapid Transit system. It's world famous, you know."

I didn't, but was touched any way. They must have known about my problems with the weather.

"Then I saw my unawrept: 'Travel is not very helpful to you today.' Again patience, I could see Miss Landslexand and the Daughters of American Song planning this together... I heaved the world.

9:30 a.m. Armed with a telephone directory, I begin the campaign. There is nothing littered under RAPID TRANSIT and nothing listed under BUS. I appeal to the operator, who refers me to information, who gives me a number.

Engaged. I try again. One of those scratched, pre-recorded under voices explains that everyone is very busy. But "don't hang up." This upsets me; are there so many people in trouble already?

Takes Empty Bus

With the seventh unsolicited encore I begin to get upset. But there's no fun in shouting abscenities at a machine which keeps endlessly repeating "Don't Hang Up."

Finally I win through. "I wonder if you could tell me how to get to the Queen Mary?" There is an almost silence, to my senses I suppose that after the streak of that pre-recorded voice people ask for all kinds of strange things.

"Take the Number 61 bus from Colorado Boulevard in Long Beach. It departs every hour on the hour and will cost you 85¢. At Long Beach get a local bus."

10:00 a.m. Luckily the bus is late, a general meeting on the benches at Colorado had concluded that I should go to Los Robles, and they were right.

The bus is empty and I stretch out on the back seat. Do you know that if you take it slowly, analyzing the advertisements and interpreting the psychoanalytic problems of the editorial writers, a reading of the Star-News will last almost exactly from Pasadena to Long Beach?

12 noon. I am just getting used to the bone-shaking bottom-bruising rhythm when, out of the corner of my right eye I notice a sign saying Long Beach. I appeal to the driver, who advises me where to get off and where to get a bus to the Queen Mary. As I leave, he shakes his head sadly: "There's really nothing to see."

12:05 p.m. I see a Greyhound Terminal and ask about buses to Pasadena. They refer me to Continental Trailways, on the other side of the street, who tell me that they do indeed run a service to Pasadena, at twenty minutes past every hour. That raises morale. I allow myself a few moments of self-indulgence.

as I imagine that air-conditioned shock-absorbing bus racing back along the Freeway to Pasadena, while I recline in my adjustable seat enjoying a well-earned siesta.

12:10 p.m. I met Beach but just an incrersifabl. Still it fills a need and crosses out of experience.

12:50 p.m. I start looking for the bus to the Queen Mary. The first man I approach advises that I ask a policeman, and in an sympathetic that I haven't the heart to tell him that those gave make me nervous. A second suggests asking at the greyhound terminal, while another

RAPID: See Page 1

RAPID: See Page 1

WEATHER		IN SPORTS
Cooler--85°	**STAR-NEWS**	Tennis
Complete Weather Report on Page 2	PASADENA, CALIFORNIA, SUNDAY, AUGUST 24, 1969 25 Cents	Smith, Lutz Gain Crucial Round. Page A-1

Officials See End of City Riots

Negro Leaders Said

Nixon Postpones Vietnam Decision

Jim Thorington

Jim Thorington

Journalist and trainer Mike Tillson pretends to push his car in the snow on Dartmoor (top); photographer Jim Thorington and I chronicle the arrival of Ugandan Asian refugees at Plasterdown Camp in Dartmoor (above); Brian Fogg (left),editor of the Tavistock Times *and former editor of the* Tailor and Cutter.

With reporter's moustache and mackintosh (top); the Gospel Oak street where I lived (above); pages from New Statesman, Drugs and Society *and* Community Care *(left).*

Barbara Greenberg

My new friend Barbara and myself behind my flash American car (above).

My apartment at Coral harbur behind the caretaker's houseboat (top) and a rare surviving copy of the short-lived Bahamas Weekender *(above).*

Keith Morris

The wedding party outside Camden Town Hall (top): my jubilant father stands at my right shoulder with his American friend Dick Goldwater behind him; articles from World Medicine *(right) with a cover featuring my future boss John Havard (above).*

A feeling for language

It's the only thing that unites medical editors,
Stephen Lock tells Michael O'Donnell

A right royal visit

Report: Tim Albert
Photographs: Ian Familton

A six minutes past 11 Her Royal Highness the Princess of Wales peeked round the corner of the BMA's new library, saw the lines of dignitaries waiting in hushed silence to greet her — and grinned.

This incident set the tone for an essentially informal visit in which she opened the New Nuffield Library, softened the hearts of senior BMA politicians, and delighted staff and their families with two impromptu walkabouts.

Many of the children in the courtyard — one of whom at least had come from as far away as Sheffield for the occasion — gave her bouquets of flowers. Some managed to shake her hand, examine (at their request) her engagement ring, and a few junior members of the accounts department were chided gently for meeting her twice.

Strict security, reinforced by several police men and women, surrounded BMA House all morning, with many members of staff (sensibly wrapped) pressed into service as stewards, and even crash barriers erected for the small crowd waiting on the pavement outside to catch a glimpse of the princess as she swept through the gates. Admission was by special invitation only, to the annoyance of one member who wanted to use the library.

The weather was cold but fine, but as the event the two members of staff designated as medical officers had nothing to do. There were only two slight mishaps once, when a small child slipped and fell, which elicited considerable sympathy, and once when a photographer did, which elicited none.

The visit to BMA House continued a royal connection which started when Princess Diana's great grandfather-in-law, King George V, accompanied by the then health minister Mr Neville Chamberlain, formally opened the association's headquarters in 1925. Her father-in-law,

Prince Philip, visited in 1966 when he was president, and the Prince's Room, now used mainly for formal entertaining, was named after him. Her husband, Prince Charles visited several times in 1982-3 when he too was president of the association.

The building was started in 1912, designed by the famous Edwardian architect, Sir Edwin Lutyens (architect of, among other things, the public buildings of New Delhi) for the Theosophical Society, of which his wife was a member.

This visit marked the end of a £650,000 programme to move the Nuffield Library from its increasingly cramped occupation of a building at the back of the main courtyard (which itself had been made possible thanks to a £50,000 gift from the eponymous foundation in 1965) to more dignified and spacious surroundings among the the columns of Lutyens's great hall.

It will free the old library building for eventual letting, and allow more of the library's 20,000 books and 1,500 sets of periodicals to be on open display.

The Great Hall, on the first floor above what is now the members' dining room and the Hasting room, and extending up another four floors, was originally intended to be a kind of cathedral for the theosophists. But its magnificent vaulted ceiling proved too expensive to finish, and it had in later years become expensive to heat, with bad acoustics, and out of tune with modern fire regulations.

It was therefore used sparingly, mainly

The imposing Tavistock Square headquarters of the BMA (top); an interview with Editors Michael O'Donnell and Stephen Lock (above); my only foray into royal reporting (left).

A nervous encounter with
my first computer (top left);
a selection of covers from my
second spell as an editor (above);
Digging my vegetables in the
lea of the first floor folly in glass
(left).

Barbara Albert

Barbara Albert

The sea front at Wimereux (above); our apartment windows inside and out (left and below); the digue *lashed by storm (bottom).*

Barbara Albert

Barbara Albert

Regis Sion

Bernard Laffaille, captain of the Wimereux cricket
club, loses his wicket (above); the boys and girls
of the junior team take tea at the stade hippique
(below).

Regis Sion

The horological windfall as advertised in the Phillips catalogue (below); a report of a writing course (top right) and my own newsletter (right); Harvey Marcovitch and I work the flipcharts on an Editors' course (bottom).

Barbara Albert

It was a world away from the *Guardian*. For a start, as the stylebook reminded us, it was *The Times*, never the *Times* (a habit I have managed to get out of for this book). The leader writers who clustered around the office of the editor, William (later Lord) Rees-Mogg, weren't just clever, but posh and clever. Some had impeccable connections, such as brothers as ambassadors, and I am they sure went away for country weekends. The reporters and subeditors, on the other hand, were more down-to-earth, recruited from newspapers and news agencies as much as from universities.

The uniform – even for the subeditors – consisted of suits, proper shirts and ties. Once I turned up in a grey polo-neck sweater. When Colin Wilson told me sternly that I was under-dressed, I unrolled my shirt carefully to show a large plaster covering what I assured them was an unsightly boil; the matter was dropped. But I made sure I wore a tie again as soon as I could.

For most of the evening we would sit around our specially designed news desk in the middle of the large and largely empty news room, chatting pleasantly and hoping for some major disaster to happen. The nearest I came to one was when the authorities activated the four-hour flood alert for London and started opening up the disused tram tunnel that was designated as flood control headquarters. I had mixed feelings when it was called off: reporters like a good disaster.

We usually had a brief flurry of work when the rival first editions came out, and if they had any good stories we had to make sure we had them too. Annoyingly the reporter who kept me busiest was David Hencke, newly promoted from the *THES* to the *Guardian*. Only a few weeks before I had been subediting his copy; now I was rousing unhappy sources past midnight to check if his stories were true. They invariably were.

On the night that Elvis Presley died the news desk was inundated with calls asking for confirmation. We also had to organise quick coverage of the birth of Louise Brown, the first test-tube baby. Another evening we were tipped off that Idi Amin, the notorious Ugandan dictator, had been ousted and was flying to England.

Stanley Baldwin, who was a law lecturer by day and had the pale complexion of someone who rarely saw the sun, found in his contacts book a number for the president. As the junior reporter it was my duty to call it, and a deep, rich voice responded.

'The president is not on his way to England', he said. He sounded very certain. I still think it might have been the president himself.

Occasionally I was sent outside the newsroom into the real world. I attended a meeting of the National Front in north London, where burly men wearing what looked like policemen's boots said appalling things about those from other races. I covered a dinner at the Law Society and my subsequent news story earned a protest from the president, a well-known and (according to my father) tricky criminal lawyer. He complained that I had not made clear that his after-dinner remarks had been made in a personal capacity.

I was a guest at a dinner given by the McWhirter twins, founders of the Guinness Book of Records and supporters of right-wing causes, to honour those who had contributed to 'freedom'. The honour that year went to the owner of a factory called Grunwick where the workers, mainly Asian women on very low wages, had been locked out for months. Everyone assumed that since I was from the *Times* I was a sympathiser; for once I kept my counsel.

A happier occasion was the evening before the Queen's silver jubilee, which I spent walking up and down the Mall speaking to grateful subjects camping out to ensure a good view of the next day's festivities. When my shift was over I changed into a dinner jacket, collected the editor's junior secretary (later a journalist and news presenter) who had changed into a long flowing gown, and together we went to an Anniversary Ball being held at the Royal Albert Hall. Working for the top people's paper had its perks.

In my non-working hours I started work on a novel based on my experiences. I have it still and it's an interesting relic. It sits in a cardboard folder, typewritten, churned out on a time-expired black ribbon and hard to read, full of written-in corrections and misspellings. The content bristles with stock figures and stereotypes, few of which would be usable today, with details from a lost world: yellowing copy paper, the battering of typewriters and even, in the London Underground, a non-smoking carriage.

The story, inspired by the pot-boilers of Arthur Hailey, combined several strands taken from my experiences: a cash-strapped liberal newspaper cosying up to a right-wing millionaire, a press conference hijacked by a participant with an axe to grind, and a tentative romance snuffed out when the hero (loosely based on my friend John Ezard) is killed by an IRA bomb.

One of the few passages I am happy to put into the public gaze describes the frustrations of night reporting:

> 'A picture, intended for the front page, had somehow been lost
> at King's Cross; a late night press conference, expected to yield a
> good strong story, had yielded precisely nothing; the lawyers had
> been unusually pernickety; and the main rival's first edition carried
> an exclusive story about an education report which, in spite of its
> intrinsic dullness, it had seemed prudent to chase up, even until

one o'clock in the morning. By then some of the printers had walked out and it all became a waste of time anyway.' (Tim Albert, untitled, unpublished manuscript, 1977)

3.10: Back to school

Between my regular shifts I was still writing articles about education, and one of them took me back to my old school Douai. It was part of a series for the *TES* in which reporters revisited their own schools.

I understood later that the school had been in two minds whether to let me come. I was keen to do it, however, partly for the money and partly to work out some of my own feelings towards the place. I was not intending to do a hatchet job, though by now, a decade after leaving, I was opposed to public schools and no longer a Catholic.

Father Wilfrid, the teacher who had witnessed my total inability to understand physics, was now headmaster. I had a stilted interview with him, though in retrospect he had been brave to take part.

He told me of his philosophy of the 'other Rs' – religion, responsibility and respect. He wanted every boy to leave the school 'a well-informed Catholic, who is also a gentleman in all senses of the word, and who is possessed of the requisite corpus of knowledge that will fit him for his future life, whatever that will be'.

There had been changes. Hair was longer and the grey suits we used to wear had been replaced by sensible sweaters and jackets. There were more clubs: canoeing, squash, radio-controlled aeroplanes and politics. More boys had cubicles and all the metal beds had been replaced by wooden ones, designed by Father Wilfrid and made by the boys.

Girlfriends were allowed down at weekends, when they ate in the refectory and stayed the night in matron's flat. Matron was still there, though her hair was greyer than I remembered it and she told me that she had taken up writing short stories for the Irish newspapers. She also reminded me of my unhappiness.

'I have just had a young boy in here in floods of tears because he was so miserable,' she said. 'I told him that you were coming to see me – that you were also miserable – but were now working for the *Times*.'

The curriculum now included general studies and computer science, but not what Father Wilfrid dismissed as the '-ologies'. Religious instruction was still prominent, though with a greater emphasis on 'fundamentals' rather than personal and social issues. When I asked some prefects what they knew about

Karl Marx, one replied that they had been shown a short film about him. He thought it all seemed 'very involved'.

I was pleased to hear that the penalty for smoking had been reduced from eight strokes of the cane to a £1 fine (proceeds to cancer research) and £5 on the second offence. There were other imaginative punishments, such as rising early to tidy the school grounds, but the head still used the cane for serious offences.

'The short answer is that for quite a number of boys the most intelligent part of their anatomy is the seat of their pants,' said Father Wilfrid.

One problem he identified was rising costs. Since I had left the school, eight monks had left the monastery and the shortfall was made up with lay teachers, who cost more. To make savings, the prep school had been moved from its Hampshire hill top to a newly constructed block in the school grounds. The Italian and Irish servants had been replaced by self-service catering. Nevertheless fees had risen from £100 a term in my day to £500 a term. I concluded:

> 'So the future may not be too bright. And in so far as that might mean the end for a single sex, single religion, independent and academic school, then I for one shall not mourn. But having said that, and having revisited the school, I am still not wholly convinced that there is not somewhere there a particular ethos that survives (even if the Catholicism is rejected) that has a particular value and which produces good conscientious objectors and community activists as well as good solicitors and army officers. I would have misgivings about losing that'. (Tim Albert, Religion, Responsibility and Respect, *Times Educational Supplement* 1975)

The school closed in 1999 and the buildings turned into homes for the well-heeled.

3.11: A specialist, briefly

In the autumn of 1977 I was approached about two full-time jobs. One was as a reporter on the *TES* and the other as deputy education correspondent on the *Daily Express*. I declined both.

The first would have barred me from writing or editing for other national newspapers. The second would have had me writing for a paper with very different views from mine, which was a pity since the job came with £100 expenses a week on top of genuine expenses. This tax fiddle, popular among national newspapers at the time, would have netted me an extra £700 a week tax free at today's prices.

Then a third offer came along. Peter Wilby, who a few years earlier had beaten me to the post of education correspondent of the *New Statesman*, was appointed education correspondent of the *Sunday Times*. (He was later to return to the *New Statesman* as editor.) With his support, the editor Anthony Howard, who had given me one of my first breaks in London and for whom I had been writing occasional pieces ever since, offered me the post.

It was a step up. I was now a specialist reporter and not just a jobbing hack. The *New Statesman* paid me a small retainer in return for regular pieces, and I had plenty of time to work shifts and write articles. As correspondent for a national publication, I became a fully-fledged member of the education correspondents' group. This entitled me to sit down at regular lunches in Kettner's restaurant in the West End along with the national correspondents and editors of the *Times* supplements.

There we would network and, after the meal, listen to an invited worthy who we hoped would give us a good story. The only contribution I still remember was a sparkling and witty presentation by Ken Livingstone, then an up-and-coming Labour politician with an interest in education.

The down-side was that the *New Statesman* did not have the deep coffers of the other publications I had been working for. I had become accustomed to the grand world of expense account living; now I was working for a cash-strapped left-wing weekly. When I covered the annual conference of the National Union of Teachers in Brighton I had to slum it in a second class railway carriage and, worse, stay in a mid-terrace boarding house. I tried to spend as much time as possible with my colleagues languishing at the Grand

and the Metropole Hotels. Anthony Howard, went one waspish comment, was as careful with his publication's money as he was with his own.

More seriously, there were not enough funds for investigative journalism. I had to seek out little-known stories that could be written without too much research, or summarise current stories in witty commentaries. But if there was no cash, there was certainly cachet. In one copy of the magazine that I carefully keep, my name appears on the front cover with Clive James, David Lodge, Malcolm Bradbury, Kingsley Amis and DJ Enright, and in the same size typeface.

I found Anthony Howard an inspiring editor, with the knack of making you go just that little bit further. Several times he sent my articles back for reworking, mainly because he thought the endings could be stronger, but the more I sweated the more I realised that his judgment was sound.

The first story I wrote for the magazine attacked one of the privileges that many of my new colleagues had enjoyed: an Oxbridge education. Under the headline **Streaming Spires**, it took as its starting point a still-familiar tale. A head teacher had written to the papers about a star pupil who had failed to get an interview for Oxford, and I followed this up. I quoted the figures: 28% of applicants to Oxbridge were from independent schools, which transformed into 39% of successful candidates.

'Of course there is a case to be made for institutions of excellence' I wrote, 'But the case for them collapses if entry to them is not on academic merit alone'. I floated the idea of a public inquiry – 'particularly if it grasps the real education nettle and declares that the best way of ensuring that excellence is kept well apart from privilege would be to abolish the independent sector'. (Tim Albert, Streaming Spires, *New Statesman*, December 9, 1977).

Peter Wilby sent me a note with the splendid compliment (and one that I have unashamedly handed out to others ever since) that he wished he had written it himself. The letter pages continued the debate, which of course is still going on four decades later, and in much the same terms.

It was not just in elite universities that the dead hand of tradition was stifling change. I took a trip up to Sutton-in-Ashfield where some fairly modest innovation had been ground down to a halt. A dynamic headmaster, Stewart Wilson, had got rid of uniforms, bells and streaming – and had introducing a new curriculum. A small opposition movement gathered, and it found its opportunity when members learnt about a lesson in swearing and complained publicly. **Parents cane the swearing classes,** snorted the *Daily Mirror*.

Normally the storm would have passed, had it not been for political changes. Control of the council had moved recently from Labour to Conservative. Urged on by a local governor, a doctor who sent his child to a private school, the council called in Her Majesty's Inspectors.

The Inspectors, who clearly weren't as hidebound as I had suggested in my article a few years before, gave the school a good report. So the parents set up their own working group to come up with the findings they wanted. But the damage was done. The head found another job and staff morale plummeted. 'We were so nearly there', one of them said to me. 'If only they had left us alone'.

I found an even more depressing story when I wrote about the Youth Opportunities Programme. Some 60,000 young people were coming out of school each year with no formal qualifications, and this vocational approach was launched with a great fanfare. (Sound familiar?) I visited one of their landmark premises.

> 'In one section a small group, mainly boys, would be spending about three months manufacturing and assembling various trolleys, ironically intended for the educational service which had so recently defined them as failures.

> 'In another section a group, mainly girls, was taking part in a huge game of make-believe, pretending that their classrooms were commercial offices and that the invoices they received and the problems they were asked to solve concerned real companies, real orders, real people.

> 'In a third and sadder section, a group of less able children were assembling tricky little light bulbs, packaging them up and sending them off to the local college where, unknown to them, another group would dismantle them.' (Tim Albert, Bright lads wanted – ready to learn about boredom, *New Statesman*, July 14, 1978)

I found the job challenging and interesting, and my stories were attracting compliments. So when Anthony Howard announced in the early summer of 1978 that he was going to the *Observer* as deputy editor, I was not unduly concerned. His replacement was Bruce Page, a tough investigative journalist (dubbed 'the Colonel' by Private Eye) who had successfully run the *Sunday Times* Insight team. The first piece I wrote for him – a court case for unfair discrimination brought by a would-be student at the North London Polytechnic – he asked me to change substantially.

A few days later on a Saturday morning, a thank-you-and-goodbye letter from him dropped on my doormat. I was fired, and it was completely unexpected. My now ex-editor paid tribute to my professionalism before adding that my attitudes were not in line with the direction he wanted the magazine to take. That night I had to go to a cousin's 21st birthday party and give a cheery toast, but (to put it mildly) my heart wasn't in it.

My head, on the other hand, told me that this kind of thing happened all the time. The job of an editor is to define the talent you want, and if you feel someone does not have these qualities then that person should move on. But it's upsetting. To make matters worse, I was no longer eligible to attend the regular lunches of the education correspondents. I was back as a jobbing freelance.

The ulcerative colitis became more troublesome and I started suffering from near-constant headaches. I was sent to a specialist and had a barrage of tests. Finally came the diagnosis: cluster headaches.

'What does this mean?' I asked.

'It means that you get a lot of headaches, in a cluster,' was the reply.

'Yes,' I said. 'That's why I came to see you.'

I continued to suffer, often walking the streets in the early hours of the morning as a way of dealing with the pain. The symptoms clustered on and off for nearly a decade, until an osteopath, working on my neck, cured them in two sessions.

Meanwhile I started applying for jobs, and one week came across a vacancy for someone to go to the Bahamas to train journalists. I spent hours preparing my letter of application, only to find that the recruiter was the new subeditor at the *THES* with whom I shared a desk a couple of times a week. We went out to the pub for a chat and he put me forward for the job, which I duly got.

I started to get ready. I had several briefings from my recruiter, found tenants for my house (with care of the cat written into the lease by my brother the lawyer), arranged to become the local stringer for the *Times*, had a briefing at the Foreign Office, bought a lightweight suit, held a farewell party, packed up my belongings in my old school trunk, was fêted at the pub by the *Times* night staff, and had a farewell dinner with my family which turned out to be more of a farewell than I realised.

In October 1978 I flew to Nassau, riding on a wave of jealousy from my now former colleagues.

3.12: Burnt by the sun

I lasted a year in the Bahamas.

In retrospect it was unlikely to be the place where a sacked white liberal could safely lick his wounds. Underneath the glittering veneer of the smart resorts (most of which were unapproachable on my salary), I found the country poor and divided. I failed to impress my employers and my co-workers. I worked six days a week and lived on the wrong side of the island. I was lonely. A hurricane with the same name as my brother smashed into the country and in the middle of the year I had to fly home at short notice.

This did not square with the image of the islands as a haven of luxury and sophistication: 'It's better in the Bahamas', went the slogan at the time. Until five years before it had been a British colony, and among the palm trees and bougainvillea it sported whitewashed colonial buildings, policemen with red-striped trousers, judges with wigs, a parliament with a mace.

It also had luxury hotels and lavish villas, though the latter tended to nestle behind security fences. For some decades the sun and the sea (seasoned with a little sin) had attracted some seriously rich people to the islands. Its reputation had been enhanced by the decision to move the Duke of Windsor there, well away from the Nazis, during the second world war and appoint him governor. Now wealthy incomers mixed with wealthy local elites: long-established white families and a new generation of mainly black politicians and businessmen.

But away from these pockets of luxury, the glitter vanished. The nondescript tracts of scrubland between the resorts were dotted with litter and rusted abandoned cars. Shops out of sight from tourist eyes were poorly stocked. For many families home was a small wooden hut, roughly the size of my brother's garden shed back in Esher. There were constant reports of violence, sometimes against tourists but usually against family members.

Earlier fortunes had been built on piracy, slavery and smuggling; current ones were being built on gambling, off-shore financial services (piracy of a sort, one might argue), and drug smuggling. Every so often the papers would run a story about a mystery plane landing in the middle of the night on a remote island, sometimes accompanied by unknown people with guns. The police looked into it, but the mysteries were never solved.

A charismatic prime minister, the London-trained lawyer Lynden Pindling, led the government. He stayed as prime minister for another 13 years, despite mounting concerns that he had been taking money from Colombian drug barons. One official report, published several years after I had left, revealed that somehow what he spent managed to be eight times what he officially earnt.

Pindling and his party had won power only after a bruising battle with the opposition party, and the struggle continued not just in parliament (though the opposition was weak), but also in the press (where the noise was much louder). The morning newspaper, the *Guardian*, was strictly pro-government. The evening paper I worked for, the *Tribune*, carried the flag for the opposition.

The *Tribune's* owner was a larger-than-life figure, Sir Etienne Dupuch. His father had founded the paper in 1903 and Etienne became editor in 1919 after returning from service in the first world war. For decades he was a valiant and outspoken critic of the worst colonial excesses, then found himself overtaken by more radical, more populist politicians.

When I arrived he was in his late 70s and the editor was his daughter, another tough London-trained lawyer. But it still felt like Sir Etienne's paper. Each day we published an angry signed editorial written by him, and rumour had it that he had piled up enough editorials to last six months after his death.

From time to time he and his wife visited the newsroom, peering out from the editor's glass fronted office and sometimes sallying forth to talk to the journalists. On one of these occasions he told me about his good friend Lord Beaverbrook. He also expounded his view that the worst thing the British had done was to give up their empire – voluntarily. As someone who had not long before turned down a lucrative job offer from the *Daily Express* for political reasons, I found little common ground. Having been a freelance for most of my working life, I lacked the political skills to cover the cracks.

I quickly lost the support of my bosses, as well as that of the two expatriates on the paper. One was an accountant and the other a former *Sun* subeditor; both disliked my relatively privileged upbringing and my fancy, liberal ways.

I worried about racism, and then worried some more about whether worrying about racism was itself racist. Like many well-intentioned innocents before me, I did not realise that sympathising with the oppressed did not buy their support (nor should it have done). I also did not realise that, while there was no love lost between black Bahamians and white Bahamians, both groups agreed that they had had quite enough of English men (sic) coming out and telling them what to do, whatever their motivation.

I did not have the compensation of a fulfilling social life, though that was largely my own fault. I had chosen to live in a spacious apartment: newly built, light and airy, with deep-pile green fitted carpets – and a large spare room for the friends and family members I hoped would visit. My enthusiasm was only slightly dimmed by the loyal colony of cockroaches that clearly liked the place as much as I did.

The downside – and the reason I found it affordable – was that it was a long way from the action, a good half-hour's drive from the capital in a place called Coral Harbour. This was intended to have been another enclave for the rich, but the developers had run out of money. They left behind a small network of canals, dotted with some completed homes, and a small network of roundabouts and potholed roads, along which I would walk at night, still nursing my cluster headaches. Looming over the area was the concrete shell of a tall hotel, originally a key part of the development but long since abandoned and looted.

Every morning except Sunday I would drive into town in my large, second-hand US car – the type used by gun-slinging cops in TV shows. The wheel was on the left but we drove on the left. In the late afternoon I would drive back, cook dinner, listen to the news broadcasts from Miami and go to bed. Occasionally I would pass an hour in the company of my neighbour in the flat above, a retired American mathematician called Truly who had called in to the Bahamas in his yacht and stayed to teach in the local college. But I spent a lot of time on my own.

I managed to mix with some expatriates at weekends. Some were sympathetic teachers and doctors and nurses, but the largest group was made up of accountants and I had little in common with them. On the night of 4 May 1979, when Mrs Thatcher won her first term as prime minister, I was among a group of British subjects and postal voters hearing the results at the British embassy. I was the only one to mourn the passing of Labour.

Despite my unhappiness, the early part of my job seemed to go well enough. The task was to train some Bahamian journalists. We picked an interesting quartet of trainees: a young school-leaver who had been a noted junior sportsman; a young man who had come back from a Benedictine college in America; a young woman who had spent some time in England while her father, an engineer, was on attachment there; and the daughter of the proprietors of the Chinese restaurant where I took my lunch.

I modelled the training on the course I had been on eight years before in Plymouth: a short period in the classroom with typing, shorthand, journalism theory and ethics. We also had practical sessions and I arranged some outside visits. One was to the new defence force being set up by a retired Royal Naval officer to limit drug-running, and another to the recently opened Club Med, then considered a raunchy addition to the tourist scene (though with a good buffet).

I had to cope with unexpected cultural difficulties. The British influence was still evident, but the Bahamas was so near the United States – most televisions were tuned in to Miami stations – that it was waning fast. For instance, cricket had largely given way to basketball and baseball. There was only one properly maintained cricket pitch and that was in the grounds of the prison.

I found the clash between the two cultures was particularly acute when it came to matters of grammar and style, a key part of what I was teaching. Should we write about 'honour' or 'honor', and were we served in shops or stores by 'assistants' or by 'clerks'? My employers insisted on English-English usage. I enforced the rules, but it felt colonial.

After about six months I heard on the grapevine that my job had been offered to someone else, even though technically I had the option of another 18 months to go. I also heard whispers that I was considered a frightful lefty – and that my name was on a list at the British High Commission of people to be watched. It might have been my (short-lived) association with the *New Statesman*, but I did not feel a threat to international order.

When the first part of the training course was over, three of the four trainees moved into the newsroom as staff reporters. The fourth, Mark Beckford, was assigned to help me launch a magazine: the *Bahamas Weekender*, a 24-page tabloid targeted at Bahamians and tourists.

Mark and I constituted the editorial team and the first edition appeared in May with a lead story about vanishing wildlife in the islands. I commissioned the cover, wrote local and national news summaries, researched and wrote some features and commissioned others, selected syndicated material, interviewed notables, wrote about coming events, did a restaurant review, and subedited the articles. The magazine went to press on the Friday evening and on the Saturday Mark and I had to report for a day's work in the main newsroom.

I ghosted a gripping three-part story about a Bahamian who claimed to have drifted for 10 days in an open boat without food or water, though later my employers told me it was not true.

Mark wrote a story that there were poltergeists in a nearby house. Sightseeing crowds gathered, with people claiming to see a tree move, a sock hit a shoe, and a suitcase converse with a policeman. Rocks started to fly, though probably not with supernatural origins, and on the third day the police had to use water hoses to disperse the crowd. The daily papers wrote it up avidly, but Mark wrote a considered piece:

'What really happened at the house? A hoax? A plot? A poltergeist? Your guess is as good as mine. But whatever happened, it was enough to make a woman who had never believed in the supernatural do so now'. (Mark Beckford, The haunted house: was it a ghost? *Bahamas weekender*, May 26, 1979)

After the eighth issue, in early July, I was told that the magazine was losing money steadily and would close. I had never seen any commercial information or any market research, but the decision was final. With several months of my contract to go, I found myself back in the newsroom, demoted from news editor (effectively the editor of the day) to subeditor.

I was sustained by regular visitors coming out from England to stay. My cousin Anthony lifted my spirits and my reputation when his tight, curly hair elicited the question of whether we had African blood in our ancestry. (My father always claimed that we had.)

I found one local ally – Larry Smith, Bahamas-born to English parents, who worked for the government communications agency and a journalist with a good style and a fine critical mind. He contributed to the *Weekender* and later we plotted unsuccessfully to raise funds to relaunch it. We fell out later, for reasons that I no longer know, but he helped me get through a difficult time and I remain in his debt.

I might have found some consolation by filing stories for the *Times*, but by now the presses were silent as its new owner Rupert Murdoch faced off the print unions. In the event there were only two international stories of note while I was there. The German Chancellor Helmut Schmidt touched down for a short visit between meetings, and held a press conference. A few months later the just-deposed Shah of Iran spent a short and controversial exile in one of the swankier properties before being moved on. But I did attend the press conferences and they brought me into contact with travelling journalists. It underlined how far I was from the London media life I was used to.

Towards the end of my stay, we received warnings that Hurricane David was moving towards the island. There was a slow build-up as it, and the damage it left in its wake, was tracked across Cuba. On the Sunday morning that it was due to strike I got up early to listen to the weather forecast, and found my neighbour Truly taping his window and making his boat safe. There was unusual tension the air, caused partly by our imagination, partly by a sudden drop of air pressure.

As the wind started to build I left the low ground of Coral Harbour to drive into Nassau. Shops had opened specially to sell emergency supplies. I had lunch with Larry and his family and we went to the shore where the sky had an eerie glow and the sea bulged with menace.

As the winds strengthened I drove to the sturdy and (we hoped) hurricane-proof *Tribune* offices, along with a lot of fresh water, some food and the other expatriates working on the paper. One of our photographers, a jolly and enthusiastic young man, joined us when the winds became too fierce for even him to venture out of doors.

That night I slept fitfully in a sleeping bag, waking from time to time to hear the winds howling and feel the building shake. In the morning we ventured out: palm trees were smashed, buildings damaged, and the rain still bucketing down. I drove carefully back to Coral Harbour to find my taped-up windows unbroken. But everywhere the electricity was out, not because of the wind but because of the incessant rain that seeped into the infrastructure.

We set about getting things back to normal, though my heart was not in it.

3.13: Lost and found

By the time Hurricane David had smashed across the Bahamas, my life had changed. This particular strand of the story started a few months into my stay, just before Christmas 1978.

My first Christmas away from home was always going to be a difficult time. I missed my family and the Christmas rituals that went with it. I found it difficult to reconcile the festive season I was used to with temperatures of 80 degrees and the bouncy versions of *Good King Wenceslas* and *The First Noel* belting out from loudspeakers high in the palm trees. My one consolation was that an unusually high influx of yuletide tourists allowed me to write the perfect Christmas headline: **No room at the inn.**

On the day itself I queued up for one of the phones at Nassau Airport (I did not have a phone at my flat) and spoke to my family as they were finishing their Christmas lunch. As well as my parents and my brother and sister-in-law, there were now two small fair-haired nephews on whom, like all good uncles, I doted and missed terribly. After a stilted conversation I drove into Nassau and flitted through a couple of expatriate functions with my friend Jane, a maths teacher from England who, like me, had gone to the Ursuline Convent in Wimbledon. But I did not feel part of the celebrations and it felt too sultry for turkey, crackers and paper hats.

But I was sustained by the thought of the trip to the Bahamas that my parents were planning for March. It was one of the things we talked about on the phone that day. But it never happened. One afternoon at the end of January I got a phone call at the newspaper. It was my father, telling me the trip was off: my mother had not been well and was going to hospital for tests (that fearful phrase again). A few days later he called again: my mother had been diagnosed with advanced cancer of the pancreas.

I wanted to fly home at once, but was advised to wait. For a couple of weeks I fretted from afar, regularly phoning home from the office for updates. Then, in the second week of March I got the call that I should come.

Before I had gone to the Bahamas, my brother David had wisely suggested that I get an American Express credit card in case I needed to buy a ticket home in a hurry. I had bought one and now used it. I flew to Miami, where I moped around the airport shops during a six-hour stopover, and then took the plane to London. During the flight I sat up all night listening repeatedly to a Mozart piano concerto.

I arrived in London early in the morning, to be greeted by three generations of family: my father, my brother and one of my nephews who, too young to realise the awfulness of the situation, greeted me with the broadest smile. I had conflicting emotions: happy to be back but devastated by the circumstances.

Later that day I visited my mother in the private wing of University College Hospital. The first shock was that the sister in charge was the friend of a friend. The second shock, much less pleasant, was my mother's appearance: painfully thin, distracted, and talking about roaming the woods in Bristol with some young man I had never heard of. I think she registered my arrival and knew who I was, but I'll never be sure.

My house in Gospel Oak was full of tenants so I stayed with my father in Wimbledon. For the next few days we went up to London together to the hospital. We did little more than sit by her bedside, sustained by the friends and relatives who came into her room, clearly distressed and saying their goodbyes. On the fifth day my mother died. About an hour before, my father and I saw fit to call a priest to give her the last rites. This agitated her greatly, but again we'll never know why. The loose ends dangle still.

A few days later we held a formal and well-attended funeral in the church at Wimbledon. My father could not bear entertaining people in the house that had lost one of its two central characters, so we held a small family wake at a cousin's house nearby. Letters flooded in from all kinds of people paying tribute to my mother's kindness.

I spent a few more days in Wimbledon visiting friends and mourning before flying back to the Bahamas. I did not go to an empty flat. Our American friends the Goldwaters had planned to visit when my parents were there, and – encouraged by my father – they had kept to the arrangement. They stayed with me in Coral Harbour and I found it comforting to show them the tourist sites – and share lobster at local prices. But I could not express emotion. Perhaps I had gone through the bereavement process decades earlier when I was sent away to boarding school?

Now the story takes a new turn. My friends in the Bahamas rallied round, and one Sunday my friend Jane encouraged me to meet her at the Sunday festivities at the Travellers Rest. She had a friend staying with her that she thought I might like to meet.

Barbara Greenberg was from New York, a television production manager – Jewish, liberal, smart on the outside and the inside, working on Emmy-award-winning dance programmes for public television. She liked England and the English, having made several trips to London in the past few years. We chatted about the media worlds of London and New York, and found that the 3,000 miles separating our upbringings did not stop us having similar views. I invited her and Jane to a restaurant (I was writing restaurant reviews at the time). A few days again I repeated the invitation, though this time without Jane.

Barbara and I had dinner and walked on the beach, though the blossoming romance was temporarily halted when she stubbed her toe. We went together to the hospital; there was a hairline fracture. After she had gone back to New York we started to correspond. A few months later, in a gap between TV productions, she came out to Nassau again. Jane had gone to England for the summer holidays and she stayed with me in Coral Harbour. When she told her mother that Jane would not be there she asked perceptively:

'What's his name?'

My father came out in October. My contract had finished and I had plenty of time to show him round the Bahamas. It was strange to see him on his own, and he was clearly devastated by my mother's sudden death. His bad leg – the one that 15 years before had triggered the diagnosis of motor neurone disease – was making it difficult for him to walk. But he was keen to do things, and my friends again rallied round.

We took a side trip to Jamaica, where at one tourist attraction he was lifted by two muscular Jamaicans onto a small boat to float down the 'rapids'. For a short while his broad grin returned. We stayed in a pink hotel in the north, full of Cuban party members, and with an extremely loud German man at the next table whom we spoke badly of – until my father noted his concentration camp number.

Once he had flown home I started to pack up. I flew to New York to stay with Barbara, the new woman in my life.

1980s: health care blues

In which I learn about the world of doctors,
import a soulmate, and wander into
the new digital age

Time line

1980   John Lennon assassinated; Rubik's cube craze

1981   New disease identified as AIDS; IBM introduces personal computers; Prince Charles marries Lady Diana Spencer; racial tension in Brixton and other areas

1982   Economic recession and high unemployment; Argentina invades Falkland Islands; Henry VIII's ship *Mary Rose* is raised

1983   Mrs Thatcher wins second term with a large majority; Griffiths reports introduces general managers to NHS

1984   George Orwell's predictions don't take place; miners' strike; IRA bomb explodes during Conservative Party conference at Brighton

1985   Miners' strike ends; Nobel peace prize for International Physicians for the Prevention of Nuclear War; riots in Birmingham and London; famine in Ethiopia; Greenpeace ship *Rainbow Warrior* is sunk

1986   Chernobyl nuclear disaster; major nationalised industries are privatised

1987   Mrs Thatcher wins third term with majority of 102; corporal punishment ends in state schools; *Herald of Free Enterprise* sinks leaving harbour; 'Black Monday' stockmarket crash; DNA used to convict criminals

1988   Pan Am flight 103 bombed over Lockerbie; Mrs Thatcher announces review of NHS

1989   Berlin wall is dismantled and world leaders declare end of cold war; students massacred in Tiananmen Square; Tim Berners-Lee invents 'world wide web'

4.1: Regrouping

As the 1970s became the 1980s, I was back in Wimbledon. Things were not looking good. At six weeks short of my 33rd birthday, I was living with my recently-bereaved father in the family house while my tenants in Gospel Oak served out their notice. Neither my father nor I had been invited to a new year's party. I had no job. I had a proper girlfriend at last, but we were separated by 3,000 miles.

For most of the last two months of 1979 I had stayed with Barbara in her Manhattan studio apartment, dodging the flailing paws of Freckle, her ferociously jealous male cat. While she went out to work I learnt how to do the *New York Times* crossword and scoured the New York newspaper scene for a job. I met Barbara's mother and her family and friends. I was taken to her aunt and uncle at Princeton where I learnt the rituals of Thanksgiving, which included meeting scattered cousins and eating what I considered to be dangerously undercooked turkey.

In turn I introduced her to the Goldwaters who had sponsored my life-changing visit to the United States a decade before. We borrowed their car and drove through New England to Canada, and back. We went to a college football game, where I ate hot dogs and struggled with the rules. We were having fun, but one day, with Christmas arriving fast, I suddenly realised that I needed to be 'back home', with my now-depleted family.

When I got back I saw how my father's life had changed. He had converted the top floor of the family house into a self-contained flat, now occupied by a housekeeper and her husband. They were no strangers: she was the sister of our long-ago Austrian au pair Mitzi and he had been a gardener at my childhood haunt of Cannizaro Park.

That year my father hosted no Christmas party. The day itself we spent with my brother David and his family, now increased to three boys. We went through the usual routine: a brief speech from Santa Claus (it was my role now to put on the white beard and red dressing grown), a frenzied opening of presents, and some sleight-of-hand with the sixpences in the Christmas pudding. But the usual orchestrator of the event was missing. We didn't talk much about my mother, but her absence filled the rooms.

Early in January I returned to my small terraced house in Gospel Oak and set about settling back. My trunk arrived from the Bahamas. It had been prised open while in storage at Nassau and everything of value had been stolen. I shouldn't have minded this post-colonial redistribution of wealth but I did.

Reluctant to return to the hustle of freelancing, I looked for a permanent job. I heard of a vacancy at *World Medicine*. I knew two of the magazine's staff members (one of whom, Geoff Watts, was leaving to pursue a radio career), and had already contributed odd pieces: the way my ulcerative colitis was diagnosed; the medical rituals surrounding the birth of a nephew; a questionnaire I had received from the Royal Free Hospital with 250 questions asking if I suffered from brucellosis and/or probed my ears with sharp objects.

I expressed an interest in the vacancy. A few days later I found myself lunching with the editor, Michael O'Donnell, in a smart West End restaurant. It went well, our joint Catholic upbringing oiling the wheels. During the dessert I was offered a job as executive editor, number three in the hierarchy. It looked as if my freelance days were over.

4.2: A new direction

My new place of work was on the fourth (and top) floor of Clareville House, a grade II listed building above a smart steak house just south of Leicester Square. For most of my journalistic career I had worked in large open-plan newsrooms. But here, off a corridor long enough and wide enough for occasional scratch games of cricket, we each had our own little eyrie. It was the first time that I had an office to myself, and also the first time I had a secretary, though I had to share her with the deputy editor.

There was a quiet, collegial atmosphere. Michael O'Donnell presided as a genial abbot, encouraging us on our chosen paths. His early life had taken him conventionally through the Jesuit boarding school Stonyhurst to Trinity Hall Cambridge, St Thomas's Hospital London, and then a 12-year career as a Surrey GP. He strayed into writing advertising copy, magazine articles, books and plays. By the time I met him, he had led a successful campaign to push the General Medical Council into the first half of the 20th century, and was appearing regularly on radio and television.

In 1980 Michael had been editor for 14 years. He had positioned the magazine between the brash medical newspapers and the serious medical journals, a blend of *Punch* and *Private Eye* with a touch of *Scientific American* thrown in. He was well aware that doctors constantly complained of too much to read, so his aim was to make *World Medicine* the one publication they would read for pleasure.

Large parts of it were written by doctors, many of whom decades later were still describing to me the thrill of receiving a letter that their submitted article would be published. For the remaining pages, Michael used his extensive contacts – many of them fellow members of the stylish Garrick Club a few hundred yards from our office – to commission a wide range of articles. These authors included barristers, politicians, media folk and actors, ranging from the *Observer* columnist Katharine Whitehorn to the actor Robert Morley. They were not doctors, but in the main understood those who were.

He nourished young writers. One article we published – about the financial pressures brought about by heart transplants at Papworth Hospital – was written by a fresh-faced tyro called Alan Rusbridger, later editor-in-chief of the *Guardian*. (Alan Rusbridger, What's going on at Papworth?, *World Medicine*, February 7, 1981).

Not all contributors wrote well and the magazine's reputation of being well written was not strictly true; it was well subedited. Some of the articles we received were dreadful: unstructured, verbose, pompous. But when we saw the germ of a good idea – or a good joke – we would spend more time than most carefully nursing it into shape.

Soon after I joined, Michael passed me a copy of Strunk and White's *The Elements of Style* (Allyn and Bacon, 1999), an American classic guide for writers. The original text was written by William Strunk Jr at Cornell University, and updated and enlarged some 50 years later by his student EB White, then a *New Yorker* writer and author of the children's book *Charlotte's Web* (Harper and Brothers, 1952). Michael introduced the verb (transitive) 'to strunk', and strunking was rife. Not all authors were grateful for this service.

'You've taken out my personality', one mega-strunked doctor once complained to me. I resisted responding that in that case I had certainly done him a favour.

Those who overestimated their talents had their bubbles swiftly pierced. One doctor complained that his article had been badly subedited and then found his letter published in full without subediting; the uncorrected errors of grammar and style did not enhance his reputation as he had hoped. The historian Frank Honigsbaum insisted that his overblown response to a moderately hostile review of his book should be published in full. His wishes were honoured – but in 6 point. (Frank Honigsbaum, Please use your *BMJ* magnifier, *World Medicine*, November 14, 1981).

One of Michael's additional missions was to redistribute the income of rich publishers among poor writers. And he felt that writing for other publications, provided they were not in direct competition, broadened the mind as much as it deepened the pocket. He was particularly proud of the time when, showing a senior executive around the building, it dawned on him that, though every journalist on the staff was beavering away at a typewriter, none of them was writing for *World Medicine*.

I found a downside, however, which was Michael's tendency to rule with a light touch – seasoned with a little divide and rule. This put me in direct conflict with Fiona, a few years older than me, the rather stern daughter of a general. She had assumed responsibility for meeting deadlines and ensuring that all articles complied with the rules and conventions of English grammar.

But she was not a copy editor and we fell into a power struggle. This often expressed itself in noisy disputes over the exact placement of a comma, but in reality was over who had the final say on articles that were about to be published. As managing and executive editors respectively, our titles did nothing to clarify our duties.

After a few months, my friend and deputy editor Colin Tudge left to write for the *New Scientist*, and I became deputy in practice though not in title. Michael agreed to have the copy flow altered in my favour, giving me in theory the last word on matters of style. But Fiona and I still argued, though the arguments now came at a different stage in the production process.

My discomfort was eased considerably one morning by a conversation with Professor Bryan Brooke, a distinguished retired professor of surgery recently appointed associate editor.

'Your problem is that you assume this place is run like a newspaper,' he said. 'It isn't. It's run on NHS lines. Michael is the consultant, you are his registrar, Jeremy' (Jeremy Laurance, later the distinguished health editor of the *Independent*) is the senior house officer, I am the old buffer who comes in to help out – and Fiona is the ward sister.'

His insight comforted me. Apart from the odd conflict in the production cycle, my life had taken a turn for the better. I had a full-time job and was again a specialist journalist.

4.3: Doctors discovered

By the 1980s the traditional medical men we had looked up to – characterised in fiction as the wise and caring GP Dr Finlay and the haughty yet brilliant consultant Sir Lancelot Spratt – were spending more time on the golf course. In their place appeared a new and younger breed of men and women trained in the sciences not the humanities, questioning current practices and current hierarchies, and with no memory of what health care had been like in pre-NHS days. It was an interesting time for the doctor tribe and its observers.

One of the first stories I covered for *World Medicine* was a vicious piece of in-fighting over plans by London University to cut down the number of medical schools in the capital. There was clearly a problem: 34 institutions of medical education – far too many. Most of them, crucially, were not within pockets of potential patients but within walking distance of Harley Street's rooms for private practice. It was convenient and lucrative for consultants in the inner London hospitals, but at the cost of being expensive and divisive.

The proposals to merge some of the medical schools caused uproar. Medical students, with the tacit approval of their professors, wrote emotive slogans and chained themselves to the railings. The professors wrote angry letters to the *Times*, and ostracised colleagues who were brave enough to say that the plans made sense. It became nasty.

One spring evening I sat with Professor Arthur Crisp in his garden to discuss the events. He was a courteous and clear-thinking psychiatrist from St George's and an early pioneer of treatments for eating disorders. He had also been one of the authors of the report. He had been vilified for his efforts, not least for allegedly making sure that his medical school, St George's, would be immune from major change. (In fact it had anticipated the problem a decade or so before and already moved out from Hyde Park Corner to Tooting). Professor Crisp was clearly hurt, though he admitted that the authors had thought their solutions were so obvious that they had underestimated the likely resistance.

It was nearly two years before a compromise was reached and London University started to put some of the medical schools – like St Thomas's and Guy's, St Mary's and the Charing Cross – on the path to merge.

Yet this was a time when doctors needed to be united. Major challenges were appearing, particularly over leadership of the health services.

Traditionally this had been the role of doctors. They had done this with the support of administrators – typically a retired squadron leader tasked with ensuring that the laundry was clean, the food was warm and the edicts of doctors carried out. Now a new group was being recruited and formed: NHS managers. They came with university degrees and many were fast-tracked along a special training scheme. They started to involve themselves in areas from which 'the layman' had previously been excluded.

Some far-sighted doctors tried to get their colleagues involved in management and I went off to report on a three-day course sponsored by the Department of Health. Its stated aim was to help consultants handle the new breed of managers; its real aim was to entice them to become managers themselves. There were 17 doctors on the course, all male. The tutors, recruited from business schools, suggested to them that they should not confine their analytical skills to clinical medicine – and exhorted them to get their house in order – 'otherwise others will do it for you'.

One or two were convinced; most were not. And those attending were only a tiny proportion of those who had been invited: most of their colleagues hadn't seen the point. One invited surgeon had written to the organisers testily: 'As you will know I have been invited to attend a seminar on management. This involves three days of clinical time. Does the region consider this essential?' (Tim Albert, Doctors fight back, *World Medicine*, May 17, 1980). This antipathy between medicine and management persists.

Doctors also started to find themselves challenged by colleagues in newly-developed professions (such as nursing and even social work) who were becoming far less submissive. Many patients were also starting to join in the questioning.

I led my own little charge by commissioning several of my fellow journalists to write consumer pieces. Craig Seton of the *Times* wrote about his experiences parenting a Down's syndrome child. Melanie Phillips, the social services correspondent of the *Guardian*, and Annabel Ferriman, health services correspondent for the *Times*, wrote about childbirth.

Annabel came up with a splendid story that I have cited ever since. A senior registrar who visited her glanced at the women's magazine she was reading and commented, loudly, that you could tell how much a patient knows about obstetrics by the magazines she reads. Annabel wrote: 'I made a mental note to come in for my delivery armed with copies of the *BMJ*, *Lancet* and *Solicitor's Journal*'. (Annabel Ferriman, Nine months of being better informed, *World Medicine*, March 7, 1981).

Doctors used the pages of *World Medicine* to take up the fight. One of the most popular sections was *Talking Shop*, which for a while was my responsibility. It consisted of half a dozen or so short pieces by doctors describing their career progression, their fights with bureaucracy, their views on care, and their encounters with patients – often with a twist in the tale and a lesson to be learnt. One piece I treasured came from a junior doctor (now of course a professor) who came up with the inspired suggestion that all junior doctors should have a label on their lapel showing how many hours they had been going without sleep (Graham Barker, Is sleep deprivation an essential part of medical training?, *World Medicine*, November 14, 1981)

Doctors also contributed with glee to a section called *Nooks and Crannies of the New Bureaucracy*, seeking out such examples as:

> 'Learners are asked to take their name with them to their next allocation. Should anyone have a name that does not belong or if someone has no name please contact the School of Nursing',

> 'Sticky labels to indicate allergy: These are to be used only in instances where the patient has an allergy'.

Alongside the jokes sat more serious matters. Barney Williams, a GP in Chippenham, wrote a blistering (definitely the right word) account of what would happen in his patch if the bombs went off. His scenario – and remember when he wrote this – started thus:

> 'A vacillating American president. A rigidly determined British prime minister. A bomb given by Colonel Gaddafi to the Pakistanis. The Afghanistan situation deteriorates and war breaks out. The Russian leaders decide to immobilise and then invade the American offshore fortress of Britain. Across the land the bombs begin to fall'. (B J Williams, Chippenham during World War III, *World Medicine*, November 29, 1980)

He went on to estimate that, within one minute of a standard nuclear bomb exploding, the population in his area would drop from 102,000 to 64,200. Within 24 hours it would go down to 24,200 and by the end of the week 19,850. To enable the three surviving doctors to cope he proposed getting the dying to dig their own graves, and recruiting shotgun-toting 'wardens' (now we would call them 'security') to protect the doctors. This programme might salvage 7,200 people in the area, he forecast – a 7 per cent survival rate.

On a more theoretical level, one postgraduate dean wrote of the danger that 'medicine is becoming a technology first, a science second, and an art third.' While saying that he did not want to turn the clock back, he wondered whether the order might better be reversed. A GP in Surrey wrote how the practice of medicine had changed (and was likely to do so even more).

> 'Nowadays doctors' telephones and waiting lists are filled with the fear of illness rather than with illness itself. It's good that many of the diseases we learned about as students are seen less often... but it does leave a gap in the lives of the older generation of doctors who feel to some extent deprived of their vocation and purpose... when the computers take over you might become even less of a doctor than you are now'. (RJ Cremer, No time for illness, *World Medicine*, March 8, 1980)'

The magazine teased out remarkable contributions. While I was there – and remember this was more than three decades ago – doctors raised the possibility that the whooping cough vaccine might have unwanted side-effects, called for the resignation of the head of computers at the Department of Health, highlighted the iniquity of culling badgers to prevent bovine TB, and called 'urgently' for migrants to be stopped coming in to the country and using NHS services for free.

Others raised the 'chilling prospect of genetic printouts becoming a prerequisite of marriage licences'; and the danger that too much preventive medicine would mean the survival of too many 'crumblies' (later to be called wrinklies). One contributor even spotted that many American homosexuals (as gay men were known in those days) were getting ill, a fact which he put down to the side effects of some new medication.

4.4: For better...

As I was settling into *World Medicine* a marvellous (and to be honest a long-awaited) change was taking place in my life: 'I' was merging into a 'we'. Since I had left New York, Barbara and I wrote regularly and phoned occasionally and briefly. In early February she flew over to stay with me in my small house at Gospel Oak.

She met my family and friends, who couldn't hide their approval, and we drove down to Tavistock to see the 'real' England. The weather could have nipped our relationship in the bud, but it was an unusually mild February and the daffodils in the Tamar Valley were already in full bloom. The weeks passed quickly. A couple of months later Michael O'Donnell sanctioned a trip to New York so that I could write some articles and develop my relationship with Barbara (though not necessarily in that order).

Shortly after that she bravely decided to take six months' leave of absence from Channel 13. On a Friday night in July she flew to England. I planned a special welcome, and booked a room at the Ship Hotel in Brighton. We drove there straight from Gatwick Airport. All went according to plan, until it was time to go to sleep, when a burglar alarm started to shriek just outside our hotel window. And continued shrieking.

I phoned down to the night porter who phoned up a few minutes later and told me the good news. They had located the offending premises and its owner. Then the bad news: he had gone to London for the weekend. I had no alternative but prophylactic action. Thus it was that Barbara, having given up her old life to make a new one, found herself sharing a bed with a man curled up with a piece of lavatory paper in each ear. I am lucky she stayed.

I still find it miraculous that two people brought up in different cultures and different religions 3,000 miles apart could connect so well. But there were more difficult moments to come. One Sunday I was invited to make up the numbers in a cricket team. Barbara and I went off into the sunshine together, me with my whites, she with the Sunday papers to read during what my past form suggested would be a very short innings.

It turned out to be an uncharacteristically long one. When we finally came off for tea I sailed past Barbara with a quick greeting and into the clubhouse with the other cricketers for the players' tea. The women stayed outside. Had she been able to drive, she said later, she would have left. I have never tried to clarify if she meant the cricket ground, or me.

It was not easy for her. Her visitor's visa would not allow her to work, so she spent her time being a tourist (which quickly palled), taking driving lessons on a car with a gearbox, and waiting for me to come home so we could do things together. All the while the clock ticked closer to the six months beyond which she would have to go back – or become illegal.

One evening, with just over a month to go, we were having dinner in a restaurant at the shabbier end of the King's Road when I suggested a plan that would keep her in the country. A few days later I told my family to keep clear December 22, which would have been my mother's 69th birthday.

'Are you getting engaged?' we were asked.

'No' we said. 'We are getting married'.

It was a small affair. The business part took place in Camden Registry Office with 16 guests, including Barbara's mother who flew over from the States, as did my – now our – friends the Goldwaters. Our activities were recorded by Keith Morris, the favoured photographer at *World Medicine,* who had taken iconic photographs of Elvis Costello and other musicians but never a wedding. In his photographs, all in black and white, our two parents stand out with the most enormous grins. We were both in our mid-30s and they had both clearly thought they were not going to get us off their hands.

After the ceremony we treated our guests to a multi-course banquet in our favourite Chinese restaurant on a barge in Regent's Park. We had no idea what the menu would be: the waiter we tried to tap had been sworn to secrecy by the owner. That evening my brother hosted a party for family and family friends, and on New Year's Eve we held a party for our own friends.

In the summer we held more celebrations in New York. We went there on the QEII, then considered to be the height of luxury and, we thought, a perfect choice for a belated honeymoon. The voyage got off to a bad start when a union strike kept the ship in Cherbourg. We had to cross the channel in a hastily-chartered and elderly ferry. By the time we had crossed over to our dream ship, fortified by the thought of a lavish meal, the kitchens had closed and the crew had gone to bed. We had no alternative but to do the same.

The service did not improve. I had hoped to be woken up each day with an early morning cup of tea, which I considered then and now to be a mark of fine living. Our steward told me to ring when I woke up which I duly did, and every day we were back from breakfast before he answered the call. In an attempt to control my ulcerative colitis, I was following a special diet, details of which I gave our waiter: it was dairy free and gluten free. That evening he proudly announced that the chef had made a dish especially for me. It turned out to be a quiche.

Three days out we hit a fierce storm, which kept us huddled on deck staring at the horizon trying not to be sick. We then ran into fog, which meant that the wind and sea had abated but there was no longer a horizon. The mournful bark of a fog horn accompanied our slow progress. However, the journey did end with a magnificent *coup de th*éâtre as, with the sun rising, the ship came under the Verrazano Bridge, passed the Statue of Liberty and Ellis Island, and came in to dock on the west side of the city of New York. Barbara, whose grandparents had made this journey as migrants from the pogroms in eastern Europe, found it particularly moving.

When we came back – fortunately by plane – we settled into the life of a young(ish) married couple. I startled Barbara by telling her that I planned to hire a carpenter to build some dressers in the dining room. It was another sign of being divided by a common language, as Winston Churchill and/or George Bernard Shaw may/may not have said. For an American, a dresser is a chest of drawers. Why would I want to keep our underwear in the dining room?

Still, she stayed.

4.5: ...for worse

My new role as a health journalist took on a personal dimension.

A few months before our marriage my father's worsening back pain turned out to be secondaries from prostate cancer. At that time the treatment of choice – which goes under the misleadingly floral name of orchidectomy – was to reduce the influence of testosterone by taking out the testicles. He succumbed to the procedure with good grace, and afterwards came up with a brave line.

'Doctor', he said, 'you have made a new woman of me'.

I fed the remark to Michael O'Donnell and he used it during his weekly radio appearance on the radio show *Stop the Week*.

As the months progressed the cancer spread and the jokes dried up. My father had several bouts of radiotherapy and for a while had to stay in hospital where a young nurse insisted on calling him Sid. A Sid he was not, and we had to ask her to use two Ys and both syllables. As a conscientious son and journalist, I started to write about his experiences.

One day I found him distressed to hear that his chemotherapy session had been cancelled because it was a statutory NHS holiday (an official day off for all staff) and no-one was available. On another day after his treatment he was sent home in an ambulance. The journey took three hours while all the other patients were dropped off first. No-one had thought of asking him if he would have liked to have paid for a taxi for what should have been a 10-minute journey.

David and I organised a 75th birthday party for him, and he presided with his old elegance, taking out his green smoking jacket for the occasion. It was a successful evening, with friends of all ages coming to pay tribute. A few weeks later he came to stay in my house in Gospel Oak for the weekend: I remember having to help him out of the bath.

But as the months went on he became more and more frail, more and more dependent, and more and more in pain. I drove regularly from north London to south to ferry him to and from hospital. When his housekeeper decided to move to Carlisle to be near her daughter, I recruited a replacement. He had sudden dips, and Barbara and I made several hair-raising drives because we were told the end might be near. My father was clearly grateful for what I was doing, though he startled me on one occasion by saying that my mother would have been surprised at how much I was doing for him.

By September 1981 his world had shrunk to the dining room. David and I carried his bed downstairs and turned it into a downstairs sickroom. There he lay, pitifully thin, surrounded by reminders of the life he was about to leave: his wife's cherished piano in one corner, an ornate clock inherited from his father on the mantelpiece, and on an oak sideboard the Asprey silver-plated, bell-shaped cocktail shaker, a wedding present from Great Aunt Alice.

He had round-the-clock nursing. He remained serene, though he told David that he had had a good life and was not afraid of being dead, but didn't rate this dying business. As with all his aphorisms, we never knew for certain whether he composed it on the spot, or retrieved it from the depths of his brain, which remained crystal clear.

As this was going on, not surprisingly my ulcerative colitis entered a new phase. Until now it had been more of a nuisance than a disease. I went to the loo more often than most, and used steroid suppositories at night, which had not been the ideal start to sharing a marital bed. But apart from that I had not felt particularly unwell.

Now I started to develop acute stomach pains, diarrhoea and bleeding, nausea, tiredness and depression. I was going to the loo sometimes several times an hour. Travel was difficult, partly because I felt weak but also because of the danger of getting caught short.

I started what became a lifetime habit: planning all journeys in terms of opportunities of finding a useable lavatory. It was not always successful. I remember with great embarrassment having to squat by the pavement coming back from a most jolly dinner party, and using a bucket in a store cupboard in Wimbledon station because the proper lavatory was locked.

I became a near-weekly visitor to the gastroenterology clinic at the Royal Free Hospital, and I started to write about my own patient experiences as well. Once I waited for two hours before overhearing one member of staff expressing to another their hope that the doctor I had come to see was enjoying his holiday. I had been wasting my time.

Another time I spotted the splendidly authoritarian sign on a door: 'If door is closed please wait'. In one incident which, probably wisely, I did not write about, I asked the clinic doctor what my blood results the previous weeks had shown.

'Your ESR is high', she told me.

'What does that mean', I asked.

'If you don't know, don't ask', responded the future professor.

Back at *World Medicine* I asked the same question of our consultant editor Professor Bryan Brooke, a gastroenterological surgeon.

'That's easy,' he said. 'It's a general index of inflammation.' On his advice I got myself transferred to another doctor.

Barbara and I added to our stress with house hunting. We decided to leave the inner city and finding a gentler place in leafy Surrey, returning to my family roots and nearer the next generation – I now had three fair-haired nephews to dote on. We scoured the newspapers and viewed houses that might suit a young couple hoping to start a family themselves.

One Sunday night, after visiting my father and a couple of houses, I became so ill that we had to stay overnight at my brother's house. I was up all night, as inevitably was Barbara. By the morning I was too weak to get out of bed. My sister-in-law called a duty doctor who came to the house before surgery, and within 10 minutes I was being manoeuvred down the stairs in a red blanket by ambulance workers, my youngest nephew looking on wide-eyed and frightened. Though not quite as frightened as I was.

I was taken to Kingston Hospital, a short drive away, though I remember nothing of it. I had dehydrated. For those who haven't experienced dehydration, it is a terrifying experience. I felt disengaged from life, unable to do anything and not interested in trying. I let myself be taken where I had to be taken. When doctors and nurses started to fire questions at me, I had trouble formulating the answers.

But soon I was hooked up (through my writing and bottom-wiping hand) being rehydrated and pumped full of steroids. Within an hour or so I was well enough to be placed on a golf trolley to be taken the short distance to my destination ward.

This turned out to be in the old workhouse, and many of my new companions seemed similarly dated. Mr Lewis was a former sergeant major with an erect bearing and a long, thin head who called the nurses 'Missy' and tried to keep us in order. Mr Mardar was confused and kept on putting on his best suit and making a dash for the exit. Mr Jackson was a former submariner with a flowing white beard who was old and blind but not confused.

The nurses were helpful and caring, cheerfully feeding and washing us, and in my case rescuing me from the fast-encroaching tide sweeping up my bed after I tipped over the bedpan. But it was clear that the real power belonged to the ward cleaner. She and her friends would colonise the day room for their break, their cigarette smoke curling contemptuously up into the sign that warned: 'No smoking. For patients and visitors only'.

Our first skirmish came on my second day when, as the notorious steroid-induced hunger pangs were beginning to ramp up, I asked the nurse if I could have a second sausage. A message came back from the ward cleaner: I had not ordered two; the request was denied. Two days' later I again asked for more (a suitably workhouse thing to do). This time she came to tell me off personally.

'What do you think this is – a hotel? I told the nurses last time: if you want extra food you must get your wife to bring it in.'

Soon after that I started to notice that while the ward cleaner came in empty-handed at the beginning of the day, she did not seem to leave the hospital during her shift – and then went home with a fully laden shopping bag.

I was not the only person she bullied. One morning I witnessed a shocking piece of abuse, which I wrote about later, carefully.

'Poor Mr Jackson... does like his brown bread and one morning, finding that he had got white bread by mistake, asked the nurse if it could be changed. The ward cleaner was again on guard duty, this time with her friend (was she really the shop steward?). No, she said, there was no question of changing. But she didn't leave it there. Our guardian of the NHS victuals went up to Mr Jackson, argued with him that the slices of white bread that all but he could see lying on his plate weren't white but brown, and then stood back, arms on hips, with her friend, watching him as he ate it up. Needless to say, Mr Jackson, and particularly his nurse, was quite upset...

'Now I'm all for a health service run by the people for the people, but we must be careful to ensure that the 'people' we are talking about are those who are sick, and not those running the service.' (Tim Albert, Health care and the withholding of sausages, *World Medicine*, December 12, 1981)

After about a week I was discharged from hospital. My relief was unbounded, but short-lived. Barbara came to drive me home and on our way we stopped in to visit my father, still hanging onto life. I sat with him and held his hand, which was not something I had done often. I talked to him, and I think he reacted. His breathing was laboured. After a couple of hours I got ready to go back to north London, but suddenly the agency nurse suggested gently that I should stay. Within a few moments his breathing stopped. His suffering was over.

David and I spent the next few days organising the funeral. I asked Father Egan, my father's former friend and former headmaster of my Jesuit prep school, if he could make a speech, but he said that he was unable do so for non-Catholics. Instead we asked a younger Catholic priest, son of one of my father's pre-war friends who had been a friend of my brother at school. He was happy to accept.

The service he designed, he told us proudly, would cover elements from Jewish, Catholic and agnostic traditions. In a phrase that went down well in the crowded crematorium chapel, he described my father as the Abbot of Lingfield Road. That afternoon we held our last party in his home, and that evening Barbara and I stayed in a hotel in Surrey to carry on our house hunting.

The following day we viewed a house just outside Leatherhead: a 1938 cottage with a ground floor extension sitting in one third of an acre of garden, with a vegetable patch and a view over water-board land with a spring and a pond. Unlike in north London the near sky was filled with trees. The couple selling the house clearly liked the same things we did – wooden furniture and water colours – so we decided it was the place for us. And then the vendor's son punched me in the testicles.

Despite this gesture we went ahead with the purchase, and started to plan our move. Within a few weeks my ulcerative colitis flared up again. The trigger seemed to be a glass of brandy reacting on my steroid-sated stomach. I vomited uncontrollably, and the clearly hassled locum, who arrived in good time, prescribed me a total of 100 suppositories. I tried one, which was not successful, so the next day Barbara bundled me along to the Royal Free Hospital where, still retching, I sat in casualty for about an hour.

Before long I was in a hospital bed for the second time in a few weeks, being pumped with more steroids. On the first day I was approached by Professor Neil McIntyre, nominally in charge of my care, who told me it was his 250-word questionnaire I had mocked in *World Medicine*. He then handed me a bundle of paper.

'I have written an article with [the eminent philosopher] Karl Popper,' he said. 'Do you think you could edit it while you are here?' I propped myself up, pulled out the breakfast tray, got to work, and stopped feeling sorry for myself. It was a particularly shrewd piece of health care.

A few months later I noticed that the tree at the edge of Wimbledon Common – the one that my father called the tree of life – had also died. We had not realised that they had had a suicide pact.

4.6: Happy Christmas – you're fired!

By the end of 1981 I was racking up the stress points. I was an orphan. I was a married man. My new wife and I had just moved house. I had been in hospital twice with a nasty disease. More was to follow.

The October 17 issue of *World Medicine* contained an article by Karl Sabbagh, one of our regular columnists, urging doctors to boycott an upcoming Medical Olympics due to take place in Israel. Karl was a successful TV producer and writer who ran a medical education foundation funded by the pharmaceutical company MSD. He was, like Michael and me, a product of a Catholic education, but his family were displaced Palestinians.

His was an impassioned, tightly-argued and hard-hitting piece (among other things labelling Prime Minister Begin a terrorist). It was also – as he signalled in the last paragraph by pointing out his family were part of the Palestinian diaspora – unashamedly one-sided. (Karl Sabbagh, The blood on Begin's hands, *World Medicine*, October 17, 1981)

We had expected some controversy. We had not expected the ferocious storm that the article unleashed, bringing us unprecedented amounts of angry mail from all over the world. A few correspondents argued calmly that Karl had got his facts and/or arguments wrong – and expressed their sorrow at his being allowed space to express them.

Most were far less temperate. They wrote about Karl's 'virulently and inflammatory political article' and of his pen 'dripping with hate'. His employers came under pressure to dismiss him.

We felt under siege, as in a sense we were. Sympathisers sent us copies of two letters from the Israel Medical Association. One urged doctors to return future copies of our magazine unopened; the other urged pharmaceutical companies to withdraw their advertising. Other letters accused Michael of anti-semitism and of taking bribes from the Palestinian Liberation Organisation.

His response was to run five pages of debate in November, and in January another two. He also wrote a calm editorial:

> 'I can understand the anger stoked by Karl Sabbagh's article and clearly we will never appease the anger of some of our more venomous correspondents. But I would remind the others, as their

anger cools, of the now rather hackneyed, though nonetheless true, proposition that free speech is really only worth defending when you disagree with or disapprove of what is being said'. (Is World Medicine anti-semitic? *World Medicine*, September 28, 1981).

I too came under personal attack, with a story in the *Jewish Chronicle* alleging that I was an anti-semite. The origin of this story, I managed to work out, was a mass mailing from an Israeli university several weeks previously asking news outlets if they wanted to receive regular releases. Since we had no news pages I had declined the offer, thinking that I would save them time and money.

Michael rushed to my defence, pointing out in his next column that I was unlikely to be an anti-semite, bearing in mind the religion of my wife and of my grandparents currently residing in the Willesden Jewish Cemetery. But I found it a harrowing experience, particularly since I had been out of the office on sick leave when the article was accepted, edited and published. I am all for righteous indignation, but it has to be right.

Then matters took a turn for the worse at *World Medicine*. Those involved at the time still cannot agree whether what happened next was an unhappy coincidence, or a direct consequence of the furore (though adherents of the latter are clearly in the majority). Whatever the truth, the consequence was severe.

Just before Christmas, the managing director of IPC Business Press gathered us all together for a meeting. He told us that the co-owners, the American publishers McGraw Hill, had sold them their half of the magazine. The IPC plan was to move us to Sutton where we would be part of the Building and Contracts Journals – and that some people would be facing 'a redundancy situation'.

He was taken aback when we laughed at this phrase, though the reaction was triggered not by the threat but by the euphemism. We were both furious and afraid, combining a knee-jerk reaction to sudden change with a reasonable fear that the spirit of the publication would suffer from a move to the suburbs. Michael wrote in a diary piece: 'The old *World Medicine* is dead. We now wait to see what happens to the new one'.

His new bosses sacked him as soon as they saw what he had written. I was still on intermittent sick leave, and on a day I was resting at home the staff, led by a furious Fiona, whipped up the contributors to impose a boycott. When I went into the office the next day I faced a dilemma. As the next in line my duty to the publishers was to persuade them to keep on writing. But this was not something I was willing to do.

By this time the press had picked up the story, and a former colleague, Dennis Hackett, took me out to lunch to prepare a piece for *Campaign,* the media and marketing newspaper. By the end of lunch I realised that there was only one thing to do. I went back to my office and gave my resignation to our acting publisher, ironically an old friend who never understood my action or forgave me.

I then phoned Barbara to ask if she could drive up to the office. I tidied up my papers, collected my belonging and said my goodbyes. Within an hour I was an ex-executive editor.

4.7: In the wilderness

Walking away from an untenable job may be life-affirming, but it's not long before the financial consequences begin to assert themselves. I soon realised I was in the shit; in the light of my ongoing illness that was an apt metaphor.

On the day after I resigned, the phone rang regularly with messages of support. I took the calls in the living room of the home in Leatherhead we had moved into less than a month before. The calls were welcome – but they soon dried up.

I had to find a job or go back to the career path I had been trying to leave: that of a peripatetic, jack-of-most-trades, freelance journalist. I asked around for permanent positions, but was particularly discouraged by the remark made to Barbara by the editor of one health services publication. Her boyfriend, a doctor and senior editor on another medical publication, had advised her not to employ me unless I had my colon removed.

Not surprisingly the aforesaid colon started to misbehave again. But now when I retched uncontrollably my new GP practice, being in suburban Surrey rather than inner London, sent a trainee rather than a locum to my home to check me out. After she had done so she knelt by my bed and gave me her home number.

'If you get into any trouble tonight, don't hesitate to give me a ring', she said. 'I can be here within 10 minutes'. The offer worked: Barbara, the doctor and I all had a good night's sleep.

Next morning an ambulance arrived to take me back to the Royal Free Hospital. It was a Surrey ambulance and the driver didn't know the route to north London hospitals, so Barbara had to drive our car in front to show him the way. I was admitted promptly this time, and stayed on the ward for another 10 days, during which time I went through the now familiar routine of being pumped full of steroids.

I 'celebrated' my 35th birthday on the ward. One of the nurses sent me a card: 'Have a super day'. Professor McIntyre, originally responsible for my care, had passed me onto his colleague Roy Pounder, who continued the policy of treatment through distraction by hauling me out of bed to give a talk to medical students on what it was like to have ulcerative colitis.

Barbara, now allowed to work in the UK, had found a job with the American television company NBC. Each day she came in after work, laden with food. We had learnt from the previous two stays that hospital fare does not stave off steroid-induced hunger.

She told me later that she had feared becoming a widow within a year of marriage. Some time later, looking back in my diary for that year, I saw that she had written on the day of our first wedding anniversary: 'We made it!'

The nation was informed of my illness. The *Times* Diary noted:

> 'Turning your back on *World Medicine* can seriously damage your health. Dr Michael O'Donnell, who left hurriedly after a row with the journal's proprietors, has since suffered an attack of shingles. Now Tim Albert, the executive editor, who promptly followed him out, is in hospital with a nasty recurrence of colitis.' (*Times*, February 9, 1982)

The steroids worked, as usual, and when I got out of hospital, shaky and unclear about my future, Barbara and I took a break. We went by ferry to Calais. As we drove south along the coast road a wintry sun came out, shining on the rolling hills on our left, and to the right on the smattering of seaside villages lining a sparkling English Channel. It was the type of scene that raises the spirits. And the spirits continued to rise as we drove into Wimereux, a small resort with a jaunty promenade, a sweeping bay, Edwardian villas and a family hotel serving lashings of *coquille St Jacques* and *coq au vin*.

After a week we returned and I went back to being a freelance, writing about Open University summer schools and interviewing the heads of Broadmoor Hospital and the Yehudi Menuhin School. Dennis Hackett, who I guess felt some responsibility for my resignation, commissioned a piece on cot death for a new colour supplement he was launching for the *Mail on Sunday*.

It was a harrowing story. 'Only four and a half weeks after I had rung round everybody telling them we had a daughter, I was ringing them up to say she was dead', one distraught father told me. I was particularly impressed by the lucid arguments and compassion of a young paediatrician based in Brighton. His name was Dr David Southall, and his subsequent involvement and researches into cot death – which included the secret filming of parents – were later to involve him in many years of controversy, including being struck off the medical register for a while.

I started researching for a book about doctors that I provisionally entitled *The Sorcerer Elite*. I interviewed the Dean of St Mary's Medical School, and he allowed me to sit in on some interviews for medical school places. My draft describes those who did not make it: the daughter of a nurse whom the panel thought would be 'a rather good nurse' herself; a student from south east Asia who was dismissed as 'rather glib'; a young woman who stressed she wanted a career and not a family and had the panel speculating afterwards whether she might have a psychiatric problem. The statement by one mini-skirted candidate that she didn't want anything to do with animal experiments was put down to the fact that she went to a comprehensive.

Then there were the successful ones.

"Two other candidates turned up looking for all the world like doctors in miniature, he in a neat suit with short hair and a serious look, she in a pale purple twin-set. They both had a parent who was a doctor. They had done the 'right things' like joining a scientific society and doing voluntary work in hospitals, and I felt they got easier interviews. She was treated with avuncular courtesy, even being signalled by the chairman before she entered the room as a promising candidate. The questions she had to face were far softer: "I see you are a very practical person... You appear to be pretty good at sciences." Both candidates did well...' (Tim Albert, *Sorcerer Elite*, unpublished manuscript).

I got in touch with Mike Averis at the *Guardian*. I knew him from my previous spell at the paper and he was now one of the senior night editors. He offered me work on the home subeditors desk which, since it did not involve going out of the office, was a perfect job for someone with a dodgy intestine.

I drove in after lunch, and started with a gentle warm-up by subediting the weather forecast or a report from an early press conference. In those days we were handed articles on slips of paper, and we had to make the stories safe, accurate, readable and grammatical. We had to cut them to as near the right length as we could (using a standard word count formula of words per inch), and then write a headline that had to fit a designated space. Our edited version would go to the 'revise sub' at the end of the table, a scholarly man with half-moon glasses who would chide us sorrowfully if he found habitual errors.

At about 9 o'clock, when our work on the first edition was over, we had a quick supper break in the canteen followed by a couple of pints in the pub.

After that we edited a few stories for the second edition and then I drove back to Leatherhead in the car arriving home at about midnight. Barbara was usually asleep. I was wide awake, however, and needed time to wind down. I was helped in this by one of our new acquisitions – a video cassette recorder that allowed us to watch television programmes after they had been broadcast. That was some progress.

As in most newspapers, reporters and subeditors co-existed in a mild state of war. Reporters saw us as too insensitive to recognise the beauty of their prose. They held us responsible for ruining their style, cutting their literary wheat and replacing it with chaff, and bothering them with stupid questions about what they had written when they were already running close to the next deadline.

We subeditors bonded like the oppressed minority we felt we were. We reassured ourselves that our actions would not have been necessary had the article been clearer and more accurate in the first place. We also knew (because we checked) how often their numbers failed to add up and names were misspelt.

Within a few weeks I was a regular on the rota. These were busy times, with the Falklands War and Mrs Thatcher's triumphant re-election. I was not on the staff, since it was not a rich paper and staffing levels were strictly maintained. But I was confident that it would only be a matter of time before a vacancy came up, and I would have a good chance of achieving my ambition of becoming a staff journalist on the *Guardian*. My ulcerative colitis was manageable again.

I felt back on track.

Mostly we had it good

4.8: A wage slave again

I never got that job on the *Guardian*. In the winter of 1984 four vacancies for a home subeditor came along like a double dose of metaphorical buses, but by this time I had moved on.

One morning, as I was stirring gently after a night of subediting, I received an unexpected phone call from a Dr John Havard. I knew who he was – the secretary of the British Medical Association. I still had on my bookshelf the copy of *World Medicine* that Michael O'Donnell had handed me when I first met him, and which featured a cover picture of Dr Havard and a lengthy profile.

He was looking for someone who might be a suitable editor of the BMA's house magazine and Michael had put my name forward. Once again I received an invitation to lunch; this time it was not in a spacious West End steakhouse but in the rather gloomy surroundings of the Oxford and Cambridge Club in Pall Mall.

Dr Havard was then in his 50s: an energetic, intelligent and bluff man with fine qualifications. He was a barrister as well as a doctor, and as a medico-legal expert had helped to bring changes in the law on seat belts in cars and on undetected homicide. He had also been an athlete of some note and held the London University record for the 100 yards, he holds it still, since the event went metric soon after. He appeared socially awkward, though this was clearly not enough to stop him – as the tabloids many years later recounted with glee – to have had a **Top Doc Love Child**.

When he was appointed secretary of the BMA five years before, the association's management style was described in *World Medicine* as 'early primitive feudal'. Dr Havard made it his priority to modernise, and now, he told me over lunch, he wanted to turn the house magazine into something that members would want to read, not criticise. He said that he would fully support an editor who could do this, even at the price of upsetting a few people in the process. At the end of the lunch he suggested that I apply.

The thought of being an editor – even of a house magazine – was tempting. So I drafted a detailed application with full details of the changes I would make. I was one of two people called for interview by a panel consisting of Dr Havard, Dr O'Donnell, and Dr Stephen Lock, then editor of the *British Medical Journal*. The interview went well, with Michael (as he told me some time later) 'lobbing up a few slow balls outside the leg stump'. Dr Havard offered me the job, subject to a medical examination and approval by the finance and general purposes committee.

This should have been a formality but wasn't. The committee members were all doctors, and some could not resist asking me about my ulcerative colitis. How long had I had the disease? Was my colon intact? (This was a thinly veiled way of asking if I had had a colostomy, which I hadn't.)

I learnt later that, after I had left the room, one or two argued that I was too sick to be employed. The discussion was resolved when Barbara Dyer, the redoubtable personnel officer (as we called them in those days), told the committee that it would be a disgrace if a medical organisation could not cope with someone with a medical condition.

A few weeks later, on a memorably bright day in February 1984, I reported to Mr O'Brien, the uniformed porter who commanded the front lodge of BMA House in Tavistock Square. He directed me through a set of ornate metal gates where I found myself in a courtyard with fountain, four imposing statues and a clipped circular lawn. Around me was a stately building designed by Sir Edwin Lutyens – architect of war memorials and New Delhi – as the world headquarters of the Theosophists, an odd but well-connected religious group that thrived around the turn of the 20th century.

It was a sprawling place, with four-storey offices flanking the courtyard, a garden of remembrance round the back, with an extra building that housed out-of-favour departments. There were wide staircases and lifts at the front of the buildings, and narrow staircases at the back, presumably designed for the servants of the Theosophists. Early on I got lost on one of these staircases and stumbled on an imposing wooden front door: it was a flat in which chief officers, such as the chairman of council and treasurer, could stay in London during the week.

Edwardian echoes remained, particularly in the lavatories, which were grand affairs of white porcelain, wood, and black and white tiles. Sadly, soon after I joined, they – as well as other parts of the building – were transformed into a style best described as Nondescript Trust House Forte.

I became an office worker, with an index-linked pension, grey suit from Marks and Spencer, blue card (holidays for the ordering of), and an entitlement to park my car in the car park not more than once a month. The pay was more than generous, mainly because it was inflated by the association's need to attract doctors onto the staff.

I held the rank of assistant secretary, which put me firmly in the officer class. This entitled me to take luncheon in the members' dining room (the alternative was the staff canteen in the basement) and have a minimum of six weeks holiday a year. I thought it was a typographical error when I first read this in my terms and conditions. But it was genuinely meant as a minimum figure, though only rarely did anyone take advantage of it.

The inward twists and turns of the building mirrored its owners. On the surface the BMA was a single-minded and united group that had seen off cabinet ministers of the calibre of Nye Bevan, Barbara Castle and Dr David Owen. But, like middle-class Wimbledon village in the 1950s, antipathies raged underneath the surface calm.

Hospital doctors still looked askance on GPs as having fallen off the career ladder, and GPs still looked upon hospital doctors as too rich and too arrogant for their own good. Both groups were clearly unsettled by the new breed of articulate junior doctors who agitated for a good night's sleep. Other groups – public health doctors, occupational health doctors, medical officers in the armed services – were looked down upon by everyone else.

They were united, just, by a complicated constitution that was so full of checks and balances that the early 20th-century socialists Sydney and Beatrice Webb praised it as a marvellous piece of democracy. An annual representative meeting (dubbed the doctors' parliament) took place every year in mid-ranking conference towns such as Norwich, Scarborough and Bournemouth. Council meetings were held at BMA House every two months and executive meetings in the intermediate months.

The medical politicians who attended these meetings took themselves and their positions seriously, week after week travelling to London for endless discussions and negotiations, speeches and disputed points of order. The longest and fiercest debates seemed to be on how many doctors from each group should be represented on each committee.

We on the staff would sit in on council meetings quietly discussing which of the doctors in front of us we would allow near our bodies were we to fall ill. This was, in retrospect, out of order. When 30 years later terrorists blew up a bus just outside the gates of BMA House with horrendous results, there were many tales of medical politicians rolling up their shirt sleeves and heroically getting on with saving lives.

Each group of doctors had their own officers, negotiators and backup staff – plus presidential chains of office. At the summit of the organisation was an elected triumvirate: chairman of council, chairman of representative body, and treasurer, with at least one at any time being a GP and one being a hospital consultant. It took a lot of effort – and a lot of paper – to make it work.

This was the function of a cadre of committee clerks. As a journalist I had until now been shielded from such people by zealous press officers. But I found them bright and young, graduates from good universities, who ran their committees with stark efficiency and reams of rococo prose. There were several 'characters': two later became councillors in Islington (for different parties), one rising to leader of the council.

There were also two – both of whom were particularly helpful to me as a new editor – who went spectacularly off the rails. One had to resign when one of his cupboards was opened to reveal dozens of unanswered letters The other was convicted of child offences. These would have been great stories for the independent journalist, but I could no longer break them.

I had gone over to the other side.

4.9: An editor's chair

The magazine I found myself in charge of went under the distinctly dull name of *BMA News Review*. The title reflected the fact that the magazine was steered more by the decisions of committees than by the demands of commerce. I thought briefly of trying to get the name changed, but quickly discovered that I had more urgent problems.

My first challenge came when I decided to get some up-to-date photographs of senior BMA figures – the 'repertory company' as we irreverently came to call them. I contacted a photographer and asked him to come in and take some. When I told the publisher what I was doing he was incandescent.

'Use the office camera', he said.

I then discovered two things. First, he had bought the camera the previous year, and its only sustained use had been when he had taken it on his family holiday. Second, I had no budget. I asked Dr Havard to settle the dispute, and within days he made it clear that I no longer reported to the publisher – but only to him. We agreed that he should become editor-in-chief, which meant that he could use his powerful position as secretary to guard my back as I tried to focus the publication on the 80,000 doctor members, rather than the 200 or so who came into the building. The protection turned out to be invaluable.

Another early challenge was the magazine's reputation for 'getting things wrong'. Since one of the selling points of a house magazine is that it represents the house it serves, this was clearly a big problem.

I started to do what my journalism training had drummed into me *not* to do: send out advance proofs of our stories to senior staff so that they could point out 'factual errors'. These negotiations were time-consuming and vexing, but it was chastening to see how many errors we had escaped making when the copy came back.

Even so, some staff members took major liberties over what could or could not be considered 'factual errors'. Capital letters became particularly controversial: like most publications we tried to keep them to a minimum for ease of readership, but every committee felt they were its due. When I turned the Central Ethical Committee into the central ethical committee their members branded me publicly as impertinent.

Nor was my concept of good writing universally accepted. This was brought home to me when I wrote my first report to the BMA Council. I decided, naively, to show these doctors and their lackeys how to write, so I used the best parts of my *Daily Mirror* training to produce an unusually short and crisp report.

I realised that I had got it wrong when I overheard one senior medical politician (later knighted) complaining to another that the report was too short and I was clearly trying to hide something. After they had debated it formally, council members voted unanimously that it should be rejected by them and rewritten by me.

I redrafted it carefully, adding no new information but putting in all the long words and circumlocutions that I had previously avoided. At the next meeting, council passed it without comment. Another lesson learnt.

I soon realised that running a house magazine had advantages as well. My new colleagues included experts who could tell us or write about matters dear to our readers' hearts – pay, working conditions and pensions. One of these was Adam Lock, son of the editor of the *BMJ*, and the only contributor I ever had who routinely wore a three piece suit and gold fob.

Adam wrote us an article on abatement – a complicated pension regulation that meant that some doctors who retired and then started working again had to give some of their money back. Over the next few weeks he received 396 letters and 127 telephone calls asking for further information. We thought it a dull subject; our readers certainly didn't.

The BMA was also a prolific producer of reports. This was largely because Dr Havard, sensitive to those who mocked that the initials BMA really stood for British Money Association, was determined to counterbalance trade union activities with those promoting public health. As far as I was concerned, it gave me a good reason for covering a range of matters unconnected with doctors' pay and conditions.

The first press conference I attended as editor was to launch a controversial BMA report arguing that boxing should be banned on health grounds. The boxing correspondent of the *Daily Mail*, not a man used to frequenting the Edwardian committee rooms in BMA House, questioned the report's contention that the main point of boxing was to harm one's opponent.

'Forgive me if I'm wrong,' said Dr Havard, who was chairing the press conference. 'But I'm ashamed to admit that I was junior heavyweight champion of my school, and I'm under the impression that I won the title by hitting the other boy harder than he managed to hit me.'

In the ensuing years the BMA's reports ranged from irradiation of foodstuffs to alternative therapies, from alcohol and accidents to living with risk. They also fought fiercely against the tobacco industry, and I joined the campaign with enthusiasm. It would not have advanced my career had I attacked the BMA, its members and its practices – but there were plenty of targets outside the association.

AIDS became a huge issue. At one stage about 30 people a day were ringing the BMA's advice line, worrying about the safety of saliva, jacuzzis, and food cooked by gay friends. One informant said that builders working on a centre for gay people had refused to continue. Another said that all the gays in his work canteen were made to sit together in one section and use disposable cups.

We commissioned the chief medical officer, Sir Donald Acheson, to write a piece for us. He challenged the current assumptions: 'Infection is not transmitted by ordinary social contact or through food, crockery or toilet seats.' (Donald Acheson, The challenge of AIDS, *BMA News Review*, July 1987).

Another health scare was the threat of nuclear war, still hanging around like a malign mushroom cloud. We covered the BMA's growing links with the various medical pressure groups that had sprung up, such as the Medical Campaign Against Nuclear Weapons and International Physicians for the Prevention of Nuclear War. What is the point, these groups asked, of providing good health services if they were to be wiped out in a few seconds of international madness?

In one of the favourite pieces I ran, a regular contributor, Mervyn Rosenberg, lampooned the idiocy of civil defence planning. He was the single-handed consultant in a 19-bed hospital in the far north of Scotland. Early warning telephones had been installed recently at his hospital and in the old people's home nearby. And a consignment of baked beans had been sent for the emergency food store.

He pointed out that he was being asked to 'prepare to look after a host of people dying of thermal burns and radiation, while I die of the same things myself', which quite reasonably he described as ludicrous. 'Call me uncaring if you like but I hereby give notice to the General Medical Council that, after a nuclear attack, they can take my name off the register. If they are still there'. (*BMA News Review*, June 1987).

As the months and then the years ticked by I took on more staff, secured larger budgets, increased the role of the magazine by running daily newspapers at annual conferences, and attracted more readers. I learnt new skills: managing people, managing committees, defending my territory against predatory managers (once using the dangerous weapon of threatening to resign). I was able to observe that the association's management style had evolved from early primitive feudal to early robber baronial.

As an editor I was sent invitations I would not otherwise have received. At one smart occasion I shared a table with the health minister Edwina Currie, who I found clever and attractive. At another I sat next to the eminent lawyer Lord Denning, who was elderly, clever and unstuffy.

'Call me Tom', he said, leaning on my arm as we moved to the dining hall.

I was invited to the *BMJ*'s 150th anniversary dinner, so posh that the invitation said we should wear our tailcoats and decorations. I thought I was being smart by wearing my Wimbledon Council coronation medal, but I learnt later that others were similarly subversive, with decorations ranging from a spelling bee medal to a beautifully beribboned sommelier's cup.

Hottest ticket of all was to the reception following the formal opening by Princess Diana of the BMA's relocated and refurbished library. I got admission to the reception, and was chatting with a small group of doctors and staff when HRH stopped to talk with us. The conversation quickly moved to public speaking and how difficult it could be to keep awake in official ceremonies.

'Someone fell asleep when my husband was talking in America the other day', she said, without guile. 'But then he had only been married to Joan Collins for a couple of weeks'. Her eyes flashed with amusement. It was this mixture of ceremony and subversion that made her so alluring: the girl next door with a coronet.

But I was disturbed by what went on around her visit: the fraught build-up, with doors and flagpoles getting a fresh coat of paint, flags handed out for waving in front of the cameras, and fierce negotiations over whose grand-daughter would present the posy. When the event was over, our magazine carried a statement from John Marks, chairman of Council, making it clear that it was the Princess's staff – not the BMA – who had chosen which groups to talk to. I can only imagine the complaints from passed-by and aggrieved luminaries.

After Princess Diana's visit I suffered my most severe case of writer's block. I got through it by writing a scurrilous poem – too scurrilous and in-jokey to be reproduced here. I then wrote the official piece of history (Tim Albert, A right royal visit, *BMA News Review*, April 1986). It wasn't a long chapter in history, however: 25 years later the library that had been opened with such pomp was moved round the back, and the room it had occupied became a grand hall again.

Throughout this time I worked closely with the press office. At the start of my tenure the man in charge was RAF Thistlethwaite, accused by Paul

Vaughan, formerly his colleague (Paul Vaughan, *Exciting Times in the Accounts Department*, Sinclair-Stevenson, 1995) of sounding like a small aerodrome in Lincolnshire. He was a gentle giant who had come from the Egg Marketing Board, and had been remarkably effective at building up relationships of trust with health reporters, often over a drink or two.

He had done this through being affable, approachable, and – a trait not usually associated with press officers at that time (or this?) – helpful. He held legendary parties for journalists, and at the end of the evening, if you were lucky, he would recite by heart large tracts of melodramatic Victorian verse.

His colleagues in the press office passed me a stream of material for my back-page column. One of the first was an inquiry from a BBC Radio 2 programme asking why men collected blue fluff in their navels; this became the subject of a competition to come up with an answer. The winning entry put forward a theory that it was due to the conductive effects of male body hair.

A tall and charming woman whose home was in Sark shared with me some of the letters and phone calls it was her job to deal with. One child wrote: 'I write to you for information for both me and my friend want to become surgeons. Please send us two copies of everything'. Another wrote to the BMA: 'Please forgive me for writing to you. You are not of this world'. Some employees might have agreed.

I received some eccentric mail on my own account: one of the most tiresome was from a doctor who regularly sent several closely written sheets in green ink (yes, there is some basis for the stereotype) arguing, often unpleasantly, that there was no such thing as a female orgasm. I sounded out some colleague editors: they too received them. We talked about whether we should report him to the GMC, but none of us did.

At times, and in retrospect recklessly, I threw stones out of the glass house and mocked coverage about the BMA that I felt was inaccurate or unfair. One journalist wrote a snippy piece about the puritans at BMA killing off its wine club; I gloated that they had not. The short-lived daily newspaper *Today* printed as news an attack on family doctors by Prince Charles; it turned out to be from a speech he had given to the BMA six years before.

On another occasion the same newspaper picked up one of our stories and published it without attribution. I wrote to the editor, David Montgomery, who had been one of my colleagues in Devon. He sent me a £60 fee and asked me to send more stories.

Like many journalists at the time I placed great store on the working (and sometimes drinking) lunch, and Dr Havard allowed me to put entertaining on my expenses. The head of finance was not happy about the arrangement, but his reservations did not stop him from accepting my invitations.

These lunches provided me with good information and good ideas. One of the most fruitful was with Sir Christopher Booth, who had just completed a year in the mainly honorific role of BMA president. We talked about one of the major issues occupying (and indeed dividing) the BMA: the long hours being worked by junior doctors.

Sir Christopher and I, with a bottle of wine weakening our caution, came up with the notion that he would go to a typical hospital and sample a night on call. Within a few weeks he did just that, and shadowed two junior doctors.

By the time he arrived there had been seven new medical admissions, and there were another five, including a cardiac arrest, before they got to bed at 4am. Two hours later they were called up for another cardiac arrest. His article concluded:

> 'No-one can function properly as a physician after 24 hours of continuous duty, with only two hours of sleep. Obviously I can only speak for the situation in this hospital on that night, but it is monstrous that we should subject any devoted young doctor to such conditions.' (Sir Christopher Booth, A knight on call, *BMA News Review*, January 1989).

The story made several national newspapers and helped sway opinion towards the junior doctors. Not everyone was pleased: I heard later that, because of this article, Sir Christopher was passed over as president of the Royal College of Physicians.

4.10: Into Europe

After a few years of marriage, Barbara and I discovered that we could have children only after a depressingly high level of medical intervention on my part. We decided not to proceed, which at least saved an unborn child from the burden of being named Victoria Ann Albert. Instead we decided to buy a flat in France as a holiday home.

It would be cheaper than having children, we reasoned, and would spare us having to worry about GCSEs and late night parties. At a fraction of the cost needed to support a son or daughter, we would have a place to which we could tempt over for weekends our nephews and our growing number of godchildren. We would lavish kindnesses upon them – and send them back to their parents just at the point we became tired of them and they of us.

We started our search in Wimereux, the small seaside resort near Boulogne that we first visited when I came out of hospital in 1982. Originally a tiny farming and fishing settlement, it had morphed with the coming of the railways into a smart resort for the bourgeoisie from Lille and the aristocracy from Paris. They built splendid villas with Norman-style timbering, local tiles, fretwork-edging under the eaves, and wood-clad belvederes and balconies nudging each other for the best view of the sea.

The place had history. In what appeared to be the French equivalent of 'Queen Elizabeth slept here', a long low house was said to have sheltered Napoleon. Some 50 metres away was a stolid Art Nouveau villa where a century and a half later Adolf Hitler is said to have slept the night.

The Germans fortified the town as part of the Atlantic Wall, knocking down some of the villas. One of the large hotels became headquarters for the *Wehrmacht* weather service. It was from there that they confidently predicted that the weather on June 6, 1944 would be far too bad for a landing by sea. This encouraged Field Marshall Rommel to drive to Germany for his wife's birthday, which caused him to be hundreds of miles away when the Allies invaded.

In 1986, when we started looking for an apartment, enough of the original Edwardian villas were still standing to give the town a rare charm. The reason they were there in the first place was the sweeping arc of a beach, along which curved a somewhat battered *digue*, part-protection and part-promenade, running half a mile from one set of high cliffs to another.

In those days only one commercial property was allowed on the sea front: the *Hôtel Atlantic*. This had been a byword for French glamour in the 1930s, within easy reach of England via ferry and tramcar. Now it was operated by a second generation of owners who were bored and resting on their laurels. Dennis Thatcher was reputed to be a regular, coming in for a snifter between rounds of golf on the nearby course, where conventional sand-filled bunkers nestled against concrete bunkers created by the Third Reich.

In winter the *digue* was a forlorn place. One February, on my birthday, Barbara and I walked along it with only a man and a dog between us and the distant horizon. At other times it was too hazardous even for three people and a dog, with icy waves crashing over the sea wall, sending water lapping at the hotel door and throwing spray high up into the air.

But in summer the town transformed, with the population jumping from 6,000 to 18,000. On fine evenings (and even some that were not so fine) the *digue* heaved with holidaymakers, seeing and being seen: Parisians with their white trousers and striped seaman's sweaters, miners' families from Bethune in jeans and flowery print dresses, a smattering of Brits in their socks and sandals and khaki shorts.

As they walked they would pass others, smugly catching the last rays of the sun or sipping aperitifs outside their wooden beach huts. These were painted white with just a small amount of blue, as laid down in the local regulations. The competition for these huts was fierce. A friend of ours, a British civil servant who was 'let go' in a change of government, spent some of his payout on a house in the town. One day he went to the town hall to find out how he could have a beach hut as well.

'You have to be resident' said the woman in charge.

'But I am', he said. 'I have a house in Wimereux.'

'*Mais non, monsieur*', came the reply. 'You have to be more resident than that.' In other words: French.

While they were reluctant to sell their beach huts to the British, the French showed no reticence in selling them their family homes. We signed up with an estate agent called Gaston who showed us the house where he had grown up, and told us about his brother who had been killed by an allied bomb. He had bucket-loads of Gallic charm and a Gauloise cigarette constantly at hand. One weekend we viewed four apartments and fell in love with the fourth. In a relatively simple procedure we bought it. We returned later to sign the papers, bringing Gaston a carton of duty-free cigarettes as requested.

Our new flat was on the top floor of one of a pair of identical villas on the *Rue General de Gaulle*, which ran between the main street and the *digue*. It had recently been converted into flats by a Parisian count whose family had owned it for generations. By leaning out of the window and turning right you could see the sea some 80 metres away. There was only one bedroom, though there was a space off the landing large enough to build a bunk for a small-to-medium sized child. Also included was a portion of cellar, carefully calculated on the relative size of each apartment.

We quickly tuned into French seaside life. Most mornings we would stroll down the *digue* and then turn inwards to stroll up the *Rue Carnot*. This contained all the shops that we remembered from our respective French school books, some in triplicate.

Three fishmongers offered mussels and crabs and tiny, ecologically unsound Dover soles that had been landed at Boulogne that morning. Three bakeries offered similar-looking *baguettes* and *croissants*, but with different grades of cakes and grumpiness. As for the three delicatessens, the first stocked everything under the sun, the second specialised in fine wines and artisan cheeses, and the third sold pigs trotters glistening with aspic and crab mayonnaise nestling in shells – and proudly displayed certificates attesting to the quality of meat the proprietor had slaughtered.

As if this wasn't enough, a small market came to town on Tuesdays and Fridays, where the horsemeat van displayed its red meat and red sausages and a van with a spit filled the square with the tantalising smell of roasting chickens. Both did a roaring trade, though our loyalty card was for the chickens not the horse. Elsewhere, in less favourable positions, the farmers and their wives would set up a small table displaying the wares of the season: turnips, parsley, dead rabbits, potatoes, irises, eggs...

When we ate out it was often at the *Hôtel du Centre*, where we had first stayed at the start of the decade. Its dining room resembled a Paris bistro in an impressionist painting, with leather benches and dangling lights. The food was cooked by the owner and served by his son. They were the classics: *moules marinières* and *coq au vin*, plus the occasional nod across the channel with cod in *beignets de bière*.

For special occasions we ate at the *Relais de la Brocante*. This occupied a smartly renovated former presbytery and was owned and run by the chef and the *maître d'hôtel*, two friends who had done their apprenticeships at the *Atlantic* in its heyday. The chef cooked the celebratory lunch for Mrs Thatcher and President Mitterand at the official opening of the Channel Tunnel in 1994.

A couple of times we splashed out on seven-course New Year's Eve banquets. Once when we came out after the meal in great good humour we found that the tyres to our car – and to a number of others – had been slashed.

The *maître d'hôtel* drove us home, and the next day drove us to the garage and the police station. The culprit turned out to have been a young man from the village who had been jilted on the last day of the year.

Many of our friends in England were sniffy about our choice of somewhere so northern and, well, so cold. But we could get there quickly. When work started on the Channel Tunnel I bought enough shares to get unlimited travel for £1 a trip, an unusually astute financial move. One summer we travelled through the tunnel most weekends. On one trip I rolled down the car window and asked how much it would 'normally' cost; about £250, I was told.

We were not the only ones to recognise the tunnel's financial opportunities. For a while we travelled late at night, when the fares were low. We queued alongside dozens of men (no women) travelling on the cheapest rate to fill clapped-out and sagging Volvos with booze to sell at large profits back in the UK, thereby preventing sizeable sums of money going into the Treasury.

4.11: The slow drip of the new

One evening towards the end of the 1980s I scrambled onto the top deck of a bus going from BMA House to Waterloo. There was only one other person on the top of the bus: a man in a business suit holding an unfamiliar piece of equipment about the size of a shoe. He raised it to his face and started talking.

I had heard of these new-fangled telephones that ran on batteries so that you could call up your loved one (or your stockbroker) wherever you happened to be. This was clearly one of them. I expressed admiration for his gadget, and he offered to let me have a go. I dialled our home in Leatherhead and spoke to Barbara.

'I am on the top of a bus', I said, by way of introduction.

We marvelled about our conversation when I got home and wondered whether it would catch on.

Electronic innovations were coming thick and fast in the 1980s, but most of us were slow to realise what changes they would bring. One exception was Dr Hugh Glanville, a writer and editor of some note, who was one of the first to invest in new technology. In 1981, when I was at *World Medicine*, we ran an article by him describing a wondrous, new possession.

> 'I type on a typewriter-style keyboard and the words appear on a small screen, disappearing off the top (into the computer's memory) a few lines at a time when I add more text at the bottom. The most elementary advantage is that mistakes do not matter. I simply overtype them, which is nice if like me you are not a very good typist. Nimble typists take advantage of this and go really fast, correcting any mistakes later. A winking square called the "cursor" can be moved about the screen and positioned anywhere and used to change a letter, delete it, or create a space for one that has been left out.

> 'Word processing programs, however, allow a much more flexible editing than just correcting errors. Any word, line, sentence, paragraph or page can be deleted, or picked up and moved somewhere else, or even reproduced elsewhere without being deleted. This electronic cut-and-paste facility enormously

simplifies original writing, revising, and editing. I drafted this article several times before I was content with it, but at the end I wasn't left with any multiply amended stick-taped draft to be typed out; I just had to press a button for the final version.' (Hugh de Glanville, My new right hand, *World Medicine*, October 17, 1981)

There was more. You could search the entire text for any word and number and change it, or store addresses, or sort lists – all for a cost of £1,500 plus VAT for word processor and attendant printer. In time, he predicted, these machines would provide a complete electronic filing system on the top of a desk, containing accounts, addresses, practice records, research papers and much else. And the largest leap of all: we would be able to exchange information via telephone lines to other word processors. 'They are likely to take over from straight typewriters much as electric machines took over from manuals – that is to say, in Britain, slowly,' he wrote.

Three years later, when I arrived at the BMA, talk about word processors had been superseded by talk of personal computers. I didn't really understand what they did and how they worked, but I sensed that they would be important. My new colleague Dr John Dawson, head of science at the BMA, was an early enthusiast, so I asked him to write a column.

His first, in May 1984, warned that there would be abuses and they would need to be controlled. His second flagged up the development of a BMA database (I had little idea of what *that* really meant) which would gather and keep daily summaries of press cuttings on health care.

Not long after, he went out to Africa with a Land Rover full of electronic equipment. Once there, and in the middle of the bush, he managed to receive on his computer messages from back home in England. He wrote:

'A satellite communications terminal can cost less than a modest medical and nursing library and can give access to large quantities of information. The... searching software can track down material in a fraction of a second that a skilled human librarian might take hours to find.' John Dawson, Towards the Global Village, (*BMA News Review*, January 1985).

I published the story but couldn't yet see the point.

John Dawson became responsible for the BMA Library and started to introduce changes. The old-school librarian, who proudly donned gloves to show me ancient manuscripts in his care, soon left. In his place came Tony

McSean, a younger man who had worked as a teacher, journalist and rock band manager before training as a librarian. He sometimes wore a white suit to work and he certainly understood computers.

His goal was to make the library accessible to members sitting at home or in their offices, and he organised courses showing doctors how to search databases and gather the information they needed. We sent a reporter on one of these courses, who reported her conversion from nervous Luddite to convenient enthusiast:

> 'In future it will be feasible to tap these databases from the computer on one's desk at home, in the hospital or the surgery... You can even carry a portable computer to the wilds and connect... through a local phone box' (Julia Bland, Fighting the fear of new technology, *BMA News Review*, July 1988).

On the magazine, our own working practices started to change. I bought some computers and we used them to write our copy. Our subeditor then inserted codes so that they no longer needed to be keyed in a second time.

A few years later we took the next step and installed a fancy programme called Windows – plus another fancy programme called Pagemaker that allowed us to go one step further and lay out pages ourselves. The BMA computer buffs had urged caution, but we decided to go ahead anyway, on the grounds that it would take them three years to make up their minds, by which time any new system would have needed updating anyway.

I was happy to approve these leaps into the future, but my own competence was limited. I identified with one early correspondent who reported being told at a conference: 'The silicon chip is the answer. But what is the question?'

On several occasions I made an observation that in hindsight seems the height of foolishness. Because *BMA News Review* was an integral part of the BMA, we regularly got to hear of breaking medical stories long before our rivals got to do so. Sadly this gave us no advantage whatsoever because, as a fortnightly magazine, we usually had a long wait until our publication reached its audience.

'If only we could find a way of writing the magazine one day and without too much expense delivering it on the next', I would muse. I had no idea what was just around the technological corner.

4.12: The NHS under attack

At about the time that we bought the flat in France I started smoking small cigars. This drastic action was prompted by a letter published in the *British Medical Journal*. A GP wrote that his wife's ulcerative colitis got worse when she gave up smoking, and improved when she took it up again. This set up quite a discussion.

At that time my colon was still troublesome, sometimes making it too tiring and too risky for me to attempt the journey to work – 90 minutes on train and bus with toilets only at Waterloo. My doctors had made it known that, unless my health improved soon, they would have to consider removing my colon. So I decided to experiment with tobacco.

Within weeks my symptoms started to ease. Of course, I knew the long-term risks, but I was pretty sure that smoking saved my colon. I was not the only one to think so. Stephen Lock, editor of the *BMJ*, told me over lunch one day that in my position he would have done the same. One delightful unintended consequence was that I could tell the more puritanical BMA members that I was smoking for health reasons; it wound them up quite wonderfully.

As my health improved, the health of the service charged with looking after it went into a steep decline. At the start of the decade the NHS had been the subject of a trickle of critical stories, to which I had made my own small contribution. Now, as we started to move into the second half of the decade, the trickle was turning into a flood.

Significantly, doctors were joining in with the criticism. One senior BMA member was so appalled by his treatment in a major London teaching hospital that he wrote a letter to *BMA News Review*. I thought his information so shocking that I honoured his request to use a pseudonym.

> 'The security guards were as surly and slovenly as the main corridor was disorderly and filthy. I certainly was not expecting taps that did not work, bent light pulls, the previous patient's belongings in a bedside locker and a bath full of water...

> 'I also had time to reflect on my own experiences: having to ask for my bed to be straightened last thing at night on the day of the

operation; having to ask for my antibiotics hours after they were due; the complete failure, at any time, to offer me any type of pain-killer; the radiographer who, when I struggled with my dressing gown because of a stiff arm, asked me to: "Hurry up because we are very short-staffed and very busy". ('BMA Stalwart', The need for a white paper, *BMA News Review,* March 1989)

As far as Margaret Thatcher and her Conservative cabinet were concerned, this kind of criticism stung. They were only too aware of how much money they were pouring into the health service, and the fact that this earned them only criticism first puzzled them, then made them angry.

Casting around for scapegoats, they focused on the BMA. They started to argue that much-needed changes to the NHS were being blocked by well-entrenched and over-privileged doctors, led by an over-powerful trade union masquerading as a professional body. There followed a battle over some of the long-established principles of the NHS itself. I, as editor of the doctors' house magazine, found myself embedded with one of the major protagonists.

The fight began – unexpectedly – in a BBC studio on the evening of 25 January 1988. Mrs Thatcher appeared on the prestigious current affairs programme *Panorama* and, in the middle of a merciless grilling by David Dimbleby about the state of health care, she made an important announcement. She would set up a review of the NHS.

The BMA immediately went into furious mode because they had not been consulted. They were not alone: several government insiders at the time have since stated that they had not been consulted either. The prime minister had fired from the hip.

A year later, in 1989, the government published a white paper outlining its plans for health 'reforms'. It was launched by the Secretary of State for Health, a young, tough and upcoming politician called Kenneth Clarke who allocated £1million on what his advisers called an 'information cascade'. In an unusually glitzy affair he travelled down the Thames from Westminster by boat to present the plans before 300 selected guests in an east London studio. The presentation was hooked up to five other centres throughout the country.

Crucially, the proposals envisaged the start of an 'internal market': some general practices and some hospitals would be given a degree of financial independence so that 'money could follow patients'. The government also imposed a strict timetable which suggested that they had no intention of backing down – or even listening.

Our reporter Martine Gallie attended and described it as a tame affair, with all questions vetted in advance. The sound-bites had been carefully scripted, including this one from Kenneth Clarke: 'The BMA, in my unbiased opinion, has never been in favour of any change of any kind on any subject for as long as anyone can remember'. (Martine Gallie, The video game, *BMA News Review*, March 1989, p14)

The next few months were going to be rough. Within a few weeks the BMA had gone into democratic overdrive, with a flurry of specially-convened meetings to discuss the proposal. BMA staff were galvanised into action, through a mixture (in various doses) of idealism, duty, and an eye on the CV.

Mr O'Brien, the head porter and a keen observer of BMA activities, told one of our reporters that senior figures were 'galloping around the place' and junior staff coming in an hour earlier and staying two hours later. (He did not note, though we saw it ourselves, that members of the personnel and accounts departments still left as usual on the dot of 5pm.)

Almost every day a succession of BMA spokespersons traipsed down to the courtyard to be interviewed by TV crews. Upstairs the press officers fielded hundreds of calls from all over the world: one of these hard-working people told our reporter that she lost half a stone in the first week because she didn't have time to unwrap her sandwiches, let alone eat them.

We did our bit for the cause by producing four newspapers overnight to report on major developments or meetings; they were sent by first class post to all members. The BMA launched a campaign, with hard-hitting posters pasted up on hoardings: 'What do you call a man who ignores medical advice?' went the most contentious. Kenneth Clarke hit back by saying that the prospect of change invariably had GPs 'feeling for their wallets'.

Just how nasty things had become between the BMA and the government became clear on an autumn day in Blackpool. I sent my friend Harvey Marcovitch, paediatrician and writer, to report a meeting that the BMA was organising at the Conservative party conference. I was being slightly mischievous since this was probably the first and last contact he ever had with Tories en masse, and he came back shaken. He described the start of the meeting as being quiet and dignified, and then:

> 'One Upholder of All That Is Decent yelled out that he was hearing a lot of waffle. A chair went flying as a member of the Safe In Our Hands tendency, red-faced with rage, shouted out that he was 'fed up with all this crap' and 'you're just full of bull. It's pure socialism

rammed down our throats.' (Harvey Marcovitch, Pier Groups and politicians, *BMA News Review*, November 1989).

Some years later Harvey told me that the BMA group was expecting reasoned debate and perhaps some disagreement: 'In fact the audience tore into them. They were utterly shocked because they were so used to deference. I think it was the first time that politicians said to doctors: "We know better than you".'

4.13: Out again

By the autumn of 1989 it was clear that the government was going to hold its nerve. As the legislation to change the NHS started to go through the normal parliamentary processes, the BMA's efforts switched to a rearguard action. There were small victories, mainly over language: 'budget holding practices' became 'fundholding practices', 'self-governing hospitals' became 'NHS trusts', and 'purchasers' became 'commissioners' – and the term 'internal market' was dropped.

Sadly one important piece of language that was not changed was the word 'reform', which was widely used, with the clear inference that something bad was going to be made better. The root problem – the persistence of politicians to pretend that you can improve public services while reducing public taxes – remained unaddressed (and still does).

In the middle of these battles my editor-in-chief John Havard retired as secretary of the BMA. We had had a good working relationship, based on a shared determination to provide a magazine that BMA members would want to read.

His successor was Dr Ian Field, a less flamboyant man who had worked for the BMA before becoming a doctor in the Department of Health. He was a committed Catholic and his integrity and kindness shone through. But his instincts were those of a cautious civil servant, with a marked reluctance to peep over parapets. Our weekly meetings started to become bogged down in detail.

When the health secretary Kenneth Clarke announced that he was going ahead with his white paper proposals, my staff and I mocked up a cover with a picture of the politician and the cover line: 'Would you buy a second hand health service from this man?' When I showed it to Ian Field he sucked in his breath and paused.

'You can't publish this,' he said.

'Why not?' I asked.

'We could have letters about it'.

The gulf between us was clear: he wanted a magazine that took no risks; I wanted a magazine that was talked about.

I also started to face pressures over funding. Our problem was that, unlike all the other publications sent out free to doctors, we could not choose our audience. We had to go to all members, which made it unattractive for pharmaceutical companies wishing to target their products to specific groups, such as GPs or heart physicians. So the BMA had to subsidise us, and every so often one set of doctor politicians would ask whether we were worth it. Dr Havard was no longer around to tell them that we were.

The more predatory members of the senior management team started to circle again, sliding out suggestions that I should no longer report directly to the secretary as editor-in-chief. The financial controller put pressure on me not to attend the scientific conference to be held in Jamaica. He was going, of course, so I suggested that he write a report of the meeting. He declined and the conference went unreported; Barbara and I spent the time revisiting our haunts in the Bahamas instead.

I started to look around for a new opportunity. I applied for a Harkness fellowship, which would have taken me to the United States studying social marketing. I was shortlisted. But the interview did not go well, with the final questioner laying on the misery by asking seven questions without drawing breath.

'That's a lot of questions,' I said, hoping he would subtract a couple.

'Choose your own priorities,' he said.

I walked away realising my hopes of getting the fellowship were slim (which turned out to be an accurate assessment). Back in the office I picked up the phone to speak to Barbara, who was happy in a newish job as co-ordinator for British Medical Television, a company producing programmes for doctors. She made the right sympathetic noises, until there was a sudden interruption at her end. Sorry, she said, everyone had been called to an emergency meeting.

It was nearly an hour before she rang back. Her news was worse than mine: the company had gone into receivership and everyone was redundant. That evening, in an attempt to console ourselves, we took out one of four bottles of 1967 Chateau Meyney that had been left in my father's cellar when he died. We had left them too long, however, and each one was corked, though Barbara turned them later into superior chicken stew.

For a couple of months I stewed also. Several times a week I would climb the stairs of BMA House to the advertisement department to share my unhappiness with Bob Hayzen, a sage and seasoned salesman who had become (though the term was not yet widely used) my mentor.

Like most journalists, I had always regarded advertising as a necessary evil. But it did not take me long to realise how much I needed not just the income Bob and his team provided, but also his long experience on how to survive in organisations. One of his first lessons was that, while passion is usually admired in journalism, in most business settings it is seen as a sign of weakness. Often in a meeting when I was about to react to some stupid suggestion (there were a few), he would catch my eye and I would climb down through the gears to a state of relative calm.

One morning things changed. The night before I had held an emergency meeting with my staff to explain that our plans for a daily conference newspaper – something we had done for five years – was under threat. My staff was unhappy – we all enjoyed spending a week being journalists on a daily rhythm, and I sympathised with them. This time Bob did not try to persuade me to stay. I signed my letter and took it to my editor-in-chief.

This was the second job I had resigned from in less than a decade, but I felt a load had been lifted from my shoulders. I was doing less journalism and more management - sorting out staff problems, fighting for budgets, and resisting attempts to downgrade the publication and my position in the organisation. The internal forces I thought I had defeated had re-formed and were marching up the hill again. To make matters worse, many of the stories we had covered were coming round for a second time, and sometimes a third.

I had no idea what to do next, though the peculiarities of my BMA contract meant that I had a six months' notice period to work it out. I did not feel down-hearted.

1990s: fronting up

In which I become a small businessman and try to persuade doctors that clear writing might have its advantages

Time line

1990   London riots against poll tax; Nelson Mandela freed; National Lottery begins; Margaret Thatcher resigns and is succeeded by John Major

1991   End of the Soviet Union; Operation Desert Storm retakes Kuwait; IRA launch mortar attack on Downing Street; South Africa repeals Apartheid laws

1992   John Major wins general election

1993   Stephen Lawrence stabbed to death

1994   First women priests ordained by Church of England; Channel Tunnel opens

1995   Barings Bank collapses; British forces sent to Saravejo; OJ Simpson found not guilty of double murder

1996   Mad cow disease hits Britain; Dolly, the first (cloned) sheep is born

1997   Tony Blair wins election for Labour party; Princess Diana dies in car crash in Paris; Scotland and Wales vote for devolution; first Harry Potter book published; Hong Kong is handed back to China

1998   Good Friday agreement establishes Northern Ireland Assembly

1999   Britain decides not to join European Single Currency; Scottish Parliament meets in Edinburgh; eclipse of the sun; London Police accused of institutional racism in Stephen Lawrence report; concern that 'millennium bug' will hit computers

5.1. Reinvention

In April 1990, after I had resigned as an editor, I waited for my phone to ring with new challenges. The calls materialised, once again with sympathy but no job offers. I now had to work out how I was going to continue to make a living.

My life-plan had never included abandoning journalism. I loved the work and assumed, as we all did then, that my first trade would be my chosen trade until retirement, death even. But after 10 years of commissioning and editing articles, I didn't have the heart to go back to the business of writing and submitting them. I was 43 and realised that now was the time if I were to have a good run at doing something different.

As I pondered my future, one idea started to nudge ahead of others: becoming a trainer. I had enjoyed studying training at Surrey University. I had benefited from being a trainee myself in Devon. I had enjoyed setting up a course for others while I was in the Bahamas.

While I was at the BMA my interest developed. I soon worked out that the best way of building a talented team for a house journal was to recruit bright young would-be journalists and give them a decent training programme. The strategy worked well, with all of my trainees moving on after a couple of years to more mainstream organisations, such as *Which?* magazine and the BBC. One BMA worthy went so far as to accuse me of running a training academy under the cover of running a house magazine.

I started to give lunchtime courses on effective writing for my colleagues, mainly BMA committee clerks. These sessions worked well despite regular skirmishes about the beauty of long words and the important role played by the passive voice. (Though I must say that as an occasional writer of official minutes I came to realise the value of the wriggle-room provided by writing 'It was decided' rather than 'We decided'.)

I tapped into a rich seam of demand from doctors who wanted to learn the skills of journalism. My involvement started when my consultant gastroenterologist asked if I could find help for Lyndy Matthews, one of his house officers who was disenchanted with medicine. I ended up offering her a part-time job for three months and she thrived, writing thoughtful pieces on cervical screening, medical negligence and junior doctors' hours. Others followed, mainly GPs and psychiatrists, and soon I started to run weekend courses for doctors on medical journalism; they were heavily over-subscribed.

I realised that if I were to become a full-time trainer I would need some formal training myself, particularly in the core skill of holding the attention of a roomful of trainees for a day, sometimes longer. I was still serving my notice, so took a week's holiday to attend a course called Instructional Techniques for Training Officers run by Guardian Business Services.

There were 10 of us – some from prestigious organisations like the Lord Chancellor's Office and the BBC. I was listed as unattached. On the first day we learnt how to start a training session – and with it the affection trainers have for using mnemonics. The first one we were fed was on how to start a training session: INTRO – Interest, Need, Title, Range, Objectives.

The course covered how to write training objectives and meet them – and how to deal with difficult people. With my self-presumed affability I did not expect this to be a problem, but this later turned out to be optimistic.

On the fifth and final day we had to devise and deliver a small training session. I chose to give my session on the Principles of Effective Writing and came up with the first of many mnemonics of my own. This one was PAPWE - write a Plan, use the Active, prefer the Positive, make every Word count, and don't forget to Edit what you have just written.

The mnemonic may have been substandard (and never appeared in any of my courses again) but there was some positive feedback: 'Good use of words', 'Nicely relaxed and open style', 'Loads of confidence and authority (not in a military sense though)'.

But there were some warnings: 'Can appear slightly threatening', 'You are projecting that it may be hard for you to let go during questioning, ie jumping in...', and (embarrassingly) 'Avoid words like *symmetricality* – especially in a section on short words!'

An important learning point came when one colleague asked me if I realised that my flies were open. I had not. Had anyone else noticed? Luckily no.

In November I left the BMA. It was a wrench, although the generosity of my farewell temporarily lessened the blow. My BMA colleagues clubbed together to buy me a flip chart and overhead projector. My own team commissioned a cartoon from Richard Willson, whom I had first met in Bucharest in 1974, showing me in cricketing whites, using a rolled up copy of the magazine to bat away a volley of writs and angry letters.

After a week's holiday in the Canaries, where I seemed to be the only English male not wearing knee-length multicoloured swimming trunks, I started work as a trainer. My first course took place four miles from my home (and now office as well) in a grade II-listed Bed and Breakfast across the road from Effingham golf course. It was the first of many courses I was to run over the next 17 years.

I had designed the course for a single participant, an enthusiastic American woman who was employed by the University of Basel to edit academic papers. She was a competent writer and editor, but did not have a science degree. In the view of the senior Swiss academics who employed her, she needed some training before she could help them with 'proper medical writing'. None of them had English as a first (or even second) language.

She had got in touch with my old friend and colleague RAF Thistlethwaite who, after leaving the BMA, had become honorary secretary of the Medical Journalists Association, and he in turn had suggested me. Then, as now, I saw no reason why 'medical writing' was any different from any other kind of writing, so I accepted the commission.

For three days the two of us sat across a green baize tablecloth in the B&B's slightly musty conservatory, where for the first time I used my new flip chart. Our sessions went well and I couldn't believe how much I was enjoying my new career.

On the second evening Barbara and I took my student to Leatherhead's finest Chinese restaurant and only theatre. When the two of us got home we turned on the BBC television news. The political correspondent John Sergeant was doing a piece to camera about Mrs Thatcher's future when she emerged from the building behind him. There followed a flustered and inconclusive interview.

This was the start of the prime minister's unexpectedly rapid decline and fall. I, on the other hand, was busy starting just the kind of enterprise she would have approved of: setting up a small business.

5.2 The joy of selling

There were three requirements for successfully launching a small business, one of my new clients once told me. First, you should be arrogant enough to believe that, if it doesn't work out, you can still make a living from something else; I was. Second, your family should be willing to give you unpaid support; she was. And third, you should be prepared to work all the hours God gave; I did, though looking back I gravely underestimated how many hours this would mean.

One immediate advantage, though, was that I no longer had to commute into, and then across, London. All I had to do was negotiate the eight yards from my bedroom to my office. This gave me an extra three hours a day.

My new office was spacious and overlooked the garden. It was the result of a decision two years earlier when, wallowing in the monthly miracle of regular salary payments, we had commissioned an extension to our house. The jewel in this project (or folly, depending on your point of view) was a first-floor conservatory facing south. It was a great place to work. In the first summer, when the sun started to blaze through the untreated glass panes, I turned to working in shorts and T-shirt, then just shorts. The grey suits I had worn at the BMA spent more and more time in the wardrobe.

I rediscovered the satisfaction of doing things for myself. One November evening I sat on the office floor preparing acetate slides with scalpel and cutting board, then sat at my computer to produce mock newspaper cuttings for exercises. However, this self-sufficiency came at a cost. I monitored the process of writing and posting two letters – and found to my horror that from start to finish it took 40 minutes with no interruptions. I made a silent apology to Sandra, my highly valued but long-suffering PA at the BMA.

I came up with a mission statement of course: a lofty affair aiming to provide training that would 'improve the standard of communications in health care'. I would also be 'the leading provider of such services'. My business plan envisaged 72 course days in the first year and 144 in the fifth; the latter figure turned out to be hopelessly optimistic.

To supplement my income, I proposed taking on consultancy work, including a regular newsletter for a royal college. I also proposed writing a book about medical journalism. I had managed to sell the idea to the publisher Andrew Bax of Radcliffe Medical Press when, in one of my final days at BMA House, we found ourselves stuck in a lift together. I hoped the book would help to define me as an 'expert'.

My bank manager agreed to give me a £15,000 loan over five years to pay for a personal computer, fax, laser printer and photocopier – and to tide me over until the income started rolling in. I showed my confidence by registering for VAT, and I showed my lack of it by taking out an insurance policy that would give me an income if my ulcerative colitis (or other as yet unknown disease) became so bad that I could not work for six months or more. Being dead, Barbara and I agreed, would have no negative cost implications, so we did not insure for that.

I reneged on the socialist principles I had long advocated and took out private health insurance. I justified it on the grounds that as a businessman I needed more flexibility than the NHS would offer. I also took out, on professional advice, the £28,000 in my BMA pension and bought into a commercial pension fund. Some years later a government-inspired investigation determined that I had been badly advised, and my advisers told me that they owed me some £68,000 in compensation. By the time I had agreed to be compensated it had gone up to £74,000.

Like all those starting up small businesses I had to take on a new role – as unpaid collector of government taxes. I had neither the experience nor the desire to qualify me for the role, but soon realised that if I were to make a mistake – however innocent – I would be hit with a large financial penalty. Collecting VAT was a particular strain, and I made several visits to the local office in an attempt to understand the regulations.

During the 14 years of my business career we had one VAT inspection – and passed. We also had an inspection from the Inland Revenue, and after two days in our one-room office drinking our coffee and poring over our figures, the two inspectors found only a minor discrepancy. The amount of money we had to pay to the Inland Revenue was much smaller than the visit would have cost them.

Like many other small businessmen before me, I soon discovered that having a good product is the easy bit; the hard part is getting people to part with their money to buy it. I had to learn to sell, an activity that previously I had held in some contempt as being greedy and exploitative. Bob Hayzen, my old friend and mentor from the BMA, gave me plenty of support and one important piece of advice: most people setting up in business do not charge enough.

I spent hours producing leaflets, doing mail shots, following up with telephone calls and driving around the country to meet potential clients. I forced myself to do some cold calling and learnt how sniffy some switchboard operators could be. One memorable conversation went as follows:

'I am phoning to ask if anyone in the organisation might be interested in talking about courses in effective writing?'

'Why on earth should anyone here be interested in effective writing? We are the Department of Health'.

Clearly being in business was not going to be easy.

5.3: Tilting at windmills

I had high hopes for my Effective Writing course. My big idea was to take a group of health professionals – initially doctors but I intended to cast the net wider – and show them how to turn their overblown prose into something that ordinary people would understand. I was confident that they would leap on my wise words with gratitude – and perhaps a touch of mild adulation.

The plan soon ran into trouble. Cracks appeared during the afternoon of one of my early courses. The dozen doctors facing me around the U-shaped table had discussed their goals, and I had been encouraged when many of them specifically listed learning how to write concisely. They had since prepared and written a short piece of writing, and now we were looking at how to polish their draft. Here was my chance to press simplicity upon them.

'Turn to page 31 in your course book,' I said. 'You will see two lists of words. On the left are the Anglo-Saxon ones, like 'about' and 'more'. These are the words that ordinary people used in homes, fields and taverns.

'Now look at the list on the right. Here you will see the longer, posher words – 'approximately' and 'additional' – that have come down from the Greek and Latin and were used in the counting houses and government offices.

'If you look again at your draft you will probably see you have used many of the posh ones on the right. If you want to make your writing simple and easy to understand, one of the things you need to do is substitute the plainer words on the left.

'Never use a long word if a short one will do. Strike out "The experimental apparatus was agitated by the present experimenter". Write instead: "I shook the test tube".'

I paused. And as I did so I heard a group intake of breath. Looks of horror swirled around the table. Then one of the braver ones spoke up.

'We can't do that. It's far too simple. We're doctors. Our writing has to be more dignified. If we do what you say it will be like a *Janet and John* book.'

'Besides,' added another. 'The words on the right are more *scientific*.'

It was on the tip of my tongue to point out that words in themselves can't be scientific, but I remembered just in time to do what trainers are trained to do. With what I hoped was an endearing shrug, I threw their dismay back to them as a question.

'If you don't want to get rid of the long words, how are you going to make your writing concise and clear?'

'We don't know. That's why we came on the course,' they said.

Stalemate – and I was to find myself in this position again and again over the next few years. Doctors coming on the course may have wanted to learn to write well, but not at the expense of abandoning long words and complicated sentences. What I called 'simple' writing (easy to understand), they derided as 'simplistic' (acessible or affectedly simple) which is not the same at all.

They found it all rather vulgar; some even found it dangerous. As one distressingly young public health physician, fresh from Oxford University, remarked one day in exasperation: 'We are doctors. We don't *want* everyone to understand what we are saying'.

I adapted my teaching to the prevailing culture, but it took a little time. It meant abandoning my commitment to the fixed principles of the Plain English mavens (simplicity at all costs and for all audiences), and adopt a relative approach. I banned the phrase 'good writing', insisting that we use the term 'effective writing' instead. The test of effectiveness, I argued, was not whether readers were impressed, but whether they understood.

I tried gentle mockery, arguing that those who felt they had to don a 'posh overcoat' whenever they had something to write should instead try on some other, less formal coats for different types of readers. A good stylist, I argued, could write successfully for the *Sun* in the morning and the *Lancet* in the afternoon.

My rallying call became a rather more graceful mnemonic than my previous and short-lived PAPWE. This was PIANO: *Put It Across Not Out,* which also made for a good slide, inspired by the time when my Auntie Stella was taken ill.

'Did she have a heart attack?' I asked my cousin.

'I am not sure,' he said. 'I asked the doctor and he told me that she had had a myocardial infarct'. A clear case of PIONA.

I brought up reinforcements in the form of a 'readability' test devised some 50 years earlier by an American professor of journalism. This was the eponymous Gunning FOG Test, with his acronym standing for Frequency Of Gobbledegook (Gunning, R: *The technique of clear writing,* McGraw-Hill International, New York, NY 1952).

Professor Gunning's big idea was that counting up the number of words in each sentence, and the number of syllables in each word, would produce an index reflecting broadly how easy to read a piece of writing would be. After doing his little calculation (see table below), tabloid newspapers have a score of about 8-10, more serious newspapers 12-14, medical journals 14-18, and the small print in insurance policies 20 and more. It is a useful test, provided you don't want it to measure 'reading age', which is going to be a far more complicated affair.

I asked participants to bring samples of their writing to the course, and I made them apply the test to their own work. Many found the results surprising.

I particularly remember one wise old clerk (he would not have liked being called a manager) whose job it was to answer letters of complaints. He found that when someone wrote in with a score of 8 he responded with a score of 8, and when someone (a *Guardian* reader no doubt) wrote in with a score of 14 he wrote back with a score of 14. He had been doing the job so long and so well that he did not realise his flexibility. He was impressed; so were we.

Others received a nasty shock. The article they had prepared for an academic journal, for instance, was written in a style more suited to a tabloid newspaper. Or, more usually, the information they had carefully crafted for their patients was in the style of a specialist academic journal.

The FOG score also showed how a piece of writing became more or less readable as the writing process progressed. Typically it would start off at a reasonable level, and then get denser and denser as the draft was seen – and 'corrected' – by colleagues, bosses and reviewers.

Some found this dynamic comforting. One younger writer, sent on the course by her professor on the grounds that she could not write, had the presence of mind to bring samples of her work and her professor's. As she analysed and compared their FOG scores I could see her shoulders lifting. Her writing clocked in at 12; her professor's a high 18. She went away realising that she was not a 'bad writer'; she just favoured a less pompous style.

I never quite figured out the appeal of dense prose for doctors, though I did contemplate some theories. Was it unconscious snobbery, or a desire to keep their knowledge to themselves? Was it because they had stopped the serious study of language at 16? Or were they suffering from what I called 'post-traumatic spelling-bee disorder': the result of being forced to spell longer and more complicated words from an early age, leaving them with the notion that long words are a sign of cleverness?

Whatever the cause, the habit had spread to other health professionals. NHS managers, for instance, were taking pompous and inexplicable prose to new heights. Their problem, it turned out, was that their documents had to satisfy so many audiences at the same time that the safest way of avoiding trouble was to ensure that no-one could understand them. Thus the simple sentence, 'Please follow the agreed procedure', became:

> 'The whole purpose of reaching agreement in respect of maintaining disagreements that occur within an internal framework have been known for many years. We would therefore ask you on this occasion as we have done in the past to continue to use the further stages in the internal procedure if you so desire in order that no accusations can be levelled at either side for failing to abide by the agreements' (memo spotted on notice board).

It took some months and a bit of help before I worked this one out.

When I started my courses in the 1990s nurses still wrote clearly. But as the years passed, and more and more of them went to university, they too started to embrace the inflated phrases that were running uncontrollably through the NHS. By the end of the decade they were writing gobbledegook as determinedly as the doctors.

I found solace in one small sub-group: doctors and nurses in the armed services. They often joined me in trying to persuade their colleagues of the advantages of clear thought and clear writing, but in vain. I once told an army doctor of my observation that they were better writers than their civilian counterparts.

'It stands to reason,' he replied. 'We want to put our messages out quickly and simply. We'd be dead if we didn't.'

HOW TO DO THE GUNNING FOG SCORE

Step one: Count out a passage of 100 words. Make sure it ends with a full stop, even if it comes out at slightly more or less than 100 words.

Step two: Calculate the average sentence length by dividing 100 by the number of sentences in the passage chosen.

Step three: Count the number of words with three or more syllables. This figure gives you the number of 'difficult words'.
Don't count:

- proper nouns,
- combinations of easy words, like 'photocopy',
- verbs that become three syllables when you add 'es', 'ing', 'ed' (eg, 'committed')
- technical words that readers will know

Step four: Add the average sentence length (step two) to the number of 'difficult words' (step three).

Step five: Multiply the total in step four by 0.4 to get the reading score.

Sample scores:

Airport novels	6-8
Tabloid newspapers	8-10
Serious newspapers	12-14
Medical journals	14-16
Obscure journals	16-18
Insurance policies	18-20

Example one:
An action group was formed within the *community* by the more *vociferous individuals* in 1999, which included local *councillors*, with the expressed object of campaigning for a local *surgery*. Following a *variety* of *incongruous* and *inconsequential* moves, the group *eventually* approached the *medical* practices whose current *responsibilities* included the village of Dudgeham. *Inexplicably* the Patients Action Group did not *communicate* with the *committee* and, therefore, the latter was not afforded the *opportunity* to explain the *parameters* of *provision* for a *surgery* for GPs nor the limited powers at their *disposal* for *negatively* controlling the *distribution* of *medical manpower* within any given *geographical locality*.

Example two:
Local *councillors* and others formed an action group to campaign for a local *surgery*. They *eventually* approached the doctors who covered the village. The Patients Action Group did not speak to the PCT, which therefore could not explain the rules for providing a GP *surgery* or its limited powers of controlling where GPs work. In September 1999 Dr Prodder asked if his practice could open a branch *surgery* in Dudgeham. Our practice *manager* inspected the proposed site and decided that, with some *internal* changes, it would be *suitable*. The PCT gave outline *approval*.

	Example One	**Example Two**
Sentence length	3	17
Number of long words	24	9
Total	57	26
Reading score	22.8	10.4

5.4: French cricket

Our flat in Wimereux continued to give us a bolthole, and by the early 1990s it had a new attraction: a cricket team. On one of our first visits, looking out of our window, we had seen our neighbour Bernard – an architect with a large, lugubrious Gallic moustache – taking his three children and a brand new cricket set down to the beach.

'Do you know how to play?' I asked.

The answer was no, and we rushed to teach him the main principles before the tide came in. From this chance encounter Bernard ended up as president, and I as honorary president-for-life, of the thirteenth cricket club to be constituted in France. We called it *Wicket Wimereux Côte d'Opale.* (We were going to call it Wimereux Cricket Club but the thought of the WC Club proved too scatological for French taste.)

Bernard knew how to make things happen. Within the year we had a team, albeit a pretty bad one, with a brisk Indian expatriate as coach. Bernard was our recruiting officer, and the team at various times included two doctors from the Boulogne hospital, an insurance agent, a teacher of English, a business student, a plumber and a tugboat captain.

He arranged for an artificial pitch to be laid in the middle of the town's *stade hippique*, at that time used only once a year by the local society promoting and showing the squat *Boulonnais* horses.

To say the team took to the game like a *canard* to *eau* may be an overstatement, but the players were keen, turning up every Sunday from March to November to practise their fielding, throwing, batting and bowling. They started to bring their children and at one stage up to two dozen youngsters were turning up for Sunday training.

At first both adults and children found it hard to keep their arms straight when bowling, and then keep the bat straight when batting. In time one or two started to develop well. But even they, if they were not directly involved, had a habit of wandering off the field if bored.

They loved the word 'Howzat!' Runs were *points* and batsmen were *eliminés* when bowled. They preferred to *lancer* a ball rather than *bowler*, and the important piece of gear slipped down the trousers for protection was not a box or even a *boîte*, but a *coquille*. An over, however, was an *over-r-r-r*, with a particularly Gallic rolling of the r.

The gulf between the two sporting traditions became particularly apparent when it came to eating. Leaving the game mid-way for a cup of tea and a slice of cake was always going to be hard for the French to understand, as a decade before it had been for my new American girlfriend. More contentious still were the arrangements for the all-important midday meal. Before one match between the juniors and a primary school team from England, I suggested giving the youngsters a light lunch – some bread and cheese perhaps?

This was scornfully dismissed as being neither light nor lunch. Instead the mothers brought a cornucopia of salads, meats and home-made desserts. Afterwards the 11-year-old captain of the junior team asked for the start of the game – which was already half an hour late – to be further delayed to give him and his team-mates time to digest.

Our first overseas tour was arranged by a friend of Bernard to a village near Bristol. A couple of carloads of players stayed with us at Leatherhead or were billeted with neighbours; we had takeaway curry in the garden. The following day, down in the west country, we flew in balloons (also one of Bernard's activities), took part in a French festival weekend, sang the *Marseillaise* and lost (though not too badly) to a local side.

Once the word got around, British teams started to ask if they could come out and play, though we had to be careful to make sure that they were of the right sort: not too good at cricket and ready to postpone at least some of their drinking until after the match.

For five years we persuaded the ferry company Sealink to sponsor an annual match, with a cup, between the *Président's XI* and the *Président d'Honneur's XI*. The first match attracted good publicity, with Bernard interviewed on the BBC Radio 4 *Today* programme by Jenny Bond, later the BBC court correspondent. It was a charming interview, enhanced by Bernard's tendency to talk about 'batman'.

That evening we had a *choucroute* banquet in the town hall with a succession of spontaneous speeches, one of which came from the father of one of the English players. He announced that this was the second time he had been to Wimereux, the first being in 1944 with the Royal Marines. He received a warm round of applause.

The team continued playing for about 20 years. One year a group of us, with children, went down to the Dordogne for a cricket week with other French teams. But in time the kids went into more mainstream activities like studying for their exams and going out with members of the opposite sex. Expatriates started to join, which edged the culture away from a family-friendly activity and towards a drinking club for middle-aged men who liked escaping from their wives.

The club is now wound up and the ground has been turned into a so-called English Garden. Bernard got the commission as its architect.

5.5: The newsletter pandemic

As it became clear that running courses on simple writing for health professionals was not going to be enough to support a full-time business, an unexpected niche appeared. I was approached by Roger Silver, a former *Guardian* journalist who had become a perceptive and influential public relations officer in the NHS. He was setting up a communications training unit and was looking for trainers. He had already filled the effective-writing slot, so I had to come up with a new idea for a two-day course: I chose running newsletters.

It was an idea whose time had come. 'Communications' was a buzz word, particularly in Conservative party circles where an alleged lack of it was considered the main reason why so many people hated their policies. And newsletters had become a fashionable way of tackling the problem.

This was partly due to a recent innovation. Until recently, any paper publication had been the province of expensive professionals such as printers, designers, photographers, writers and editors. Now all you needed to publish your own newsletter was an off-the-peg personal computer with a desk-top publishing package. It appeared to be a remarkably cheap solution, though this was misleading since few people bothered to factor in the time it would take.

Newsletters started to stream out from surgeries, hospitals and NHS offices. Most ended up in dog-eared piles scattered about waiting rooms and reception areas, untaken and unread. In some ways I found it encouraging: a clear endorsement of my insistence that putting messages out rather than across could waste a lot of time and money.

Their failure was not surprising. Most newsletters were badly designed, ranging from sheets of paper covered with close-packed courier type (the one traditionally used on typewriters) to those cursed by what I called polyfontophilia – the love of many typefaces. I still have one showing eight variations of type on one page of A4.

Most of the articles were dull, and littered with capital letters. They would sing the praises of those in charge ('The Senior Management Team is delighted to announce the appointment of a new Chief Accountant...'), or give instructions on how to behave ('As the Human Relations Department has noted earlier, all those members of Staff who have been issued with a Photo ID should now wear it on duty...'). Any empty spaces were filled at the last moment by articles prised out of friends of the editor, often irrelevant pieces with headlines such as **My best holiday in Ibiza** or **How to cook prunes**.

What few illustrations there were consisted mainly of primitive clip art or grainy shots of a Member of the Senior Management Team (initial upper case, please) presenting some trumped-up award to a bemused employee (lower case). These pictures had often been taken by someone in the post room (definitely lower case) with a camera.

It was a classic case of technology outrunning the available skills. As one of the first to attend this course, a genial paediatrician called Tom Hutchison, wrote in my own newsletter (I felt I couldn't avoid the trend):

'As editor I felt about as in control as a 17-year-old learner driver. Each issue felt like another trip taken gingerly around the block. There was much anxiety, no style or speed – but at least the vehicle had not yet crashed...

'I had never turned an article down and had hardly dared suggest alternatives. I was prone to nightmares, in which no-one sent me any copy and I had to write everything. Yet I would invariably end up trying to squeeze in too much.' (Tom Hutchison, How I learned to love white space, *Short Words*, summer 1992)

One of the first tasks of the course was to help participants work out what being an editor actually meant. I convinced them that it involved more than collecting articles and laying them out. They needed clear objectives and sensible planning, though the good news was that that once they had them in place their work could be more straightforward, and even more enjoyable.

We discussed the importance of measuring their performance. Questionnaires and focus groups were the obvious first choice, but these could be expensive and hard to organise. Individual feedback from colleagues and readers was free, but invariably biased. But there were other, less formal measures: having to turn away articles because of lack of space, for instance; fighting off others in the organisation who wanted to take the credit; producing immediate results, such as a pencil case being reunited with its owner within hours of a lost property notice appearing in the newsletter.

Tom Hutchison concluded his article:

'Things have changed. I have settled on a house style of length, layout and lettering... I have a budget... The newsletter is quarterly for the first time, with a pre-published series of printing dates and copy deadlines... I have become more confident in asking for articles, rewriting them to length and style and inventing headlines... I think I can dispense with the L-plates.' (*Short Words*, ibid)

I started to publish newsletters for various organisations. My first client, when I started my business in 1990, was the College (later the Royal College) of Ophthalmologists, whose chief executive Margaret Hallendorff took a personal interest. She also showed what a keen hands-on editor could do. But she had to be tough, facing up to those with power and influence who wanted their photos to appear in each edition, or expected her to publish 600 words even though she had specifically asked for 200. She had her reward when the newsletter took second place in a national newsletter competition; the winner was published by Sainsbury's and had a much, much larger budget.

RAF Thistlethwaite turned up again. He had found himself volunteered as public relations officer of the Royal Medical Benevolent Fund. He commissioned material for their quarterly newsletter while we handled subediting, layout and production. We held our editorial planning meetings in the local pub. It was fun, enlivened by such moments as spotting in an article the proud statement that when one of their members became sick the organisation had 'elevated the discomfort'. We changed it to 'alleviate', though with some reluctance.

Some of those we worked with remained blissfully unaware of how newsletters worked. One client expressed surprise that there was always just enough news to fill each page exactly. Others, finding that space had forced us to cut copy, demanded that we reinstate their golden words without being able to suggest what should go instead. I once suggested we could put a flap on the bottom of the page to accommodate the extra copy, and to my horror the client embraced the idea enthusiastically.

The administrator for a group of medical professionals sent back a dummy we had mocked up because she thought it looked rather vulgar.

'This is quite wrong,' I was scolded. 'It looks like the *Daily Mail* but our members read the *Times*.'

I waited a few days (I didn't want her to think the answer was too easy) then changed with one keystroke the typeface we had chosen for the headlines: **Doctors in pay row** became **Doctors in pay row.**

'That's much better,' she said, delighted with her contribution.

In 1991 we produced 16 newsletter pages; by 1995 the number rose to 106. It started to bring in some income, though sadly not huge amounts because the work tended to be far more time-consuming than most clients realised – and therefore wanted to pay for. And I had to hire staff, which brought a new set of problems.

There was one particularly unwelcome consequence. As I was in full-flow training-mode extolling the benefits of some basic editorial principle, a hawk-eyed participant would pull out a newsletter we had published.

'You haven't done it here!', they would gloat. I tried blaming it on the client, but it did undermine the message.

5.6: A mended heart

In 1995 our household witnessed another burst of ill-health, but this was Barbara's turn. She started to have bouts of feeling very sick. In April she had a particularly bad turn on holiday while we were walking back to our hotel after a lazy day and a fine, though hardly lavish, meal. She blamed it on the heat, but decided to get it checked out on her return.

At the time she was working in the office of the medical school of St Thomas's and Guy's, having been lured there by a friendly client. They kindly sent her to one of their top doctors, who was physician to the Queen. After the consultation he wrote to Barbara's GP that she was 'overweight, premenopausal and depressed'. She did not find that enormously helpful.

As the months progressed Barbara became worse, and she resigned from her job (not just for health reasons, but they were a major factor). We went to the Italian resort of Viareggio for a few days where I was speaking at a conference of GPs, and after a splendid day walking around and lunching well she was taken ill again. This time she suspected the olive oil.

When we got back I played the private insurance card and we went to our local gastroenterologist for a second opinion. Unlike the first doctor, he took out a stethoscope.

'Has anyone told you about your heart murmur?' he asked.

No-one had, of course, and with that sentence the world – and Barbara's relationship with the health services – changed dramatically. That evening we were back in the same private hospital, this time with a cardiologist. After the usual array of tests it emerged that Barbara had a hole in her heart, undiagnosed when young. Her turns were holiday-related, but caused by too much exercise. When she exerted herself, her liver was overwhelmed by blood, and this caused the pain and the nausea.

Within about six weeks, and just before Christmas, Barbara had open heart surgery to patch up the hole which, the surgeon proudly assured her, was the size of an old 50p coin. Hers was not an uncommon story; we heard that others of our generation were coming forward with the same hitherto undiagnosed problem.

I would like to write here that my part in this adventure was heroic, but it was not. Dealing with one's own illness is straightforward: the only focus is your own recovery. Dealing with a partner's illness is much harder, because so much of it involves looking on, powerless.

During one procedure I waited alone, increasingly worried, as other patients came back and went home. As it turned out I was right to be worried because Barbara's blood pressure had suddenly plummeted. She was wheeled back looking much worse than when she had been wheeled out.

I had to assume a phoney insouciance the day before she went into hospital for the operation, and a brisk cheeriness as I left her propped up on her bed, in the care of strangers. When the hour came for the operation, I stayed at my desk trying to work, jumping at every phone call in case it was the one saying the procedure had gone well, or not.

That evening I visited the recovery room, where Barbara lay pale but remarkably normal among an array of tubes and a mask that didn't fit. My joke that it was a Catholic hospital and the mask probably didn't fit Jewish noses was in retrospect particularly ill-judged. I thought I was remarkably cool throughout; others told me a different story.

When Christmas came two weeks later it was a real, if sober, celebration. Barbara was in pain but recovering. A short-lived setback came when she opened a present (not from me) which turned out to be a book on homoeopathic medicine; she saw it as a rebuke. One of her cousins came over from America to keep her company over the festive season and her aunt came over to keep her company once I had gone back to work. The aunt was slightly aggrieved that by the time she arrived Barbara was no longer the bed-ridden invalid she had been expecting.

Within a few months Barbara realised that simple tasks that had left her breathless, such as walking the half mile into Leatherhead, she could now accomplish more easily. Her energy levels rose considerably, which was a good thing because we were about to make some major changes in our business – and lifestyle.

Our GP took it upon himself to write to the Queen's physician; 'You may be interested to know that my patient who you diagnosed as overweight, premenopausal and depressed has just had the hole in her heart repaired.' I suggested he should add the PS: 'By the way her husband is a medical journalist and her brother-in-law a solicitor', but he did not take it up.

5.7: The business rises, the business falls

We both needed good health because we were about to steer into some trouble. In a light-hearted moment my client Geert-Jan told me of the old Jewish curse: 'May you employ lots of staff'. The curse was about to strike.

For the first few years the business had shown steady progress. I know this because at the end of each year I wrote myself a report, a habit that I kept up until my retirement 17 years later. In the first one I concluded, rather smugly in retrospect: 'The goals were met.' In the second year I reported an increase in the number of courses I was running, and in the number of newsletters I managed.

To help with the latter I took on Jane Donovan, the daughter of a cousin, first on work experience and later as a trainee. As demand continued to grow I recruited Lyn Knights, an old friend from Wimbledon days, to do part-time secretarial work. By this time the conservatory was feeling overcrowded, and Barbara was beginning to feel her home was no longer hers.

In late 1993 I started looking for an office. We saw some places in the middle of Leatherhead, varying from the run-down to the smart and expensive. In the end we settled on one that was larger than we needed, but 'good for expanding into'. It was half a mile on the other side of Leatherhead on the fringes of the industrial estates, overlooking a small garage and a large builders' merchants. We took part of the ground floor: one large room and a smaller one.

Moving into an office changes the game. Premises come with landlords, and ours proved to be particularly grumpy, cutting us no slack on anything and suddenly turning up to wander round his property looking for damage.

Premises also come with other tenants, who have their own cars to park in the limited space available. I got off to a particularly bad start on the first day when a worker from the office above ours stormed down to tell us I had parked in their space. They were right, but it was where the landlord had told us to park.

As owner of the business I had to take on all kinds of extra duties, such as health and safety checks and overseeing security. We installed a security system that was connected to the local police station. On several evenings I had to rush from home late in the evening to deal with what – on every occasion – turned out to be a false alarm.

But the business continued to do well and at the end of 1994 I was able to give staff some healthy Christmas bonuses. We continued to expand: in 1995 we ran 60 courses a year and produced 148 pages of newsletters. I added a part-time associate trainer, Peter Moore, and we engaged freelance journalists to do shifts on the newsletters. I recruited a third member of staff to run courses, though it took three attempts to find the right person.

At this time I decided to split the business into two: TAA Training and TAA Newsletters. (We decided not to have TA Training because of potential confusion with the Territorial Army, encouraging people to assume that our training would involve tramping over Welsh mountaintops.) Turnover reached nearly £250,000. But the margins were not so good, and we had been hit with a big tax bill. In 1995 I reduced the Christmas bonus. I received complaints.

'It's not as much as last year.'

'We haven't made as much money as last year,' I replied.

My relationship with my staff started to deteriorate, exacerbated by what was clearly a blunder on my part. I had installed myself in the small office where I could have quiet and privacy (and status, too, perhaps). But it proved to be divisive, with two cultures existing side by side: one with me in it; the other without.

I felt I knew far less of what was going on than anyone else. This not only put me at a psychological disadvantage but, since owners of small businesses are effectively job-sharing with everyone else, it was also inefficient. I started to leave home to go to work with a sinking feeling in the pit of my stomach. Since I owned the business this seemed (to put it mildly) rather silly.

I talked the situation over with people who knew about business and strategy, and realised that I had to make changes. I had left the BMA largely because I did not enjoy managing people and wanted to be a hands-on trainer. But I had become a manager again, this time at my own expense. So I decided to sell the newsletters, keep the training, and move into a smaller office. For this I would need one assistant, preferably working full time to keep continuity, and everyone else would become redundant.

Down-sizing in some ways is harder than growing a business. After plenty of phone calls to the lawyers at the Institute of Personnel and Development, of which I was now a member, I announced on a Friday morning that there would be a meeting in the afternoon. (Making the announcement on a Friday was part of the advice but I can't remember why – perhaps to give people the weekend to calm down, though in this case it had the opposite effect).

The staff had not seen the redundancies coming, and I found telling them a dreadful ordeal. I tried to assuage my guilt by offering a package above the minimum (or as I would have liked to have put it: extremely generous terms).

Most accepted my decision and were gracious about it. However, one of them was not. On the last day before it would have been too late, I received a letter from her solicitor summonsing me to an industrial tribunal.

The first lawyer I spoke to said enthusiastically that the case would raise an interesting legal issue; I swiftly found another one. I felt I had been unfairly judged and was determined to have my day in court. It was not to happen.

Five days before the tribunal I started to vomit uncontrollably. I assumed it was stress, but the GP I persuaded to visit said that projectile vomiting is rarely stress-related. Whatever the cause, I felt terrible, and decided to settle a day before the case was due to be heard. It cost me a friendship, £750 in a cash settlement and several thousand pounds in legal fees.

I sold the newsletter business to some former colleagues who were setting up in business and I was pleased to find them a good home. I stayed around in the near-empty offices for another couple of months, seeing out the lease with the help of a succession of temporary secretaries. At this time another saying came back to haunt me, this one from my old mentor Bob Hayzen:

Question: 'How do you get a doctor to run a small business?'

Answer: 'Give him a large one and wait.'

I wished I hadn't been so quick to laugh at that one.

5.8: A clock strikes

In the midst of all this we decided to 'sell off some of the family silver'. We contacted the auctioneers Phillips who had an office in Guildford – and an incredibly snooty-sounding telephonist to control access to it – and asked for a home visit to see if we had anything of value. As if.

We spent the Thursday evening before the visit pulling things out of cupboards that we hadn't used since we first put them in. The 'expert' turned out to be tall and charming, with a clipped moustache and a military bearing. He must have been through many grand houses trawling for treasure, and we felt guilty suborning him to our suburban home. We gave him free range of the cupboards, and he gave most things a valuation of about £30. At one stage he pulled open the dresser doors in the dining room to be confronted by a variety of different china sets.

'It looks as if you have several inheritances in here,' he said.

Then he looked up. Just above this dresser was a clock that had presided over the mantelpiece in the house in Wimbledon. It was large and heavy, sitting on a long black base with a frieze of griffins, cherubs and laurel wreaths, with an eagle astride the clock and lions guarding it on either side. Such opulence wasn't really our style and when we were dividing up the furnishings after my father's death we nearly left it for the general sale. My brother David didn't want it and said I might as well take it, so I did.

'That might be interesting,' said the expert, easing a camera out of his pocket. 'I think it's French. You might want to speak to our clock expert.'

Soon afterwards he left, leaving us feeling deflated because we had been unable to provide him with a long-lost Caravaggio. But I took his advice and called the expert. I described the clock as best I could.

'Clocks are doing well at the moment,' he said. 'There's a particularly fashionable English clockmaker called Vulliamy – one of his clocks went recently for £5,000. You'll know if you have one: his name will be written on the back.'

After the call I explained this to Barbara. I then lifted the clock down. It wasn't an easy job. I turned it around, looked at the back, and developed a stammer:

'Barbara', I called. 'It's a V-v-v-v...'

I rang the clock expert who was round in his Land Rover first thing on the next working day.

'It's a Vulliamy all right,' he said. 'How did you get it?'

'I don't know much about it. My father always claimed it was one of a pair, with the other belonging to some prince or other. My grandfather bought it. I know that because I have his notebooks and he's written down the purchase.'

The expert paled. 'You have the record of purchase,' he said. 'Can I see it?'

In a short period of time we agreed that we should put the clock into a sale. He wrapped it carefully in a blanket, and as he was about to leave, I asked:

'By the way, we have its glass cover in the attic? Do you want me to fetch it?'

He grew paler still; fortunately for his health, however, the cover proved to be not an original but a late Victorian make-do.

Some weeks later we received the catalogue. Our clock was on the cover. They had clearly done some research, and the following text appeared:

> 'This clock was supplied to the Marquis of Bath on 21 March 1811 at a cost of 75 guineas...It is not possible to ascertain when, but at some time it passed into the collection of HRH the Duke of Cambridge. On the Duke's death, it was sold at Christie Manson and Woods on Friday 17 June 1904 by order of his executors, where it was purchased by the vendor's grandfather for 24 guineas... A similar clock [was] supplied to the Prince of Wales in 1808.'

My father had always claimed that the clock had a brother (or should it be sister?) in one of the royal palaces. I would like to take this opportunity of apologising for not believing him.

To our delight the reserve on the clock was £6,000-£8,000. Barbara and I thought this would justify taking an afternoon off, and we took the train to London and the Phillips sale room in New Bond Street. The only other auction I had been to was in Tavistock, where I had bought some model railway lines for a friend. Here we felt out of place, surrounded by expensive antiques and opulent people; even the chairs we sat on in serried ranks seemed smart. But our new friend the clock expert was there and greeted us warmly. We sat down to await Lot 320.

As the lots moved smoothly into the 300s several people started to drift in to the sale room, including a nice young couple, moderately well off and probably newly married. A couple of employees came in also, each sitting by one of several phones. We sat self-consciously in what we hoped would be an anonymous place in the middle of a row.

The bidding started briskly. We reached the upper limit of the estimate in no time. The pleasant young couple joined the bidding and, after a little skirmishing, reached their limit and pulled out. Then employees of the auction house started to wield their phones. The skirmish had turned into a full-scale war.

'Twenty thousand, twenty-one thousand, twenty-two thousand...'

We started to giggle. The people around started to glance in our direction. They twigged that the clock was ours and they smiled encouragingly.

'Thirty, thirty one, thirty-two...'

Our giggles had stopped, our mouths had opened and we were holding hands.

By the time the gavel smacked down, the bidding had reached £55,000. By this time almost everyone in the room was looking at us, and we got a round of applause. Some people came and shook us by the hand. Two well-funded people – one an interior designer working on a new embassy and the other a businessman building up a collection with his newly-acquired fortune – clearly wanted the clock.

That evening we shared a bottle of pink champagne in the West End and went for a furiously expensive Japanese meal in what used to be Madame Prunier's restaurant just below my old apartment. We savoured every over-priced morsel – and the fact that for once we could afford it. A few months later we flew out to Barbados for a week's holiday. And then we became sensible again.

The final twist to this already heart-warming story is that the Inland Revenue classify clocks as machinery. And there is no tax to be paid on profits from machinery.

5.9: Science to the rescue

The windfall from the clock was not going to last forever. I had taken a risk in down-sizing the business, but again a new line turned up to save the bank balance. It was a course on how to write scientific papers, something I knew little about, having been banished from the world of science at 14. But that turned out to be an advantage: I was able to look at science writing not as a scientist but as a writer.

I had come to the notice of a medical communications company based in the Netherlands. They asked me to run a course on 'medical writing'. The course was not a success, which was not surprising since the new managing director, an Australian, had unwittingly positioned it as some long-overdue remedial training.

After a couple of hours battling against a sullen and obstructive multi-cultural audience, I flipped.

'You don't know why I am here,' I said. 'I don't know why I'm here. But we've got to sort something out that will get us through the next 36 hours.'

We had a 'frank discussion' for 15 minutes, and then the course continued in a slightly different direction with a slightly improved atmosphere. That evening I went out to dinner with a small group of the participants, and found myself seated next to Geert-Jan van Daal. He was a former artillery officer and anaesthetist with a clipped moustache who had become an entrepreneurial deviser of 'medical communication' projects. And he had a proposition.

At the time he was working with an organisation called Postgrade. It had been set up by the pharmaceutical company Smith Kline French (as it then was) to provide Dutch doctors with free training in the so-called soft skills, such as making presentations and managing time. He had noticed a demand for a training course on writing journal articles, and asked me to develop one.

I enlisted the help of Bill Whimster, a genial professor of pathology who came recommended by my old friends at the *British Medical Journal*. He turned out to be a constant source of support, a great enthusiast and a lively travel companion. He had a remarkable zest for life and among other interests was a keen roller-blader. Sadly he died from a heart attack a few years into our collaboration at the disgracefully premature age of 60.

Together we designed a two-day course and started off by delivering it six times in two months. Postgrade were wonderful employers. This was largely due to its head Ruud Weustink, a pipe-smoking and piano-playing former sales rep. He understood that happy trainers tend to produce happy trainees, and organised everything down to the smallest detail. He even flew us club class.

The programme we designed was pretty conventional. The opening lines of the course book were:

> 'The scientific paper is part of a long tradition. Physicians have been writing down their observations, interpretations, recipes and instructions at least since the Code of Hammurabi, which was engraved on a diorite monument in 2250 BC. (*Write a paper coursebook*, TAA Training, 1993)

After this history lesson (which years later helped me win a key point in a pub quiz), we laid out the formal requirements of a scientific paper. First came the four main sections – Introduction, Methods, Results and Discussion – and then the extra elements, such as tables, titles, references, abstracts. This took up most of the first day, though I did have 40 minutes to talk about the writing process.

We then adjourned for eight weeks. Geert-Jan's plan was to give participants time to write up a paper and send it to us for comment. When we reconvened for the second day, I brought with me a different tutor, a professional journal editor, who gave one-to-one feedback to those who had sent in manuscripts. Meanwhile I kept the bulk of the participants occupied with talks and exercises.

The first time we did the course we made an interesting observation. It was just before Christmas and the country was in the grip of a flu epidemic. Those who were able to come to the course were mostly those who had sent us a paper; those who had not sent us a paper called in to say they had flu and were unable to come. Was this evidence, we wondered, that writing scientific papers had protective properties?

Bill and I discussed this and other issues as we wound down after each course. Our conversations began to become more serious as we started to hear stories that challenged our hitherto rosy view of the world of medical publications.

Most of our participants were young, bright, conscientious junior doctors or researchers. They came on the course because they felt (or had been told) that they needed to have some articles published if they were to advance in their careers. Many arrived anxious, confused and blocked.

That was not surprising when we thought about it. On the one hand they had this pressure to publish; on the other they had little advice, support, time or training to help them to do so. What was worse, after struggling their way to a first draft, those who were meant to be supporting them took out their red pens and showed them how many 'mistakes' they had made. A nurturing environment it wasn't.

We also started to hear that some senior colleagues were, to put it bluntly, cheating. Several young authors told us that, while their paper was being finalised, someone they had never heard of was added to the list of co-authors. Others told us that, after they had left for a different department or gone on maternity leave, the paper they had been working on was published – but without their name in the list of authors. Others, though thankfully not many, told us that they had been persuaded to make claims that they knew the data did not support, or even put in data that they knew was false.

We started to wonder whether our course was really helping. And just at that time my now friend and patron Geert-Jan changed his job. He managed to get financial backing for a second-generation course, which he asked me to design and teach. This was a great opportunity to counter the pressures we had seen, and I seized it.

We launched the new version, keeping the two-day format, but focusing less on what papers should look like, and more on how they could best be produced. We insisted that participants should bring some data to the course so that we could guide them through a writing process in 10 easy stages. Not everyone understood this: some brought papers already in draft; others brought papers that had already been published.

'Why have you brought this?' I would ask the latter. 'It's published. What more do you want from it'.

'Well, you can always do better, can't you?' they replied.

That went to the root of the problem: writers were being encouraged to settle for nothing less than a 'perfect' paper, though there were strong disagreements over what that perfection was. We built our course on the notion that they should aim for a paper that was 'good enough' – and that they could measure this quite simply by whether or not the editor of their (sensibly chosen) target journal accepted it for publication.

'You are in marketing,' I would say. 'Find out what your customer – the editor – wants, and write it. If they accept it, you have done what you set out to do. Consider that a success.'

'But it seems rather seedy', some would say. 'Surely we can come up with a nicer definition'.

'Perhaps,' I would counter, 'but it won't help you to get published. What do you want to choose – the definition that makes it difficult, or the one that makes it manageable?' That usually worked.

There were other sticking points. An essential part of our 10-stage plan was that writers should have a clearly defined message before they started to write. This, we felt, would give the focus that many papers – and their writers – seemed to lack.

'I don't know why you keep banging on about messages,' a researcher once complained. 'A lot of what we write doesn't have one.' Quite.

Medical sociologists seemed particularly wedded to the idea of writing as a voyage of discovery.

'I never know what my message is until I have finished,' one insisted. He later undermined his case substantially when he complained that his supervisor constantly asked him for rewrites. I did not point out that he could have avoided these if he had done some more thinking in the early stages.

Occasionally a fierce tug-of-war erupted for the hearts and minds of the participants. These generally occurred with mixed-ability groups. Supervisors and mentors with more than 100 papers to their name weren't going to change their writing habits now, nor were they going to admit to their juniors that their way might not have been the best.

'You have made it all too easy,' one professor once complained, and he wasn't joking.

We ended up trying to separate the two groups and launched a course on 'How to improve your department's publication rate', which we dubbed the 'Professors' course'. We added some bits on handling writers and setting up publication policies but, as my colleague Peter Moore quipped, it was mostly the same course, but slower and with better wines.

Despite these difficulties, the course on writing scientific papers turned out to be my most successful product. I ran several hundred over the next 10 years and trained others to do the course as well. Our feedback told us that it took much of the fear out of writing, and made it appear manageable. It also gave participants confidence.

My own mission, as someone with a chronic illness, was to help doctors cut down on the time they spent writing papers, and get them back to helping patients. The moment I treasured above all was when a charming country GP in Holland came up to me at the end of a course and shook me warmly by the hand.

'I much enjoyed myself,' he said, 'and I know now how to write a paper. But I have decided that I don't need to write one, so I will take my son fishing instead'.

5.10: On the move

I did not expect that my new trade would take me to so many foreign parts.

I started to spend four weeks a year and sometimes more in the Netherlands, mainly in Utrecht, but also travelling to most of the main cities. I usually gave the course in mid-market chain hotels, though occasionally we used the lavish training centre of the Dutch Football Association, often sharing queues in the canteen with famous players (or so I was told).

I liked the Dutch, though I found them unreasonably tall. They were open and friendly in the training room, not surprisingly for a people who lived in homes with huge windows where the curtains were never drawn. Their command of English was extraordinarily good, though they did come up occasionally with such delightful 'Denglish' phrases as, 'Your room is in the backside of the hotel'.

I started to extend into other countries. I ran a few courses in the Flemish part of Belgium. Their English was less serviceable, but the lunches were much better. Instead of the open sandwiches and croquettes served in the Netherlands we sat down for three courses with cream sauces and wine. The afternoons were tough.

I ran some courses in Spain where, like the Belgians, they took their food seriously, which was fine by me. One was held in a castle, and we filed down a spiral staircase for a splendid buffet lunch. In another we started after the siesta, went on until 9.30 in the evening when we had supper, and were back again at 8.00 the following day for a morning's work followed by lunch.

In Italy my main memory was adjourning to the hospital coffee bar for a large jolt of caffeine in a tiny cup. Language was a problem in these two Latin countries, and I had to slow down at frequent intervals to allow one of the participants – usually someone who had studied in the UK or USA – to translate for the others. This made it hard going. I never found out whether I would have had the same difficulty with the French; they never showed any interest in my courses.

My training career in Germany was relatively brief as I unwittingly collided with the unspoken rules of academic hierarchy. I was invited to run the course on writing papers because, as one professor had told me, they felt that the English-speaking editors were treating German authors unfairly. It turned out not be a question of discrimination, however.

What emerged was that the professors were pushing their juniors into writing the kind of papers that *they* wanted to see, which were very different from the papers that the English-speaking editors wanted to publish. I tried to point out that it was a marketing problem – quite simply their young authors were writing for the wrong audience – but it had little effect and my invitations started to dwindle.

In Scandinavia I felt I had something to offer. Writers there assumed that their biggest obstacle to publication was their poor knowledge of English. They were surprised when I told them that they were worrying about the wrong thing. It was far more important to have a clear and well-supported message that the journal would find interesting and agree to publish. Then the journal's technical editors would tidy up the English.

'And anyway,' I added as extra encouragement. 'You should see the kind of English that the native-English speakers write'.

However, sometimes my humour caused difficulties with the Scandinavians. One participant chided me in the feedback form for showing 'attention-seeking tendencies', which upset me for a while until my co-tutor remarked that he thought that was the whole point of the job. After a particularly tough course, as my friend and co-tutor Harvey and I rode back to our hotel in a taxi, we started to discuss how no-one seemed to share the British sense of humour. At this point the taxi driver, who clearly understood more English than we imagined, tilted his head towards the rear seats.

'We like Mr Bean,' he said. Slapstick, however, was unlikely to be a serious option.

I never ran any training courses in eastern Europe, though I did have doctors from that region on courses elsewhere. One earnest participant, with a solid background in Soviet Union certainties, found our training particularly confusing.

'If A happens and then B, with a background of C, should you do D or E'? I was teaching with Harvey at the time and we paused, reflected and then both shrugged our shoulders.

'You could do either', we said. 'Try it and see'. Such a liberal approach to science was a challenge too far; he pushed his chair back and withdrew from the rest of the course.

We faced different challenges in Singapore. We took the cultural differences seriously enough to have asked for – and got – a briefing from the British Council. As we were warned, participants were scrupulously polite, but not keen to answer questions. This was, we were told, because it would for them be a no-win situation: those giving right answers were seen as overly pushy; those giving wrong answers lost face.

Occasionally we did some social engineering, and put participants in small groups at different tables so that they could compete for a prize (chocolates, or a book). This unleashed their competitive juices and they lost their inhibitions. The training room started to hum.

I never ran any courses in America. Unlike in Europe, there was already a thriving market for the type of courses I was running. I attended two conferences of the American Medical Writers Association, and discovered that medical writing was already a profession, with plenty of formal training. At Johns Hopkins Medical School, for instance, there was a medical writing programme with a full-time coordinator, six instructors, seven courses and a proud record of 1,000 'attendees' over the year.

At the time, as far as I knew, there were only two people with (part-time) medical writing appointments at UK universities, and (with a visiting fellowship at Southampton University) I was one of them. The travel was often fun and certainly broadened the mind. But it had its price. Humping course books up and down stairs did my shoulders no favours, and the ulcerative colitis brought an added strain. Most of the time my innards behaved themselves, but when they didn't I had to plot my journeys carefully past places where there were likely to be reasonable loos.

Pubs and restaurants were generally good in an emergency. I carried a Can't Wait card provided by the National Association for Crohn's and Colitis, but I found it really embarrassing to use it. Airports and motorways had good facilities but railway stations were bad: at best dirty and at worst firmly shut.

It was a solitary life. Once, after I was getting over a dose of flu, Barbara drove me to the hotel I had been booked into the night before a course. As we walked in to the restaurant she noted the number of single people seated at small tables reading paperback books and eating their meals alone.

'That's sad' she said.

'That's usually me,' I said.

5.11: The downs and ups of a peripatetic trainer

'There are people who have been sea-sick and people who have not yet been sea-sick,' an American navy captain told me on a particularly lumpy ferry crossing across the North Sea. The same principle could be applied to running training courses. Some trainers have run courses that have gone disastrously wrong; others not yet.

In my 17 years and some 1,000 courses as a trainer I had about half a dozen such courses, and most stick in my memory still. My first was the one in Amsterdam where I had been drafted in to teach a group of professional medical writers how to write. The second had a remarkably similar origin, though I didn't realise it until it was too late.

Again my client was a company providing writing services for pharmaceutical companies. As part of my preparation I visited their headquarters in London twice, and though I felt some hostility to the notion of training (and to me), I couldn't quite work out why.

The course was to be a two-day residential affair, and prudently I drove to the venue the night before for a good night's rest. After a pleasant meal I fell asleep easily, but the anticipated quiet hours of the early morning turned out to be anything but.

It was a loud clunking from underneath the floorboards, close by the radiator, that first woke me up. And the clunking continued, ensuring that the one thing I did not do was go back to sleep. I played with all the knobs on the radiator. I stamped on the floor. I made a cup of tea. I even tried my old trick of stuffing tissues in my ear. But I stayed awake fretting as the early light of dawn crept past the curtains. It was a bad start.

An hour or so later the cohort of participants arrived. We soon started to disagree. The first major upset to my normal in-course routine came when I tried to convince them that the best definition of good writing was a piece that produced the desired reaction by getting the message across to the target audience. That was not good enough for them. They insisted that there was an ideal of good writing, but no, they couldn't actually tell me what it was. I had trodden this path before.

Foolishly, I kept trying to win them over with humour, but humour depends on context and the little jokes that worked so well on other courses were here interpreted as insults. In one well-honed routine I asked participants to look at a particularly dense piece of writing and then identify the message. When they couldn't (because there wasn't one), I asked the rhetorical question: 'Does that mean you are all stupid?'

Most groups at this stage laughed and exclaimed of course not, it was obviously the writer's fault. This group did not.

'How dare you call us stupid,' they said.

The coffee breaks gave little respite. The participants formed little huddles, muttering together and glancing over in my direction. That evening, desperate to catch up on my lost sleep, I went to bed as soon as supper was ended. They stayed in the bar until the small hours, and (from comments they made the next day) having a great time criticising me and my course. The second day was an ordeal for all of us, and at the end of the course the 'happy sheets' were anything but. I usually got scores of 8-9 out of 10, but this time they were down between 4 and 6. I reduced my fee.

I discovered that the course had been arranged following pressure from the company's project managers (those selling the writing and editing services the company provided) who felt that the writers and editors were not good enough project managers. As an extra twist, the project managers were all men and the writers and editors all women. Had I realised this before the course I would have suggested that the last person they should hire for the task was yet another man in a grey suit.

As I write this 15 years later the insecurities return. But that's the nature of training: sometimes you receive almost embarrassing outpourings of gratitude; at other times you become a lightning rod for other people's pain. Sometimes the trainer ends up being bullied and labelled a bully at the same time. But it's hard to get rid of the feeling that you should have been able to make it work. My last resort in times of difficulty was to recall the mnemonic told to me by my former collaborator Bill Whimster, who had heard it from a tour guide: TOMAS - Think Of the Money And Smile.

Even TOMAS had failed to cheer me up on this occasion. So when a few weeks later I saw an advert for a Master Trainers Course near Geneva, I decided it would be worth spending what appeared to be a large sum of money. The course was run by John Townsend, a former corporate trainer and author of the pioneering *Trainer's Pocketbook* that, as I write, has sold more than 100,000 copies, is in its 11th edition and has inspired a range of similar well-selling pocketbooks from his publishers (Peter Townsend, *Trainer's Pocketbook*, Management Pocketbooks).

He had set up a train-the-trainers business in a small French town just over the border from Geneva. I stayed in a small hotel – along with trainers from the United Nations, Reuters, PricewaterhouseCoopers and Novartis – and each day walked across town to the state-of-the-art training facility that John had designed and had built. It was a comfortable and airy space with large windows looking out over the Alps, a far cry from the NHS basements that I normally inhabited.

At the start of the course I defined my goal as 'wanting to get up steam again'; I did. The course turned out as training courses should: stimulating, and supportive and a lot of fun. John was a showman and used all kinds of devices to keep us engaged, like fanfares for a card-full of action points. Many of his routines were orchestrated by a kind of magician's assistant sitting at the side of the room. The role was played brilliantly by his brother, a former colonel in the military police.

John covered the whole range of training, from working out needs to evaluation. He gave us the formula of 10 hours preparation for each hour of active training and of course had an armoury of acronyms. Some were extremely tenuous, like the Icelandic airman B GUNNAR EDEG RAF(R), though if you did manage to remember it you had everything covered for a training session.

We did a test of learning styles which showed me that I learnt not by experimenting but by reflecting. Finally I had insight into why I had had such trouble learning science: while others stormed ahead I was still thinking.

I flew back to England after the course with a set of goodies in a miniature Master Trainer Institute plastic case, a CD of 'music and sounds for focused learning' that John had composed and performed, and a pile of yellow feedback slips that my colleagues had given me. They praised me for being funny, brave and (rather to my surprise) a good team player.

I also had 139 action points, some eminently practical, such as greeting people at the start of each day and making sure the last sentence 'ends with a bang'. Other points were more personal: 'Don't be a junior clown', 'Don't even pretend to be scary', and 'Smile more'. My final two action points read: 'Go to a toyshop' and 'Be positive, be positive, be positive.'

I got an early opportunity to use my new-found skills for handling difficult people. John advocated 'mental judo', and he taught us tricks such as inviting difficult people to heckle, and know-alls to teach some of the course. Soon afterwards I found myself faced on a course by a doctor who interrupted, dominated, disagreed and even poked fun at the proceedings. At the first break I took him a copy of John's book on difficult people.

'I can't decide which one is you,' I said. Throughout the next session he was engrossed in the book, which allowed me to make rapid and unchallenged progress. At the next break I went back:

'Well. Which one are you then?'

'I think I'm all of them,' he said.

Thereafter he toned down his act, not completely but enough to take him back down the scale from being grossly disruptive to edgily stimulating.

I wrote and told John about this, and he asked if he could add this to his suggestions. I agreed, and wrote back: 'The most extraordinary thing has happened. The calibre of the participants has miraculously improved while I was away.'

5.12: Deeper still in the world of science

One lunch-time in the middle of the 1990s I strode up the imposing staircase in the Regent's Park headquarters of the Royal College of Obstetricians and Gynaecologists. Half way up I realised that something was amiss. On the wall, among the pictures of college presidents, each dripping with gravitas, was a dust-lined gap as stark as a newly extracted tooth. The portrait of Professor Geoffrey Chamberlain, until recently president of the college, had been taken down.

Professor Chamberlain had found himself in disgrace, not for any crime involving hands in the wrong places (bodies or bank accounts), but for the relatively new offence of publication fraud. As editor of a prestigious medical journal he had been imprudent enough to fast track (without sending out for peer review) a 'breakthrough' paper from his colleague, Malcolm Pearce. He had also allowed his name to appear as a co-author.

After a tip-off, it emerged that the successful resolution of an ectopic pregnancy, as described in the landmark paper, never happened. Malcolm Pearce was struck off the medical register. Professor Chamberlain was stripped of his presidency and went into exile at a university in Wales. These events startled the medical establishment, and pushed me deeper into the world of science.

My new area of interest was going to be medical journals. These had boomed since the end of the second world war. One of the beneficiaries had been the publisher Robert Maxwell (later proprietor of the *Daily Mirror* and embezzler of the pension funds of some of my former colleagues) who later disappeared off his own yacht. His great achievement was realising that here was a business that obtained its raw material - academic and scientific papers – without having to pay the producers.

By the 1990s, his and other journals were making billions of pounds in profits and playing key roles in the world of medicine and health care. In particular they influenced the careers of doctors and the funding of research. This is why Pearce and others felt they had to cheat; this is also why some of the more responsible editors realised how important it was to retain public confidence.

In the UK the charge was led by two new and dynamic editors, Richard Smith of the *British Medical Journal* and Richard Horton of the *Lancet*. They encouraged research into journal custom and practice, and set up an ethics committee to look at breaches. They also asked me to design and run a course.

The first one took place in 1996 at Nottingham University and the second a year later in a nondescript hotel (chosen for its cheapness and location) in Retford. I had invited a distinguished faculty, including the two Richards and my old friend Harvey Marcovitch, and we attracted about 25 editors to each course.

The faculty riffed gloriously and were immensely entertaining. At the end of the course participants were on the whole enthusiastic. But in both years the post-course questionnaires identified two problems. The first was that the faculty came from profitable general journals with large staffs and a stream of high-quality submissions. Most of the participants, on the other hand, were part-time editors of smaller specialist journals, struggling for profits and papers. As people told us in the feedback afterwards, the issues they were concerned about weren't always the same.

The other problem was that my carefully prepared programme ended up being largely ignored. In both years we ran out of time for two sessions: one on press releases, and the other – much more embarrassingly – on time management. 'Stick to the programme', a participant urged.

For the third year I sacked the learned editors who, to their credit, did not make it the disastrous career move it could have been. As editors they clearly understood the horrors of having responsibility without power, and they both continued to support the course, for which I remain grateful.

But it left Harvey and me on our own. For a start we resolved that the timetable was going to be sacrosanct. We reduced the number of talks and increased the number of exercises. We stopped having plenary sessions and breakout groups, and instead arranged the editors in teams of 5-6 seated at round tables in 'cafeteria style'. I introduced some of the techniques I had learnt from John Townsend, such as setting up 'talking walls' (where participants put up their ideas on sticky notes), introducing short bursts of music, and shuffling the groups around – an unsettling trick that they tried to resist.

The course ran for many years, taking in Scandinavia, Sydney, Christchurch, Addis Ababa, Barcelona, and Chicago. Each September until well into the new millennium we ran it at the Spa Hotel Tunbridge Wells. The hotel was a rambling Edwardian building with long corridors lined with sepia photographs of chefs in tall hats and waitresses with starched aprons. Our training room was hot but bright, with one wall devoted to a gentle mural of shoppers in the city centre.

I found the start of each course a nerve-wracking business, not least because the pre-course questionnaires always showed that what they were expecting to learn was not necessarily what we wanted them to learn.

Their main interest was how to increase the Impact Factor of their journal. This was (and sadly still is) a metric that ranks journals on the basis of how often an article is cited in other journals. The flaw, of course, is what I was told by economists is Goodhart's Law: when a measure becomes a target it ceases to become a good measure. The sassier editors were doing all kinds of things to help them rise in the rankings, including one shameless wheeze that involved accepting papers for publication only on condition that the authors included several references to their journal.

Harvey and I took the high ground, arguing that the best way of rising in the rankings was to make a journal well-read and discussed. The best way to do this was to publish papers that would engage their readers, and we identified all kinds of techniques for attracting people who would write them.

We also spent a lot of time – about a quarter of the course – looking at ways of increasing the chances that these articles, once published, would be read. This included how to structure the journal, design the pages, add 'page furniture' like summary boxes and pull-out quotes, and unravel impenetrable prose. We also looked at how editors could encourage people to get involved with the publication by putting interesting things on the front cover.

This got us into trouble on one occasion. We were in Stockholm with a group of Scandinavian editors, who were horrified by the suggestion. They made it clear that anything other than a title and a date on the front cover would be inexcusably vulgar. But on the whole editors found these sessions stimulating, and I was encouraged one day when one of them came up to me and said: 'I have been an editor a long time, but I have never before thought of the readers'.

Nor had many of them thought much about what editors did, other than be a kind of chief reviewer. We hit them early with an exercise which provided them with several years' worth of annual reports from a journal editor, ending up with a request for more funding. A careful reading of the papers showed that the editor was deluded – and clearly running the journal into the ground. So the winning team in our view was the one that had invested least. In what we thought was a nice twist, we revealed that the editor was now a professor and a knight of the realm. But most got the main point that editors could only edit if they had sufficient funds.

In one of the early courses one of the participants, who came from New Zealand, came up with a novel solution to this exercise. Why not save money – and the editor's career – by abolishing the paper edition and going out to subscribers electronically? At the time we thought the idea intriguing, but improbable. Within a couple of years we were spending as much time on electronic journals as we had on paper ones.

Our most popular sessions proved to be variations of the in-tray exercises that I had devised while serving out my notice at the Central Electricity Generating Board 30 years before. These provided a range of ethical dilemmas, which some of the editors thought were a little far-fetched; in fact they were all based on real-life situations.

One was directly inspired by the Chamberlain-Pearce scenario. It was a brief note to the effect that a recently published paper was based on false data. We added a bit of spice by providing two different versions: two groups had an anonymous letter to consider, while for the other two the message was signed.

That stirred up a grand argument. Some suggested that if the letter was anonymous they should throw it away; others said that because it was anonymous didn't make it untrue, and anyway would anyone in their right mind want to be a whistleblower? There were varied suggestions on how to proceed, from making an official complaint to the dean to having a quiet chat with an old rugby mate to ask if he could do some digging on the quiet.

There were few easy answers. One exception was a letter purporting to come from a firm of solicitors (with offices in several capital cities and a long list of partners on the letterhead) claiming that their client had been defamed. There was only one sensible course of action here: forward it to the journal's lawyers without delay.

Our fear of not being seen to satisfy the editors' needs proved groundless. As one editor wrote: 'I came here deeply suspicious of being lectured to, but found myself being provoked and stimulated'. They all went away with their own to-do lists, which included such sensible (and basic) actions as asking their publishers for a contract, conducting readers' surveys and composing better letters for would-be authors.

We only touched a small minority of journal editors, however. This was a shame. I like to think that if Professor Chamberlain had attended, he would have realised that the days of running a journal on trust were over.

5.13: Equilibrium

As the 1990s came to a close, the business was flourishing and I was enjoying the work. Then Barbara and I moved on to a new and dangerous arrangement: we decided to work together.

After the trauma of downsizing , the assistants supplied from a local agency were of mixed ability, left regularly (not my fault, I was assured, though not always with conviction), and were expensive. One failed to turn up after Princess Diana was killed in a motor accident in Paris, and her hastily drafted successor spent the morning in tears.

Barbara, now recovered from her heart surgery and approaching life with new-found energy, was working for the same agency. When we compared what I was paying them and what they paid her, the difference came to £100 a week. If we ran the business together, I pointed out, we would keep all we earned. The argument was strong and prevailed, though with a proviso from Barbara that we should work in an office and not from home. Otherwise, while I was away travelling, she would be stuck in the house seven days a week.

We scoured the area and found a small, recently renovated office over a shop selling windows in the Surrey town of Dorking, five miles away. Each morning we would drive past Box Hill, the tree-lined local beauty spot (later site of Olympic cycling), revelling in the passing of the seasons as the leaves changed and fell and budded. Our landlord was a local surveyor who knew how to take care of a building and its occupants. He even gave Barbara a small gift at Christmas to thank her for being a helpful tenant.

We had one small room where our desks were placed head to head, but if we turned to look out of the window we saw vines tumbling down a south-facing slope of the North Downs. Unlike Leatherhead, which about that time was nominated on a TV programme as the most boring town centre in the UK, Dorking still had a heart, a High Street, striking views, a gentleman's outfitter (run by Mr Pratt, where I bought my one and only tailored suit, now used mainly for funerals), and a thriving Friday market.

We had only ourselves to answer to, so Barbara and I would do civilised things like close the office and have lunch together, pop up the road to a garden centre, or stroll around the antique shops looking at unaffordable furniture. We joined a dining club of local business people, organised by the proprietor of our favourite sandwich shop and her friend the local chiropractor who commuted from Switzerland.

I stopped my flirtation with 'growing a business' and concentrated on running one that was small, stable and simple to control. I obtained a qualification: a fellowship of the (now Chartered) Institute of Personnel and Development. To do this I had to assemble a 13-page submission, supported by an existing fellow whom I hardly knew, showing how my work experience qualified me for this role. I could not help thinking of the articles I had written three decades before about fraudsters offering bogus degrees using a similar process. But the doctors I taught were impressed by the new set of letters after my name.

Barbara reckoned that we survived working together because her job was to get me out of the office earning money. By the end of the decade – and for several years afterwards – I was running about 60 courses a year. When I told people this, there was one of two reactions:

'Is that all you do?' said one group.

'That sounds like an awful lot,' said the other.

The gap between the two suggests that it was probably the right amount.

I still missed the monthly miracle by which money appears regularly in a bank account, but business was steady and we made a reasonable living. One good piece of luck was working in the health sector. It did not pay high rates (with the exception of the pharmaceutical industry) but in 17 years we did not have a single bad debt. The nearest we came was a doctor whose accounts department was taking so long to pay us that she gave us a personal cheque.

I started to find it easier to charge what I considered high fees. I blamed my early reluctance to do so on my Catholic upbringing and a residual fear of the sin of greed. Later I started to put the fees up, not just because I didn't want people to think I was a failure, but because I realised that if people were happy to pay what I asked they thought they were getting value.

I also learnt an important lesson about the dangers of doing something for nothing. One year an editor at the *BMJ* asked me if I would consider giving a free place to a doctor from Iraq who wanted to attend the course on editing medical journals. This was the time of sanctions and the Iraqi health services needed support. I agreed. I found out later that the doctor in question was Saddam Hussein's brother-in-law.

Though I was clearly in danger of becoming successful, my anxiety dreams still turned up from time to time. These were of two types. In the first I turned up for an examination and clearly knew nothing about the subject. (In my later life as a trainer this insecurity re-emerged as being clad only in a towel and late for a course I was giving, or finding a pillar in the training room between me and a posse of professors.) In the second I arrived at school on the first day of a new term and looked at the notice board; I was still not a prefect.

There came a turning point. One week I found myself lecturing on a course for GPs. Also on the list of tutors was Professor Anthony Clare, distinguished psychiatrist and broadcaster. One evening, after chatting about Catholic education (he had been subjected to the Jesuits) we sang duets from Rogers and Hammerstein along the shuttered streets. I then had a great night's sleep. In the morning I reported to the good psychiatrist.

'I had a dream last night. I went back to my old school. And I bought it.'

'I think you've cracked it,' he said. 'Move on.'

Postscript: January 3, 2000

There's nothing like a change of millennium for a spot of retrospection. A group of us, mainly born in the 1940s and 1950s, had spent the last few days of 1999 together, marking the changing centuries. We had dined and walked together, watched on TV the fireworks progressing around the world, and noted with relief that our computers still worked. And then one of us raised an interesting question: which innovation in our lifetime had affected us most?

Answers came fast. The internal combustion engine, because it had given us the ability to travel 50 miles or more simply to have lunch with a friend. The telephone wire, because it had enabled us to have conversations with our family, even when they lived on different continents. The radio wave, because it allowed us to listen to news or live music in the comfort of our own front room.

Then someone pointed out that, though these had impacted strongly on our lives, their introduction came before most of us were born. We quickly came up with an alternative: the personal computer and the world wide web, both invented in our lifetime and bringing previously unimaginable changes. One of our group personified this change: she had trained as a librarian but was now a teacher of computer science.

At this point the conversation became a little silly. One of our party mentioned video cassettes, which enabled him to watch movies at leisure. Another mentioned chill technology, which allowed him to eat all kinds of exotic and well-prepared food. I cited the channel tunnel, which enabled us to get on and off our British isle in half an hour. One wag (male) suggested the invention of women, while another (female) countered with the invention of tights.

Our contributions became serious again. We turned to health care in general, and to the products of the pharmaceutical industry in particular.

'Statins have had an enormous effect on my life,' said one of us. 'My father had his first heart attack aged 48. I can now lead a pretty normal life – and eat all kinds of things I wouldn't otherwise be able to do.'

'The contraceptive pill,' said his wife, a mother of two and a business consultant. 'My life would have been completely different without it.'

Barbara chimed in with the fact that without surgery she would be at best an invalid, and at worst no longer with us. I noted that without steroids I would probably not have made the new century either.

The conversation moved on to different topics and it was not until later that the enormity of the changes we had witnessed began to sink in. But these innovations were just a part of it. Thanks to the accident of birth we had found ourselves in an extremely privileged position. In our prosperous and privileged western bubble we had been able to enjoy five decades of peace, rising wealth, freedom of thought, consensus – and a succession of interesting events that, through fast-developing media, we could all share. We were indeed the lucky ones.

Thank you

The research and writing of this book has occupied me for several years, and I am intensely grateful to those many people who have supported me in this task.

I am particularly indebted to those who read and commented on various drafts; their comments were both sustaining and useful. These included: Deborah Takiff Smith, Michael O'Donnell, Ric Papineau, Mary Banks, Mary Tapissier, Jane Smith and David Albert.

Many others have helped with readings of various chapters, and with information. They include: Elizabeth Allen, Dudley Buchanan, Christine Gowing, Angela Donovan, Neil MacHugh, Susan Mills, Michael Medath, Anthony Albert, Dominic Farmer, Susan Holmes, Lucy Vignoles; Nick Stobbs, Anthony McLean, Abbot Geoffrey Scott, Tim and Sue Haigh, Bob Matthews, Jennifer Greenfield; Esther Ripley, Peter Wilby, Fred Kavalier, Jane O'Nions, Jo Rogger, Frances Verrinder, Richard Soper, Jon Ford, Sally Watson, Harvey Marcovitch, Doreen Warner, Mervyn Rosenberg, Margaret Hallendorff, and LucyAnn Curling.

I would also like to thank those who have helped in turning my manuscript into a published book. I am grateful to Elizabeth Gowing and Robert Wilton for inviting me to become part of their Elbow publishing family. I am also grateful to Jane Donovan for her proof-reading, and to Sally Witon, Su Jones and Paddy McEntaggart, Magda Pieta and Paula Charles for easing my path through the production process.

Most importantly, my thanks to my wife Barbara, who has not just supported my crabby behaviour when writing, but also provided an invaluable line of support, feedback and an invaluable pair of extra proofreading eyes.

Finally I would like to thank all those – whether they appear in these pages or not – who have made my life what it has been. You are an essential part of the story.

Illustrations

Picture credits have been shown where available. In addition I would like to thank the following:

Roger Morton for the photograph of Ditcham Park taken by his father Cyril

The Douai Abbey Archive for the photographs of Douai School

University of Surrey Archives for the photograph of students on campus (UBL/Z/45/23) © University of Surrey

The Thorington Archive, Tavistock Museum for photographs of Mike Tillson and his car, and Brian Fogg

The BMA Archive for the photograph of BMA House

Regis Sion for the photographs of the Wimereux Cricket Club

Every reasonable effort has been made to identify where copyright permission is required and to obtain that permission when necessary. If anyone sees any errors or omissions they should contact the author so that amendments can be made in any future edition.